BEHIND THE MOSS CURTAIN

BEHIND THE MOSS CURTAIN

For my friends
Dick & Debby.

Welcome back
to Savannah!

[signature]

14 AUG 04

BEHIND THE MOSS CURTAIN

AND OTHER GREAT SAVANNAH STORIES

MURRAY SILVER

Collected and Edited by

CRISTINA PIVA

Savannah, 2004

BONAVENTTURE
books

Copyright © 2002 by Murray Silver

Photographs:
Jacket Photograph and Design: Kirt Witte
Model: Heather Witte
Murray Silver: Heather Madras Johnson
Piano Red: Chris Strachwitz
Dr. Cleckley, courtesy Medical College of Georgia
Thornwell Jacobs, courtesy Oglethorpe University

Bonaventture is a proud sponsor of
"The Mystical Arts of Tibet" and
Drepung Loseling Monastery.

Library of Congress Cataloging in Publication Data
2002112233

Silver, Murray.
Behind the Moss Curtain

ISBN 0-9724224-0-4

Printed and bound in the United States of America
Fourth Edition, 2004
Third Edition, 2003; Second Edition 2003; First Edition 2002

ACKNOWLEDGMENTS

The Author is grateful to Charles H. Morris, Chairman and President of Savannah Media and Morris Newspaper Corp., who—for all too brief a time—published Connect, a free weekly newsmagazine in a newspaper format, that allowed contributors to stretch out in a manner seldom afforded by other publications; and to Peter Jackson, Director of Product Development, who so patiently fostered "Behind the Moss Curtain" in its original form, "The Butcher Murder of '45." Five other stories contained herein were also originally published in Connect: "A Piece of the Action," "One for the Road," "So Deep, So Wide," "The Saga of Silent Stafford," and "The Case of the Snakehead Smugglers," for which the author is also appreciative.

The Author is greatly indebted to Charles J. "Buster" White for having so generously provided the stories which make up the great weight of "A Piece of the Action," "Buster White's Big Fight Night," and "The Saga of Silent Stafford." Clearly, Buster White is the Author's favorite subject.

The Author is also indebted to Tony Yatro, Joe Dinerman, Sir Charles Grossman, and all the boys down at McDonald's on DeRenne for countless hours of convivial companionship, stories, anecdotes and details which color many of these great Savannah stories.

The Author thanks Maggie Hall, niece of Shoeless Joe Jackson, for so generously providing the photographs of Joe that adorn this text. Thanks also to Ed Fitzgerald, Jr. for providing the photo of his father.

This book is dedicated to the memories of Wolfe Silver, Shoeless Joe Jackson, Ed Fitzgerald, and the many characters both great and small whose legends loom in these pages.

CONTENTS

INTRODUCTION

Murray Mendel Silver, Jr., writer, photographer, concert promoter, professor, entrepreneur, human rights activist was born in Savannah, Georgia, in 1953, into two large and prominent families—one German and Russian Jews, and the other Irish Catholic; that he is today a practicing Tibetan Buddhist says something about the way in which he has gone about negotiating the choppy waters of his life: sampling a little from each experience and, as he says, "trying to keep the wagon in the middle of the road."

His family had moved a dozen times before he was seventeen years old, from Savannah to Jekyll Island to Atlanta, and having been uprooted from his home and extended family at critical points during his development was the reason why he continued to move a dozen times more before he was 45, until, at last, he returned home to Savannah where he thought he should have always remained.

In returning to Savannah, Silver moved into the house where his family resided from 1963 until they left town in 1966, and in habiting these rooms for the first time in 35 years he went back in time to when he was a kid attending Jacob G. Smith Elementary School across the street, when his father was a struggling lawyer, and when his grandfather took his own life; tumultuous times buried before he was able to take a long look at the events that shaped his young life. It was as if he could not face an uncertain future until it becomes the past; that he develops some of his stories about the good old days in the present tense may be a desperate attempt to avoid drifting back into a past that would be better left undisturbed.

Writing a retrospective column for Connect, Savannah's free weekly news magazine, provided Silver with an outlet for this very personal process. When in December 1999 a young tavern keeper named Mark Castrillo ended his life in oddly similar circumstances to that of Silver's grandfather, it struck a raw nerve in the writer who had been at a loss in figuring out why people take themselves out of a game before it's over. The result, "One for the Road," is Silver's contemplation upon these twin tragedies, and a throat-clearing introduction to what became a series of stories about Savannah in the Roaring Twenties, Thirties and Forties.

No sooner had Silver's first essay appeared in Connect than he heard from Buster White, who had been Savannah's premier promoter for more than fifty years, and who presided over a daily meeting of old timers at McDonald's on DeRenne. Silver spent many an afternoon in the company of men who had known his grandparents and great-grandparents and just about everybody else, for that matter. All of a sudden, finding stories about old Savannah was no longer a problem for Connect's retrospective writer, who had his hands full sorting fact from fiction between bites of French fries. It is no surprise then that four of these stories involve a cast of colorful characters—often favorably compared to Damon Runyon's guys and dolls—that once made Savannah a lively place to live, indeed.

"A Piece of the Action" afforded its author the chance to return to a place he had never been: Bo Peep's Billiard Parlor on East Congress Street, where his grandfather held court from 1929 until 1958, and in raising his cast of characters back to life from the dust of Bonaventure Cemetery, Silver happened upon a garden of good stories which the local populace had somehow forgotten—or never knew in the first place. For instance, Silver was surprised to discover that Shoeless Joe Jackson, perhaps the greatest baseball player that ever lived, called

Savannah home throughout his playing days and for ten years thereafter, while popular views held that following his disappearance after the Black Sox World Series Scandal of 1919 his ghost had been seen wandering around an Iowa cornfield. Why Joe Jackson moved to Savannah, what he did here and why he left, is the subject of "In Search of Shoeless Joe," in which Silver traces his every barefoot step.

Following the publication of Bill Harris's "Delirium of the Brave," in which Harris fictionalized the more sordid and seamier side of Savannah, Silver's editor at Connect, Peter Jackson, suggested that there might be a story in the real-life tale of Jesse McKethan, who murdered his best friend back in 1945 and will forever be remembered as "The Butcher Murderer." At first glance, it was not a subject that Silver cared to consider: its gruesome nature aside, the details of the crime, its prosecution, and Jesse's execution left little for Silver to expound upon. But in ways which made him think that there is much more than meets the eye—or finds its way into the local newspaper, for that matter—Silver stumbled upon facts of the case unknown at the time that are perhaps more shocking than the story itself.

For six weeks in 2000, Savannahians waited at Connect distribution points throughout the city for the latest installment of "The Butcher Murder of '45," and letters to the editor poured into the paper's offices, including a rave review from Pat Conroy in which he said that he "wouldn't be surprised if Connect's retrospective writer was nominated for a Pulitzer Prize." Silver promised that the story of Jesse McKethan was far better than that of Jim Williams, and readers tended to agree, with the exception of those who thought Silver had gone too far in picking a fight with John Berendt in the introduction, "Why Tell the Story of Jesse McKethan After All These Years?"

That Silver skewered the sacred cash cow that "Midnight" had become both angered and amused Savannahians who were forced to reconsider their fondness for Berendt's book: was it worthy of all the hoopla, or was it the "cloud with a silver lining" Silver spoke of? Can any town promote Murder to its lasting benefit?

In answering these questions, it is important and interesting to note that Murray Silver has denied all requests to turn his story of The Butcher Murder into a major motion picture. Disregarding the windfall profit to be made, he did not think Savannah could withstand another blood-soaked biopic. Besides, he had already gone through the process of watching his first book, "Great Balls of Fire: The Uncensored Story of Jerry Lee Lewis," made into a movie and found the process wanting.

This is not to say that the Author spends his days with his head lost in the clouds of yesteryear. Having satisfied his nostalgic cravings, he turned his razor-sharp wit on current affairs, such as the Savannah harbor deepening project, the Snakehead Smuggling case, and the debacle of the Pulaski monument renovation. In perfecting these records, Silver walks a fine line between editorial opinion and objective fact-finding, sometimes blurring the lines between fact and fiction so that it is practically impossible to tell where one leaves off and the other begins. The end results, however, are just plain funny.

It's all here: guys and dolls, the great and near great and the almost forgotten, set against that most picturesque of backdrops Savannah, Georgia. With a map of the city in one hand and this book in the other, visitors and residents alike will be enthralled with Murray Silver's intensely personal guided tour.

Cristina Piva

ONE FOR THE ROAD

On any given Sunday, from the first of September until the end of January, a gang of regular customers gathers at Coach's Corner Sports Bar on Victory Drive to watch pro football—not just the one or two key match-ups but all the games—blaring from a bank of monitors to rival the stock exchange. The gang numbers roughly a dozen members, led by Darren the computer wiz, Tony the electrician, Big Mark the baker, and Frank who's in the paper business. So regular are they in their habits and traditions that each member has his own place at the table, and waitresses know each man's preference in food and drink, whether he takes sugar in his tea or prefers hot wings to mild.

Between games confidences are exchanged among these close friends who, oddly, never meet away from their group rites at Coach's. Matings and pending marriages are run through the gauntlet of gang approval; none of the brothers dare bring a date to the party lest the fraternity greet the couple with a boisterous rendition of "Camptown Ladies," the anthem of the whipped and pecked. Do-dah, do-dah.

Baskets of chicken wings and pitchers of beer scatter the tabletop terrain and there is the flurry of flying fingers as plays are punched into the QB1 interactive game board. The Sunday ritual beginning around noon is in high gear by the first kick-off at one o'clock and breaks up some eleven hours later at the end of the late game—and this on top of having spent all day Saturday watching the colleges play.

Brother Frank is asked if he'd like to quit his job making paper and run his own sports bar. He tears his attention away from the screen long enough to shoot a look back over his shoulder that reads "stupid question."

"Don't you think you'd get tired of sittin' around all day watchin' sports on teevee and eatin' wings, Frank?"

"No," he replies, reflexively. "I could do this all day, every day, twenty-four seven."

"Really?" the questioner asks, with mock surprise. "And how long do you think you could keep up this sort of thing?"

"Forever," he answers, without having to think about it, and returns his attention to the screen.

To own a sports bar is the dream of practically every red-blooded American male. Mickey Mantle owned a bar, Jack Dempsey owned a bar, and Archie Bunker and Sam Malone owned bars on two of the most popular shows in the history of television. Even the most popular movie of all time was set in a bar, Humphrey Bogart's "Rick's Americain," in *Casablanca*.

So there is ample precedent for what Frank dreams of doing one day. A lot of time and money could be wasted by a government-funded study to determine why this condition exists in the American male and still come no closer to the truth than Samuel Johnson, the great 18th Century English man of letters, who reasoned, "There is nothing which has yet been contrived by man by which so much happiness is produced as by a good tavern."

In his desire to own a sports bar, Mark Castrillo was no different from Mantle and Malone, Bogart and Bunker, or Frank who's in the paper business. Castrillo moved to Savannah in 1985, following a stint in the U.S. Navy. He worked for a beer distributor until he learned the business and everybody in it, then tended bar on River Street with the dream of owning his own place someday. He had his eye on the old Malone's site on Williamson Street, which had been vacated in 1986. The owner intended to turn the space into condos, using city bonds to refurbish the building. When the city turned him down, the building sat vacant until the Callen Trust bought it.

It took Castrillo nearly 10 years to amass the kind of money needed to transform the 18th Century warehouse into a state-of-the-art pleasure palace accommodating up to 1,000 patrons. He spent hundreds of thousands of dollars on a truckload of teevees and wall-to-wall pool tables. And when he was finished, he opened the doors of Sports Fan Bar & Grill just in time to reap the rewards of an Atlanta Falcons team headed for their first Super Bowl appearance.

Somewhere along the road in its second year of operation, something changed for Mark Castrillo at Sports Fan. The dream of owning a sports bar dissolved into the long littleness of micro-management and the nightmare of a Falcons team gone to hell. Too busy with the crowded hour to fear to live or die, he gradually spent more and more time away from home until, at last, he moved into an apartment above his bar. And now, whether he wanted to or not, Castrillo was sittin' around watchin' sports on teevee and eatin' wings all day, every day, twenty-four seven.

Everyone who knew Castrillo loved him, and there isn't a person to be found that will say a discouraging word about him, including his competitors. His closest friends remember seeing him at Malone's in City Market on Saturday, Dec. 4, 1999, and he was his usual, convivial self. He hadn't the slightest complaint; he was, after all, living every man's dream. And that is why those friends experienced an incredible sense of loss and bewilderment to have learned six days later that Mark Castrillo had been found dead in a parked car at the Marriott with a self-inflicted gunshot wound to the chest.

* * *

Four-tenths of a mile from Sports Fan's front
door and 40 years ago, Savannah's premier sports bar
stood on the corner of Congress and Drayton, fronting
Christ Church. Bo Peep's Recreational Parlor isn't there
anymore, and there isn't a plaque pointing out where it
used to be, or a monument to its owner. But it's the place
many old-timers still remember most in a city that is a
walking tour of three centuries of history.

In its day, from 1926 until 1958, Bo Peep's was
the best-known hangout in Savannah. Located in a three-
story building, it was a taproom and luncheonette
downstairs and the Victory Hotel above. Bo Peep's was
known for having the best roast beef sandwich in the
civilized world, the place where wives could find their
husbands when they couldn't be found anyplace else. The
main attraction was the pool tables, and every character in
the vicinity—from the crowned heads of Europe to the
baldheads of Broughton Street—stopped by Bo Peep's to
rack a few balls and catch up on the latest scores.

That it was the only place in town where a guy
could bet a few bob not only made Bo Peep's popular but
also made the owner a pot full of money.

The proprietor's name was Wolfe Silver—born in
London to an English mother and a German father who
had immigrated to Savannah in 1902. The family lived
above their grocery store on the corner of Williamson and
West Broad (just a few short paces from the building that
later housed Sports Fan), and Wolfe had to quit the third
grade to shine shoes in order to help his parents make
ends meet. He was 21 years old when Prohibition was
enacted, and living among a large Irish population
thirsting for what was not-so-laughingly referred to as the
"water of life" created a demand which he decided to fill.

Wolfe went to New Orleans where he hooked up
with an up-and-comer in the underworld named Bugs
Moran, who imported hooch into one of the last outposts
flying in the face of the 18th Amendment. Wolfe started

out bringing in pint bottles by the suitcase then barrels by the carload, needed a point of distribution, and rented the Mendel Building on Congress Street. He made a lot of money quickly, enough to buy the building and a fleet of cars so that runs to New Orleans could be handled with greater efficiency.

Wolfe bought a dozen Cadillacs—not so much for fashion as for function—a big car with a big engine. Before setting out on the road where a caravan of new Caddys would be noticed, Wolfe led his fleet to a dirt track in Daffin Park where they drove around in circles all night until the new carriages were covered with a camouflage of dust. Then they set out for the Crescent City to load up. Somewhere in Alabama, between Blight and Boogerflick, Wolfe was busted—or rather, his men were nabbed. He managed to escape in the lead car. Wolfe high-tailed it back to Savannah alone, wheels on fire, where a pundit of the pool room casually remarked, "Little Bo Peep has lost his sheep." Thus, a nickname was bestowed upon Wolfe by which he was known—even by his wife—until his death, in 1963.

He was industrious and he was clever, maybe the greatest judge of human nature since Freud, and crossed the firmly established boundaries between Savannah Jews and gentiles, the Irish and the blacks. He was a Jew married into one of Savannah's largest and oldest Irish-Catholic families, and realized that his success stemmed from simply knowing how to relate to each on their own terms. A Jewish patron once asked Bo Peep about the Irish stew served in his luncheonette. "It's just beef and peas and carrots in gravy, Bo. What's Irish about it?" And Bo Peep replied, "In a town full of Irishmen, *this* is Irish stew."

Being one of few men of great wealth in Savannah during the Depression made Bo Peep an attractive target for anyone in a position of power looking for a payoff. The mayor, the police chief, and the municipal court judge made frequent visits to Bo Peep's house on Washington Avenue to shake the money tree. Even the preachers who railed against drinkin' and gamblin' from the pulpit of Christ Church were not above passing the collection plate across the street at Bo Peep's. "Let me hold some of that money," Reverend Wilder said to Bo Peep on one famous occasion. "The devil has had it long enough." And during the holiday times of the year, and seemingly at all times in between, the truly needy lined up in the lane in back of Bo Peep's where he distributed free baskets of food.

Bo Peep owned a string of Vegas-styled slot machines in several locations throughout Savannah. He took bets on everything from horse races to ice hockey— "Any game you can name, any amount you can count"— and even made odds on whether the sun would shine the next day. If he said it once, he said it a thousand times: "The town is full of guys who think they're mighty wise," and the fact that they held these differences of opinion on all matters sporting and were willing to put their money where their mouth was, made Bo Peep a millionaire.

Naturally, a man in Bo Peep's position found his share of trouble; it simply wasn't possible to attract his type of clientele without occasionally suffering the consequences. On the occasion of his oldest son's engagement to be married, Bo Peep sprang for the ring, a rock the size of a clear carbon cue ball that one of the pool hustlers just happened to be carrying around. "And if you like this deal, wait'll you see what else I got," the hustler told Bo Peep. "I'm in the business," he said, but he didn't say exactly what business he was in.

True to his word, the hustler delivered a sack of ice at unbelievably low prices. Bo Peep couldn't handle it all, and so he did favors for his friends the mayor and the judge and the bank president, arranging for them to buy nice presents to give to their wives. The jewelry business did so well in Savannah that someone tipped off the Georgia Bureau of Investigation, who was wondering where a large collection of stolen jewelry was being fenced. The fence unwittingly turned out to be Bo Peep.

His arrest came as a complete surprise to Bo Peep. What surprised him even more was that it would cost him an absolute fortune to buy his way out of this mess: he had purchased diamonds at ten cents on the dollar and sold them at cost to friends who had the pieces insured at retail values, and these same gifts could not be retrieved from wives and girlfriends unless Bo Peep agreed to pay for their replacements. At that rate, it would cost him a million dollars to buy back jewelry that hadn't earned him a nickel. And that, as they used to say down at the poolroom, was a whole new proposition.

When he bought back as much jewelry as he could find and could not account for the rest, Bo Peep was forced to fight the charge of receiving stolen property in the federal courts. He hired the judge's son, who agreed to represent him for a reasonable fee and promised to keep him out of jail. Where the proposition would get pricey, though, was the payoff to the judge. In the end, the process wiped him out and still didn't keep him out of jail: when Bo Peep couldn't come up with a $25,000 bribe on demand, the judge banged the gavel on two years to serve.

The poolroom foundered with Bo Peep gone away. It was still a popular spot, but there was no one to run the gambling concession, which was how he milled the big sugar. The place just wasn't the same without its proprietor, and by the time Bo Peep won his release from prison it was too late to salvage. Worse yet, when he went back to all of the people who owed him a huge debt—the politicians he had sponsored and the businessmen he had fostered—his friends fled like rats from a sinking ship. He lost his business when he was forced to sell the building on Congress Street. He was too old to start over, and with a third grade education and a resume that read like a rap sheet, he had outlived his heyday and headed toward retirement with nothing to his name.

Bo Peep died alone in a rented room across the street from where his business used to be. He spent the long, lonely last night of his life looking out the window onto the street he once strolled when he was king and his pockets were filled with cash. He counted up his wins and losses and tried to make sense of it all, but in the end he couldn't figure out why it was that when he needed them most all of the friends he had helped wouldn't lift a finger to help him, as if they secretly delighted in his downfall and disgrace. If he had made a million dollars in his lifetime he gave away a million-and-one for he died broke, and for want of a cup of kindness costing nothing, suicide was the natural, consistent course dictated by the logical intellect.

The coroner said Bo Peep strangled himself, but his family knew that he had died of a broken heart.

You can't go inside the building where Bo Peep's used to be because it's been torn down. Before he died, Bo Peep vowed that no one after him would ever move onto his site at 17 East Congress Street and run a going concern, and it's been paved over for the Christ Church parking lot. But old-timers sitting on park benches in Johnson Square can still see the place with its window painted "Finest in the South," and can detect a faint hint of roast beef in the air, a parade of spectral visions with familiar faces passing by where a marker ought to be. The vision that is clearest is the face that is missed most, the little man with the big heart who used to run the place, Bo Peep.

The vision lingers a moment longer and then returns to that place where shadows play until summoned again—call it a heaven of harp music and cotton candy clouds or a sports bar that serves the world's best roast beef sandwich—and before Bo Peep vanishes he can still be heard to say, "The town is full of guys who think they're mighty wise."

Bo Peep's Pool Room on Congress Street
Bo Peep in center, in white shirt

A PIECE OF THE ACTION

MARCH 2000

Sunday, February 13th, was a particularly foggy day. There was no sky, only a transparent tent that draped the tops of the oaks sheltering Savannah's squares and avenues. The world was black and white and shades of gray. No one was on the street. It seemed as though no one lived here anymore—they had all gone long ago, leaving lighted houses to be covered in time by shadows and fog.

It was intriguing, this fog. It crept in everywhere, into doorways and remote corners of rooms, and into the pockets of my raincoat. My breath was visible, like cigarette smoke. With a failing, despairing energy I started blindly down the dimness of Congress Street, looking for a way out of this fog. I might be lost in here for days.

It was getting darker now and darker; time went fast and then slow, moments that seemed to be ultimately sorting and resolving themselves, an order unto itself. I could still see my white breath in the darkness, and pale faces peering out a window across the street from Christ Church.

I was drawn to a wealth of golden light, comforting warmth. A faintly familiar icy-cold face welcomed me, and then I was in a group of friendly faces; I was shaking hands. The scene had a historic quality to it—sweeping over me with a vast nostalgia—as if people I knew to be dead were moving about. I made my way inside, dazed by the magic.

In the great smoke-filled room with the dark and fog shut out I took a seat at a bar on a stool near a billiard table, and the evening's oppression instantly lifted. Light played on gleaming nickel taps. For a moment, I thought I had lost my mind. Thoughts had been snapping inside me lately like little hooks on a dress—my mind runs down like an old clock—and as my gaze moved around the room and came to light on a calendar for 1947, I felt as though the last hook had come undone. A jukebox in the far corner struck up "Ole Buttermilk Sky," which echoed muddily, as if over a stretch of water and through fog thicker than cotton.

A small man with a round face wearing thick glasses appears next to me. He is busy unfolding little scraps of paper with scribbled notations written in code, what looks like bets on sporting propositions. He reaches for a ballpoint pen, makes a few calculations, and then returns the pen to his pocket without retracting it, streaking his white dress shirt with ink marks. Two guys are standing over by the billiard table talking about this and that and who's doing what to whom and whether it was the first or second time when suddenly the room goes silent as a huge man in a dark trench coat enters. He walks up slowly behind the little man seated next to me, and taps him on the shoulder.

"Are you Mister Bo Peep?" the man in the trench coat asks.

"Who wants to know?"

"Your cousin Hymie from New York sends you his regards, and tells me I should make it known to you that I am upon the scene and available for whatever you may require."

"What's your name and what's your road game, friend?"

The man in the trench coat reaches into an inside pocket with a hand as big as a ham and draws out not a gun or knife but a pitch pipe. He blows softly into the key of B-flat, and then he begins to sing:

24

"My name is Kayo Rosen,
and cf all the boxers chosen
to spar with the Champ Jack Dempsey,
I'm the only one ain't gimpy."

"Well, friend, Jack Dempsey is not around Savannah to be sparred with," Bo Peep says to the stranger when he's done singing. "But why don't we step around the corner and discuss some form of employment for you."

The scene changes, and suddenly we find ourselves in a place that by all appearances seems to be a casino. There are tables for black jack, craps, poker and roulette, and Bo Peep explains to Kayo Rosen that although he has no need for a sparring partner, he could use a "keeper of decorum," or bouncer, at this, the Owl Club. It is a hidden spot in the dead of night, and a brilliant and mysterious crowd of society types and shadowy underworld figures are in attendance.

Kayo Rosen surveys the scene and agrees to the proposition, and in no time at all the decorum of the Owl Club is improved 100 percent. There are no more arguments, no bickering, no shouting, no cursing, no drunks, and no stiffs. In fact, all the fun seems gone out of the place, and many of the regular customers are finding the new atmosphere to be too sterile for their taste and longing for the old days—that is, until trouble comes staggering into the Owl Club intent on causing some type of disturbance.

Kayo Rosen leans over and quietly instructs the intruder to "pick it up and get it out of the club," and here's where the intruder makes a tactical error for he tells Kayo where he can go and what he can do when he gets there. But before he can fill in the details, Kayo grabs the intruder by the throat and squeezes until his mouth flies open like a trap door and his tongue jumps out like a jack-in-the-box. Kayo grabs the guy's tongue and releases his choke hold to pull out a knife, turns to Bo Peep and says, "Mister Bo Peep, you want I should make you a tongue sandwich?" The whole crowd is hushed and breathless.

"No, Kayo, tongue is not on my diet," Bo Peep replies, and in one swift move, Kayo dropkicks the intruder out of the Owl Club and into Congress Lane. Play is resumed at the games of chance, and Kayo returns to his seat by the door where he is joined by a dapper gentleman named Buster White, known to one and all as the local promoter of such cultural events as boxing and wrestling, and is sometimes referred to as "Snow" White— not for any resemblance to the fairy tale character—but because he is always giving patrons the old "snow job" on his next Stellar Fistic Attraction; it is not an uncommon thing for Buster White to advertise that he has "Sugar Ray" Robinson on the card and up pops "Sugar Boy" Robinson, a midget piano player, as a last minute replacement. And whenever revenue agents ask him about the gate receipts, Buster's stock answer is, "We may break even." If there's one empty seat in the house, Buster points to it and says, "We lost money." In fact, the only time Buster White is forced to admit making a profit on a promotion was the night Chief Sanouk, the Indian heavyweight champion, wrestled the Black Monster from places unknown. There were so many bodies packed into the city auditorium that the last lucky few to gain admittance were assisted by a shoe horn, and still Buster sold tickets to stand outside and look in the window. "Of course, street level windows are more expensive than the ones on the second story," Buster said, and then laughed as if it was the funniest thing he'd ever heard.

"I like the way you handled yourself just then," Buster White says to Kayo Rosen. "Obviously, you are a guy who mixes it up every now and then for fun and profit, and I was just thinking that I have an open slot for someone to fight in the main event at my next Stellar Fistic Attraction."

Instead of reaching for his pitch pipe and crooning his resume, Kayo claps a hand over Buster's mouth and stops him in mid-proposition. "I don't dance in the squared circle no more," Kayo says, "but for a piece of the action I can deliver a first-class act to round out your main event."

Now Kayo Rosen, being new to Savannah, has no one in particular in mind for the job, but for a piece of the action he intends to launch a citywide talent search to fill the bill. Before setting out on his way, Kayo needs to know who the opponent will be, which is like asking Buster who is going to be the next premier of China; one never knows who will get into the ring at one of Buster's Stellar Fistic Attractions.

"The main event will feature none other than Steve Snolesky, who is in need of a tune-up bout before challenging the title later in the year," Buster says, though he never says which title or whether it's for a boxing match or oyster-eating contest. Kayo has never heard of Snolesky, but Buster assures him that Snolesky is the current OTCOMBA champion, which sounds impressive and official, even if it does mean "Off the Coast of Madagascar Boxing Association."

And so Kayo takes off in search of an opponent for Steve Snolesky. In making his rounds, Kayo happens upon Johnny "Black Tom #1" Thomas and his brother Tommy, also known as "Black Tom #2." The Thomas brothers are called "Black" because they are very dark about the hair and whiskers and even when clean-shaven they appear to have coal dust on their faces. The Black Toms own a honky-tonk strategically placed just beyond Savannah city limits so as to avoid certain ordinances regarding business hours and activities that can legally take place upon the premises.

"I'm looking for a palooka to get in the ring with some guy named Snorinsky," Kayo explains to the Black Toms. "The guy don't have to be Joe Louis, but he should know his left from his right and be able to get into the ring without tripping over the announcer's microphone cord. I can teach a guy enough moves to make a match out of it, and if you can help me find a guy, I will give you a piece of the action."

Black Tom #1 confers with Black Tom #2, and together they come up with a solution. "There's a guy hangs around here always gettin' into scrapes," Black Tom #1 says. "His name is Angel Romero, and he's gone a few rounds in his day. The thing is, he's just off the boat from Puerto Rico, and his English ain't too good. But for a piece of the action, I can come along and act as his whaddyacallit...interpreter."

This news comes as revelation to Black Tom #2, who did not know his brother could speak Spanish. Furthermore, in Black Tom #2's opinion, Kayo Rosen has a better chance of beating Steve Snolesky with Mrs. Romero, known to the police as Shopping Bag Betty, for her penchant for entering department stores with an empty shopping bag and departing with it full, without paying. Black Tom #2 has seen Angel Romero go a few rounds with Mrs. Romero, and considers that Shopping Bag Betty takes a better punch.

From out of the back of Black Tom's nightclub comes a Latin-looking bruiser who is rattling off something that would be understood in Miami or Havana but not Savannah. He is very excited and his voice is strong. Black Tom #1 explains in a cross between Spanish, sign language and Pidgin English that he has gotten Angel Romero a fight for which he will be paid hard cash, although Black Tom #1 neglects to mention how hard this cash is going to be. First, it is going to be very hard to get this cash from Buster White, and second, it's going to be a lot less once Kayo Rosen and the Black Toms have taken their piece of the action. After more yelling and gesticulating, it appears to Kayo Rosen that he has in Angel Romero a promising challenger for Steve

Snolesky. In fact, Kayo figures if Angel can fight like he can yell, then the match with Snolesky should be a real humdinger.

The scene changes, and we are back at Bo Peep's on Congress Street. It is the afternoon of the big fight, and everyone has gathered here to find out the latest line and get their bets down. An argument has divided the room into two camps: on one side we have Irwin "Prominent" Price, who runs the cash register at Bo Peep's, and makes Angel Romero the odds-on favorite, and on the other side we have Costa Alfieris, also known as Gus, who favors Steve Snolesky.

Prominent Price's opinion is seconded by John Sutlive, editor of the Savannah Evening Press, "Irish" Billy Dyer, Walter "Statesboro" Crawford, Rocky Tarantino, Gus Gottlieb, Julius "The Champ" Kaminsky and his nephew Sol "The King," Harry "The Chicken Man" Barr, Dazzy Carroll, and Johnny "The Roo" Rousakis. Costa aka Gus is backed by Reuben "Chooley" Cooley, Johnny "The Golden Greek" Chiboucas, Joe "Little Horse" Mooney, Allie "T" Anderson, Walter "The Road Man" Howard, Lewis "Super Jew" Kooden, Johnny "Hard Rock" Hiers, "Booger Red" Patterson, Tracy "The Trigger" Matheson, Hansell "The Gas Man" Hillyer, and lastly, Joe "The Rubber King" Kent, who received his colorful moniker during the war when he made his living riding a bike around Savannah and peddling condoms to teenagers.

Before Bo Peep begins scribbling cryptic notes of betting wagers on little slips of paper, Buster White steps into the middle of the fracas and announces a last minute change in the card: Steve Snolesky is a no-show, and his replacement will be none other than Sailor Jackie Bumpinsky. There is a collective groan from the assembly, and while no one is surprised at this development, it will bear a remarkable effect on the odds. Prominent Price still says Angel Romero is a 3-1 favorite, and has no end of pleasure in making fun of Costa aka Gus's side for backing a boxer who is a figment of Buster White's imagination.

The scene changes, and we are transported to the city auditorium. The dressing room of Angel Romero is a regular carnival as Darby Hicks from Hicksville, acting as trainer, is wrapping Angel Romero's hands with gauze and tape. Kayo Rosen is watching over Darby's shoulder, and Black Tom #1 is on hand for whaddya-callit...interpreting. Darby Hicks from Hicksville is looking around the dressing room and in and out of his trainer's bag as if something is missing. Black Tom #2 is guessing that Darby is looking for Vaseline or Q-tips, but the object of Darby's search is a lead fishing sinker to put inside the hand wrap to give Angel Romero a more solid punch.

Kayo Rosen points out to Darby Hicks from Hicksville that the use of foreign objects such as lead sinkers is frowned upon by the Savannah Boxing Commission, although Darby Hicks says this rule went out with bare knuckle fights and that he customarily includes a lead fishing sinker in many a boxer's hand wraps. Black Tom #1 concedes that Darby Hicks from Hicksville is one mean hand wrapper at that, while Black Tom #2 states that he thinks Kayo Rosen is taking too much heed of some antiquated rules.

"I am also very sure that had Prominent Price known there would be a lead fishing sinker in Angel Romero's gloves," Black Tom #2 adds, "the odds on Sailor Jackie would be considerably higher."

So Darby Hicks from Hicksville finishes wrapping the hands of Angel Romero without the sinker and pronounces him as ready as he'll ever be, just as Buster White elbows his way into the dressing room and announces that the crowd is ready for the fight to commence and that we should be making our way into the ring.

We exit the dressing room and make our way toward the arena. It is very dark under the bleachers where the dressing rooms are located, and we can hear a band playing something that sounds like "La Cucaracha." Angel Romero breaks into a rumba step, Kayo Rosen is trying to get the shag to work with his big, flat feet, and Darby Hicks is doing something called "Peckin' All Around," which is a dance step that is very popular in Hicksville, and Darby Hicks is the Peckin' champion of three states. And as we make our way down the aisle, the crowd from Bo Peep's rises to its feet, yelling at our entourage. Some discouraging words can be heard from a few wisenheimers, although they are careful not to direct these comments directly at Kayo Rosen.

We climb into the ring and Angel Romero is jumping up and down like he's happy to be here. From the other side of the ring we hear some noise, and the band strikes up "Anchors Aweigh" as Sailor Jackie Bumpinsky makes his way towards us. Sailor Jackie enters the ring with the hood of his robe pulled low over his face, and is jookin' and jivin' with his back turned to our corner. Referee Joe McGhee summons both sides to the center of the ring for instructions, and at a glance it looks like a gang fight is going to erupt: Angel Romero is accompanied by his manager Kayo Rosen, his trainer Darby Hicks from Hicksville, and Black Tom #1, his whaddyacallit...interpreter. Black Tom #2 has tagged along as assistant interpreter, but Buster White claims he is only trying to avoid paying for a ticket and thereby cause him not to break even. On the other side, Sailor Jackie Bumpinsky is backed by his manager Sleep-Out Charlie Nofkee and his second "Scarface" Tony Backala; there are more people onstage than at an Ebba Thompson dance school recital.

As Referee Joe McGhee is running down the rules in English, Black Tom #1 is going through a pantomime for the benefit of Angel Romero, who all of a sudden goes from a dark tan to a Marcel Marceau in make-up white as Sailor Jackie's hood is pulled back to reveal a face that has taken more stitches than grandma's needlepoint sampler. Sailor Jackie has so many scars that he looks like he's had 100 fights and lost 99 on cuts. Even Kayo Rosen squints at the sight, and I figure Kayo Rosen has seen some ugly kissers in his time.

Referee Joe McGhee concludes his lecture and everybody bails out of the ring except for Joe and the two fighters, one of whom—our boy—is paralyzed with fear.

The bell rings for the first round and both fighters cautiously move to the center of the ring. The pace is so slow that Referee Joe McGhee cracks, "What are you slug nutties waitin' on, an invitation?" This provokes Sailor Jackie into throwing a wild left hook at Angel Romero that misses by more than a Gimmee putt. Angel Romero ducks and runs for cover, then goes into a peek-a-boo defense, which is a lot of peeking out from behind his gloves and a lot of booing from the audience.

Sailor Jackie unleashes another wild swing and in trying to avoid it, Angel Romero throws up his hands and accidentally brushes Sailor Jackie's hair. Much to everyone's surprise, Sailor Jackie's eyes roll back into his head and he hits the deck like he's just been kicked by a mule. He rolls over on his back and is lying spread eagle on the mat as if he's enjoying the rays on the beach at Tybee.

Angel Romero is so stunned that he stands stock still in the middle of the ring until Referee Joe McGhee pushes him into a neutral corner, then begins the count to ten. The crowd from Bo Peep's is on its feet, screaming at Sailor Jackie Bumpinsky for taking a dive. Joe McGhee picks up the count at three and counting four threatens Sailor Jackie, "You don't get up, you don't get paid! Five! No more fight, no money! Six! You heard me, Sailor Jackie, either you get up or I'm withholding your purse!"

Sailor Jackie's eyes are now wide open and he's beginning to stir, although he's in somewhat of a dilemma for Sailor Jackie has taken the odds and wagered his purse on Angel Romero to win; if he gets up and beats Angel Romero, Sailor Jackie loses everything.

Angel Romero is hyperventilating in the neutral corner, moments away from a first-round one-punch knockout, when Sailor Jackie Bumpinsky hops up before the count of eight, intent on giving the crowd a show before he takes another dive. In fact, Angel Romero is still hyperventilating when Sailor Jackie crosses the ring and bangs a solid right to his jaw that sends Angel Romero through the ropes and into Mrs. Romero's lap seated on the third row. Referee Joe McGhee counts him out; had he kept counting, it would've been eight o'clock the next morning before Angel Romero awakens.

The scene changes, the crowd returns to the Owl Club where there is the usual settling of the ledger and accounting for the winners and losers. Buster White has absconded with the gate receipts so as not to have to entertain the thought of refunds, but not before Kayo Rosen has extracted Angel Romero's purse. By the time Kayo Rosen has taken his piece of the action, then Darby Hicks from Hicksville and the Black Toms, Angel Romero would've made more money had he been scrounging for loose change beneath the bleachers of the auditorium. And Sailor Jackie Bumpinsky walks away with nothing, having lost his winnings on his bet.

In the aftermath of Buster White's Stellar Fistic Attraction there looks to be a better fight among the gang at Bo Peep's, who are still arguing the pros and cons of a one-punch prizefight. I am pushed further and further from the center of the action until I am elbowed out the door onto Congress Street, where I am narrowly missed by a passing car.

In a blaze of light the scene is over. It was too bright and blinding to comprehend all at once, and it flashed before me so fast that from the very first I felt I had missed things. The Owl Club was gone, and the crowd was nowhere in sight. I looked for Bo Peep and thought I saw him sitting on a park bench in Johnson Square, but I couldn't be sure. Struggling to remember the scene that was slipping farther and farther away from me, I turned toward home along cobbled streets, through parks and squares. Starting at River Street and heading south, Savannah is a living time line, each block more recent than the last, so that it is a walk through history, from past to present. At the end of my journey, Habersham and the Sixties, I am back among the living and firmly rooted in the Now.

My wife greets me at the door; she's been worried. She takes my raincoat, shaking the fog out of the pockets. Feeling something strange, she reaches in for a heavy object and studies it closely. "What is this?" she asks.

"A lead fishing sinker," I reply, and leave it at that.

Bo Peep (left) playing Dice

GREAT SAVANNAH STORIES

WHY TELL THE STORY OF JESSE McKETHAN AFTER ALL THESE YEARS?

Last year at the height of the tourist season when the museum houses were running low on staff, I joined the merry band of distinguished men and women who conduct tours of the Juliette Gordon Low Birthplace located on the corner of Bull and Oglethorpe streets. I considered it my civic duty to lend a hand, and help visitors to our fair city appreciate the finer points of one of our first families. I was given a biography of Juliette—we call her Daisy, as did her family—and a 50-page description of the house and its contents, and while mastering the material I was surprised at the wealth of information about Savannah's history that I picked up along the way; I am glad I did it.

It didn't take long for the senior staff members to realize that I was much better at giving good porch. That is to say that I was of great assistance entertaining people who have to wait as much as 30 minutes on the front porch for the next tour. Oh, I tried to show off my astounding knowledge of the Gordons but I was soon reduced to a human weathervane, pointing in which direction lay The Lady and Sons, Mrs. Wilkes, and Clary's. It seems that the only thing tourists want to do is eat, and for many visitors eating is all they can find to do.

If I heard it once, I heard it a thousand times: there's nothing to do in Savannah. Once a tourist has ridden around the squares in a trolley and taken a tour of one or two museums, they wander around until they end up at City Market or down on River Street...and we're back to eating and drinking.

Here's a fun fact: in 1999, tourists spent more than $900 million in Savannah, but the average length of stay was only a day and a half.

So I conducted a survey of tourists to find out what they came here expecting to see and did not find. The overwhelming majority of them said that they came here—some from halfway around the world—just to have a "Midnight in the Garden of Good and Evil" experience.

Unfortunately, they found out there is no "Midnight Experience" to be had here. You can't tour Mercer House, the primary cast of characters is dead, and unless you want to watch Lady Chablis careen through a tired routine of disco and dishy repartee at Club One, then you're down to swattin' sand gnats while searching for Danny Hansford's grave—which isn't where Clint Eastwood's movie moved it.

I don't get it, really. Maybe I'm all alone in this world but I don't understand what all the "Midnight" fuss is about. I read the book when it was first published. I wanted to like it, but before I was halfway through I could no longer recognize my hometown. I never heard about drag queens and voodoo priestesses when I was growing up here, and as far as the tragedy of Jim and Danny is concerned, I thought it was a cheap and nasty story about sad and pathetic people.

It seemed to me that John Berendt came to Savannah from New York with his skewed "Gone with the Wind" sensibilities and "Cat on a Hot Tin Roof" perceptions, found a freak, a fairy and a fool and attempted to elevate them to a stature befitting the Gordons and Mercers. Apparently, while reading Berendt's words, these readers from around the world conjured up such a gothic vision of this town that they just had to see it for themselves.

It was only after Clint Eastwood, of all people, made a movie based on Berendt's book that many readers saw for the first time how cheap and nasty the story really is. Of course, Savannah photographs beautifully, and that is reason enough for tourists to visit here even after all the "Midnight" mess has died down.

The heirs to Jim Williams' estate are still trying to milk "Midnight" for all its worth. Jim's sister paraded him before the public in a second book, "More than Mercer House: Savannah's Jim Williams and His Southern Houses," as if he were the patron saint of preservationists. She put Mercer House on the market for an unheard of sum of $9 million, as if it were a national landmark instead of the scene of a national disgrace. I mean, you can buy half of Savannah for $9 million. How does shooting a poor street hustler in the parlor warrant asking $9 million for this dwelling? If an indoor firing range is the criteria, then there are lots of $9 million houses around town.

I always thought that if the heirs of the Williams estate wanted to make millions, why not open Mercer House to tourists who complain of having nothing to do. Although, if I owned Mercer House, I wouldn't want a steady stream of strangers tromping through my living room searching for blood stains on the carpet, even at $5 a head. There's just something very sad, very desperate and rather distasteful about the whole sordid affair.

Of course, it doesn't help matters when the mayor bellies his way into a public ceremony in Forsyth Park and makes loud proclamations about what splendid things John Berendt has done for our city. The mayor even went so far as to suggest that Berendt buy a house here, instead of remaining a mere honorary citizen. To which Berendt retorted that Savannah should "give" him a house, out of appreciation. Perhaps Berendt should take some of the money he made from the book and film and buy Mercer House for $9 million. Now *there's* an idea.

As a writer, my chief complaint with "Midnight" is that it's a lousy murder mystery. Actually, there's no mystery here. That Jim murdered Danny is common knowledge throughout the world except among four juries in Chatham County. There's more suspense in playing a game of Clue than in reading Berendt's book, and for fans of true crime there are far better stories out there than this one. Why, there are tales of debauchery and murder that took place in Savannah to make "Midnight" look like Mother Goose. And to prove it, just to put my money where my Midnight is, I'm going to relate the shocking story of Jesse McKethan.

Anyone living in Savannah in 1945 will know whom I'm talking about, because the nature of the crime he committed is unforgettable. Less than 90 days following the horrors of dropping atom bombs on Hiroshima and Nagasaki, Savannah was shaken to its foundation by the Butcher Murder near Daffin Park. In a brilliant piece of detective work, police apprehended the suspect in a matter of days. The suspect confessed to the crime and was found guilty of murder at the end of a trial that lasted two days. He was sentenced to death in the electric chair, and it was many years before the subject of the Butcher Murder ceased to be a topic of conversation around town.

Which is why one of the relatives of the victim in this case asked me pointedly, "Why bring it up again now?"

That is a very good question, and one that better have a very good answer.

My purpose in reminding us of the story of Jesse McKethan is also an attempt to remind us of what we were like before "Midnight in the Garden of Good and Evil" robbed us of our senses. Back in 1945, even though we had survived a world war during which crimes against humanity created Hell on Earth, Savannahians were not so calloused by the daily horrors on the front pages of the newspaper not to be disgusted by the Butcher Murder.

When it was all over, when justice had been served, no one wrote a book about the Butcher Murder. And no one made a movie about it, either. And neighbors didn't shamelessly go into business conducting tours of Kehoe Ward, nor did the McKethans attempt to prosper from the tragedy by putting their house on the market for millions of dollars. No, what we did was tear down the house and bulldoze the land into a vacant lot, to put the very sight of the place out of our collective memory. Apparently we did a very good job of it, because we have also forgotten what it was to react with decency towards acts of gross indecency.

People have quit asking surviving family members about the Butcher Murder. They don't discuss it for the amusement of strangers, and they don't sit before the Arts & Entertainment Channel's cameras to gossip about this quaint little town and its quirky little murder mysteries; not discussing it—especially for lowly profit—is what decent people do.

Sometimes I think I must be crazy to do this because I fear the shitstorm of criticism from my neighbors who think "Midnight in the Garden of Good and Evil" is the greatest thing ever to happen here. But I happen to love my hometown, and I hope I'm not the only person who thinks that "Midnight" is a dark cloud with a silver lining that hangs over this town like moss.

It concerns me that the two aspects of life in this town that are best known throughout the rest of the world are an annual celebration of public drunkenness and a cheap and nasty murder. Yet the daily news is chock full of accounts of a rising rate of murder and mayhem, of drunken brawls and DUIs

We cannot have it both ways. We cannot celebrate a fashionable murder on Monterrey Square at boozy parties on a Saturday night, and then complain about the rash of killings on the West Side—or the robbery/murder of a tourist—in the harsh, sober light of Monday morning.

So, that is my answer to the question why bring up the Butcher Murder of 1945 again. Funny thing is, when I made this explanation to the sister of the Butcher's victim, she wished me luck with my assignment; she just so happens to agree with me. And after reading this story, maybe you will, too.

Oh, one other point before we get started: as you read these accounts, don't be too quick to rush to judgment. The case of Jesse McKethan isn't as easy to understand as Jim Williams. And as much as you old-timers think you know about it, believe me, I've turned up a few facts that will shock you even more than the crime itself; it was a rush to judgment 55 years ago that put a poor soul in the electric chair and the charred remains in an unmarked grave.

And I think we ought to take another look at that, too.

Jim

Editor's Note:
When ~~John~~ Williams died in 1990, he left the bulk of his estate to his mother. Upon her death, Mercer House and all its contents passed to Jim's sister, Dorothy Kingery, who wasted no time in taking inventory and culling 400 items to be sold at Sotheby's auction house in New York on October 20, 2000. The sale, entitled _Mercer House, Savannah: The Collection of the Late James A. Williams_, grossed a cool $1,708,040 for Dorothy, who decided to remain in residence at Mercer House until someone agreed to her exorbitant asking price. Less than four years later, with no sale pending, the heiress finally opened the newly renamed Mercer-Williams House to tourists at $12.50 a head, citing "enormous city and county taxes, escalating insurance premiums, and a hefty budget for maintenance" among her reasons for turning Savannah's most notorious den of iniquity into a tourist trap.

BEHIND THE MOSS CURTAIN

PART I
THE DISCOVERY

We wind the tape back to October 1945. In the aftermath of world war, proud veterans are returning home from Europe and the Pacific, just as the Nuremberg trials of Nazi war criminals are beginning. The City of Savannah is bounded by 60th Street to the South; DeRenne is a dirt road, and beyond is the old farm lots of Anson Ward. President Street Extension, the future home of hotels and industry, is Twickenham Plantation. And from Liberty Street to Gwinnett, between Paulsen and East Broad streets, is the Atlantic Coast Railroad yard.

A peaceful Monday morning around 8 a.m., and Roger Coursey of 1310 East 38th Street, is exercising his hunting dogs, a setter and a pointer, in the high grass of a vacant lot on the corner of 38th and Cedar streets, before heading off to work. The pointer stops dead in his tracks, sniffs, then jumps back and shies away from a mysterious object. Coursey wades through the weeds cautiously, thinking the dog has found a snake nest. He blanches at the sight of a severed human leg, mottled and moldy. He staggers back to his house and telephones police.

Detective Chief John McCarthy is among the first officers on the scene. He oversees photography and recovery of the leg, and then sends orders to the city lot for a crew to cut the grass in an effort to discover any other clues. Then he calls local hospitals to find no record

43

of any amputation that might shed light on the incubating case.

The severed leg is delivered to Dr. Emerson Ham, acting coroner, for examination. Dr. Ham pictures the victim as a white male from 25 to 35 years of age, about 180 pounds, rather chunky, with brown hair. He estimates that the amputation has been performed within the past ten days, and notes that there are no scars to indicate its removal by surgery.

"It's a complete circular cut with a slight angle," Dr. Ham tells McCarthy. "The bone has been sawed practically all the way through. Evidently the weight of the leg snapped the remaining portion. There is no indication of a doctor having made provisions for a flap of skin to cover the stump, and so we can definitely rule out medical procedure."

The conclusion of the coroner is the beginning of a murder investigation for McCarthy. It is on this slim thread of evidence that detectives start to unravel what will develop into the most heinous crime this city has ever seen.

Detective Chief McCarthy returns to the corner of 38th and Cedar streets with Detectives E.A. Fitzgerald, J.F. Brennan and W.J. Perkins to survey the scene where the leg had been discovered. Cutting back the grass reveals nothing. Starting from the vacant lot, the detectives spread out in all directions searching for clues.

On 41st Street between Cedar and Ash streets, the detectives find two large bloodstained paper bags in a second vacant lot. These are large, unsealed multi-walled bags of a type commonly used for fertilizer or cement. Detective Fitzgerald notices that the bags are incomplete, sort of factory rejects.

"Find out where these bags come from and you find your suspect," McCarthy says to his men.

"If the blood on the bags matches the leg, then I'd say the slayer works at Union Bag," Fitzgerald deduces.

"No one but an employee of the bag factory has access to unfinished bags."

Detectives Brennan and Perkins search the missing persons file and turn up the name of George Luther Aids, a 17-year-old boy, reported missing since October 8th. After sizing up his description, Brennan and Perkins make a personal call to the home of Mr. and Mrs. George W. Aids at 819 East 36th Street, to determine if the leg could possibly be their son's. They are greeted at the door by Mrs. Aids, an attractive woman in her mid-thirties, and she is so charming and pleasant that Detective Brennan decides to ease his way into the mission rather than lead with the shocking news of the discovery.

"When was the last time either of you saw your son?" Brennan begins.

"Sunday evening a week ago," says Mr. Aids. "I own the Shipyard Inn, at the corner of Bay Street Extension and Lathrop Avenue. It's a restaurant and a package shop. I lent Luther my car, and he dropped by in the evening. I don't know who he had with him. The next morning around 7:30, I saw the car parked next door in the middle of the street, but Luther wasn't here. And the keys to the car were gone. All I found in the car was my wrench on the floor in the rear."

"Who was the last person to see Luther?" Brennan continues.

"That would be an old acquaintance named Jesse McKethan," says Mrs. Aids. "We call him Mac, and they have been friends forever. Mac is such a sweet boy. He's terribly concerned about Luther. He calls or comes by just about every day to see if we've heard from him. But, to answer your question, officer, on Tuesday morning I called over to the McKethan's around nine and woke Mac up to ask him if he knew where Luther was, and he said he hadn't seen him since late Sunday night."

Mr. Aids cuts in. "The strange thing is, later that same day Mac came over here and told us a story about Luther running off to North Carolina with a lady in a Buick automobile. He said he thought the lady was a French teacher over at the vocational school where Luther wanted to enroll in a night course. Mac said Luther had met her at Johnny Harris's barbecue stand on Victory Drive, and that she had been trying to get him to go away with her for some time but he wouldn't go. But Mac was pretty sure Luther had gone away with her Sunday night."

"Has Luther ever run off before?" Perkins follows up.

"Yes, and that's why I wasn't too surprised to hear Mac's story," says Mr. Aids. "Luther's only seventeen, but he's run off here and there since he was fourteen. He and Mac have been all over the state. They ran off to Florida, and over to South Carolina. Luther has only recently returned from spending about two years down in Panama City, where he worked for a cousin. It isn't like him to be gone this long without telling us where he is. But if anyone knows where Luther is, it's Mac. He always knows where Luther is."

"Do you know where this McKethan boy lives?" Brennan asks.

"He lives with his father, Peyton, at 1101 East Thirty-eighth Street," Mrs. Aids says. "Mr. McKethan used to work for the power company, but I think he works for the city or county now."

And before Brennan and Perkins can get another word in edgewise, Mrs. Aids is off again.

"Now, Missus McKethan died back in July, poor thing. And all three of Mac's brothers are dead from the same heart ailment that kept Mac out of the army. Did either of you gentlemen know Mac's brother, Linwood? He was a policeman, and he died all of a sudden, back in June of Forty-three."

46

Brennan and Perkins exchange glances.

"Yes, ma'am, we knew him," Perkins says, and then the room lapses into an awkward silence.

"You wouldn't happen to know where the McKethan boy works, would you?" Brennan asks, changing the subject.

"Mac works at Union Bag," says Mrs. Aids.

Brennan and Perkins exchange glances, only this time a different look registers on their faces. A red flag goes up, a bright light has switched on.

"I have some rather unpleasant news that you should know about," Brennan announces. "We found part of a man's body in a vacant lot near here this morning."

There is a gasp from Mrs. Aids as her hands cover her gaping mouth. Her husband sits in stunned silence, a sickening sensation coming over him in waves.

"Now, we don't know who this leg belongs to," Brennan quickly adds, trying to allay their fears. "We haven't found anything else. But the coroner says it's a young man with brown hair, and that the incident happened about ten days ago. You might want to go over to the coroner's office and see for yourself if it might be your son."

And it is usually at this point in these procedures that police officers like to take their leave and give families a chance to come to grips with the possibilities. After giving Mr. Aids the phone numbers for Detective Chief McCarthy and Dr. Ham, the detectives excuse themselves and make a bee line back to police barracks to inform Detective Fitzgerald that a visit to Union Bag might begin and very well end with talking to Jesse McKethan. The detectives save themselves a trip downtown when they happen upon Fitzgerald and McCarthy five blocks from the Aids home, surveying the lot on 41st Street where the bloody bags had been found.

"Small world," Fitzgerald says, when his partners mention the name Jesse McKethan. "He was just by here with some old lady, and they stood and watched us for awhile. I recognized him as Linwood's brother, but I didn't say anything to him."

"Which reminds me," McCarthy chimes in, "we got some complaints about Jesse from some of the mothers of younger boys around here that he was putting their kids to sleep or trying to hypnotize them by rubbing a nerve in their neck. It's a technique magicians use. But because Jesse's brother was a cop, the chief took him aside and gave him a warning. Told him if he didn't cut it out, the chief would put Jesse in a padded cell."

"So what do you want us to do?" Fitzgerald asks McCarthy. "Do you want us to bring McKethan downtown?"

"No, I don't," McCarthy says. "I believe if we just watch and wait, he'll lead us to the rest of the body, if it's him. If it ain't him, I don't want to go off half-cocked because that boy and his daddy have had enough grief to last a lifetime without accusing him of something like this. Being employed by Union Bag ain't a crime. They's lots of people employed by Union Bag. It may just be a coincidence. For now, we watch and wait."

And speaking of coincidences, later in the evening after George Aids has gone to work at the Shipyard Inn, Jesse McKethan drops in on Mrs. Aids to make his daily inquiry as to Luther's whereabouts. For the first time she appears distraught, and Jesse senses something is wrong before she can tell him what it is.

"The police were by here earlier today," Mrs. Aids tells Jesse. "They found a man's leg a few blocks away in a vacant lot. It has me very upset, Mac. You don't think it's Luther's leg, do you?"

"Absolutely not," Jesse says. "I'm tellin' ya, I saw him leave with his teacher in her Buick. I think what we should do is go look for them. I bet if we drive around

48

we'll find 'em. We can ride out to the Gold Star Ranch where I last saw them and look around. You'll have to drive, though. I don't know how to drive."

"Alright, Mac, that sounds like a good idea," says Mrs. Aids. "I just knew you'd have a solution."

Mrs. Aids and Jesse McKethan drive out to the country, bringing her daughter Marjorie and her friend Lester along for the ride. They cruise along White Bluff Road, just south of the globe gas tank, to where the Gold Star Ranch is situated, between Hunter Airfield and "the fields" where rednecks go to shoot rabbits. The Gold Star is a popular hangout where teens slip away to watch midget automobile races and play at amusements, grab a bite to eat and sneak a few beers. The drive does Mrs. Aids no end of good, and even though they do not find Luther or his new flame, her mood brightens. Jesse feels better, too.

After returning home, Jesse promises Mrs. Aids that he will stop by again tomorrow, as usual. It's around 8 p.m., and Jesse meets up with friends and they walk over to Pop Payne's place on 36th and Waters Avenue to have a few beers. The evening breaks up around eleven, and Jesse leaves alone. He meanders through Kehoe Ward, wandering past the freshly mown vacant lots. He crosses the grass plat dividing Victory Drive at Live Oak Street and makes his way to Daffin Park, where he continues around the edge of the pool. He makes his way across the bridge to the island in the middle of the pool, disappearing briefly from sight into the bushes. Emerging from the underbrush. Jesse walks home along the same route he came.

Every step he takes is counted, every move he makes carefully observed from a distance by Detective Fitzgerald.

* * *

Early Tuesday morning, Mrs. Aids arrives at the McKethan house as Peyton McKethan is having his coffee. She and her husband are on their way to meet Detective Chief McCarthy, and they want Jesse to come along to provide details about the mysterious French teacher who absconded with their son. Peyton finds it impossible to rouse his sleeping son, and tells Mrs. Aids that the boy isn't well. He promises to send Jesse right over, as soon as he's feeling better.

Jesse arises around eleven, and makes his way over to the Aids residence. They are not home, so he sits on the front porch and waits for what seems like hours. Mr. and Mrs. Aids arrive around 3 p.m., and they are not even out of their car before Jesse presses to know details of their whereabouts.

"I saw the story in the morning paper about finding the leg," he says. "So, did you see it?"

"No, we didn't," Mr. Aids says. "We spent the morning with the detective. Wish you could've gone with us. Feelin' better?"

There was something about Mr. Aids' tone that Jesse did not like. But then again, he had always felt that Luther's father did not like him. He ignored the question about his health and quickly shifted the attention back to the news.

"The paper said the leg was found by Mr. Coursey in the 1300 block of East Thirty-eighth. That's just a couple blocks from my house. I know exactly where it is," Jesse says, excitedly. "But the paper said the victim was 25 to 35 years old, and Luther is only seventeen. Like I told you yesterday, I bet it isn't Luther's leg. Why don't we go over there and look around, see for ourselves?"

Mr. Aids studies the boy's face intently. "Yeah, Mac. Why don't we do that? Hop in the back, there. I'll drive us over."

At the vacant lot on the corner of 38th and Cedar, Jesse jumps out of the car and leads Mr. and Mrs.

Aids to the exact spot where the leg had been found the previous morning. Roger Coursey spots the activity from his house just a few steps away, and walks over to introduce himself.

"My boy is missing," Mr. Aids tells Coursey. "I think the leg is his. I'd appreciate it if you could tell me what it looked like."

"It's hard to say because it was in pretty rough shape, but it looked to me like it had a scar here and here," Coursey says, pointing to places near the knee.

At the mention of scars, Mrs. Aids whitens. She has been fighting the feeling deep inside that whispers over and over, "Your son is dead," hoping this is all a mistake. But the placement of the scars convinces her that this is no coincidence. Her heightened anxiety charges the air with a static electricity that causes Jesse McKethan to circle the lot in an agitated manner, like a child frantically searching for a four-leaf clover.

Mr. Aids nods his head, thinking. "Mr. Coursey, I wonder could you let your dogs loose again and see if they find anything else," he asks.

"No, I don't mind," Coursey says, haltingly. "The thing is, I'm just on my way out. I got to run up the country, but I tell you what: I could do it tomorrow afternoon, if that's alright."

"Sure, thanks," Mr. Aids says, but he can tell Coursey doesn't mean it. Tomorrow means never, and Coursey has already seen more severed body parts in his neighborhood than he wants to; he does not want to upset the dogs.

Coursey expresses his condolences, turns and walks away. Mr. Aids goes over to his car where his wife is slumped in the front seat with a faraway look in her eyes.

"You all right, Mamma?" he says to her.

Mrs. Aids makes no response. She is watching Jesse hunting through the grass in dizzy circles.

51

"Yeah," he says loudly, as if to clear his throat. "The party who brought the leg here was the same party that drove my car home...and he didn't know how to drive, neither," he says, in Jesse's direction.

The comment startles Jesse, and causes him to break off and head down the lane that runs along the back of the lot in an opposite direction from the car.

"Yeah, whoever drove my car home left it parked in the middle of the street," Mr. Aids says, his voice rising in volume. "It was turned sideways to the curb. It wasn't parked straight! Luther didn't drive it home!"

Jesse pretends not to hear. He just keeps walking. For the rest of the afternoon, he wanders throughout the entire ward looking for body parts and clues. Mr. and Mrs. Aids follow behind closely, watching Jesse more than anything else. Late in the day as it nears time for George to go to work, he calls off the chase.

"Maybe you should come down to the police station and tell the detectives about this French teacher," he challenges Jesse. And to his complete surprise, Jesse agrees to go.

They arrive at the police barracks and Mr. Aids is disappointed to find none of the detectives in their offices. They are on the street conducting interviews at Union Bag and in Kehoe Ward. From the barracks, Mr. Aids drives over to Henderson Brothers Funeral Home.

"I guess I gotta see this leg," he says to his wife. "I don't wanna do it, but I guess I gotta. I hate to say it, but I think it's Luther."

One look at Dahlia and George can tell that it would be better for his wife if she does not go inside with him. "I tell you what," he says to her, "you take Mac here back home. I may be awhile."

George turns away, but before Dahlia can slide behind the wheel he turns and says to her, "If you don't feel like drivin' maybe you should let Mac drive. Oh, that's right. You don't drive, do you, Mac?"

"No, sir," Mac says, from the backseat. "I don't know how."

Mrs. Aids moves behind the wheel and drives without realizing where she's going. Jesse is still sitting in the back seat and is so quiet that she forgets he's in the car. She is startled when he speaks.

"Mr. Aids hates me," Jesse says.

Mrs. Aids looks at him in the rearview mirror. "You're always saying that, Mac, and it isn't true. Mr. Aids doesn't hate you. He's just upset. I'm sure you can understand that."

Jesse thinks awhile. "Miz Aids, do you recall a murder case here some years ago when a woman killed her husband for the insurance? She got by with it. Do you remember?"

"I seem to recall something about it," she says. "Why do you bring that up, Mac?"

"How much insurance does Mr. Aids got?"

"Well, I don't know, Mac. We don't talk about it."

"Why don't we kill him?" Jesse suggests, as easily as if he's asking for the time of day. "We can get by with it."

"Why, Jesse," she says, "I'm shocked to hear you say such a thing. What in the world has gotten into you?"

"He said the person who put the leg in the vacant lot was the same person who drove the car back to the house and left it parked in the middle of the street. He thinks I did it."

"Don't be foolish," Mrs. Aids says.

Mrs. Aids drops off Jesse at his house and goes home to wait for her husband. She knew if he had bad news that he would come home and tell her face to face, but that if it was good news he would call because he wouldn't be able to wait. So when the telephone rang and Dahlia heard George's voice, she was elated.

53

"I looked at the thing and couldn't tell," George said to her. "It could be anybody."

It isn't given to us to know those rare moments when people are wide open and the slightest touch can wither or heal, but George Aids knew his wife better than most men know theirs, and with a grace that comes from a higher power he gave her one last deep breath of relief before a harsher reality sets in.

PART II:
THE ARREST

October 16, 1945

Tuesday evening, while George Aids is tending his bar at the Shipyard Inn, his wife is at home making dinner for their daughters. Dahlia is glad to have something to take her mind off of the gruesome discoveries of the severed leg and bloody bags in their neighborhood. When she looks up to find Jesse McKethan standing in her living room, she is actually glad to have his company. Now that she is almost 100 percent certain that the severed leg is not her son, Jesse seems like less of a suspect and more like the old family friend she always relies upon to find Luther when no one else can. And if Jesse appears less threatening, perhaps it is because he is in the company of another young man.

"Miz Aids, this is Carroll Hendrix," Jesse says. "Carroll was with me and Luther on Sunday night. He was with us the whole time, weren't you, Carroll?"

"Yes, ma'am," Carroll says "I met Mac and Luther at the skating rink. We went over to the fairground in Thunderbolt but it was closed, so we went over to the Bamboo Gardens and then over to Cleve Ellis's place for a drink. Then we went out to the Gold Star Ranch."

"Tell what happened next." Jesse says, prompting him.

"Luther left with a girl," Carroll says, and Jesse nods his head vigorously in agreement. "He was gone a long time, maybe forty-five minutes. Then he came back and got us so he could take us home. He said he had a late date."

"See?" Jesse says, emphatically, to Mrs. Aids. "So here's what I think we ought to do: there's a fortune teller in Port Wentworth who is real good at finding out things about people no one else knows. I think we should all go see her right now."

Mrs. Aids is completely caught up in the excitement of the moment. She grabs her daughter, takes Jesse and Carroll by the hand and jumps in the car on her way to Port Wentworth. The Shipyard Inn is on the way, and Mrs. Aids stops to tell her husband what she's up to.

"Are you out of your mind?" George shouts at Dahlia, snatching her by the arm and squeezing tight. "You take Margaret and git on back home right now. I want you to lock the door and don't let anybody in, especially Mac and this guy."

"Why? What's the matter, George?"

"I just don't trust that kid, and until we find Luther, I don't want you riding out to the middle of nowhere with him. Now, I want you and Margaret to go out the back door. I'll handle Mac and this guy."

Mr. Aids walks outside to the car parked at the curb in front of the Shipyard Inn and instructs his daughter to get out and go inside. "Mrs. Aids will not be going to any fortune teller tonight or any other night," he says to Jesse. "The police are handling this matter, and they don't need no tea leaves and crystal balls. You go on about your business, and let the police handle it, hear?"

Jesse and Carroll take the bus back to Kehoe Ward. They stop in Pop Payne's place where they meet up with a couple and have a few beers. They are talking about the same topic everyone else in town is talking about: the discovery of the leg and the bloody bags. In a corner of the room a man in a dark suit sits alone, listening to their conversation.

"Hey, Mac," the man calls out to Jesse. "The newspaper says them bags they found were a type used by fertilizer companies."

"Yeah, that's what the paper says," Jesse responds.

"That means they were made at Union Bag," the man says, stubbing out a cigarette. "Don't you work at Union Bag?"

"Yeah, I work at Union Bag, but that don't mean nothin'," Jesse says, defensively. "I gotta idea. Why don't we all go over to the vacant lot and look around?"

Jesse pays the tab, and leaves with Carroll and the couple. As they walk up Cedar Street toward 38th, Jesse looks back over his shoulder and notices a man sitting in a parked car and gets the distinct impression they are being followed. At the corner of 38th and Cedar, Jesse conducts a tour of the site just as he had done earlier that day with Mr. and Mrs. Aids.

The girl has not had as much beer to drink as the boys. Standing in the vacant lot in the dead of night gives her the creeps, and she wants to go home. The boys tease her, then escort her to Waters Avenue and wait with her for the bus.

Jesse walks home alone, taking the long way that meanders through Kehoe Ward, past freshly mown vacant lots. He crosses the grass plat dividing Victory Drive at Live Oak Street, and makes his way to Daffin Park, where he continues around the edge of the pool and across the bridge to the island. Emerging from the underbrush, he walks home along the same route he came.

Every step he takes is counted, every move he makes carefully observed from a distance by Detective Fitzgerald.

* * *

When Peyton McKethan wakes up Wednesday morning he discovers that his son has already left for the 7 a.m.-to-3 p.m. shift at Union Bag. And when Detectives Fitzgerald, Brennan and Perkins come calling mid-morning, Peyton does not have to ask who they are; he

57

can spot a cop a mile off; his son, Linwood, had been a cop. Peyton tells them Jesse is at work, and that he usually comes home around four. He's certain his son will do everything in his power to help the police find Luther Aids. And later that afternoon, Jesse shows up right on time.

Jesse knows Fitzgerald on sight, and the detective need not introduce himself or show identification. "C'mon with us," Fitzgerald says to Jesse. "Let's us go for a little ride."

Fitzgerald puts Jesse in the front seat with him; Brennan and Perkins ride in the back. He drives to the end of 38th Street, and parks under the spreading arms of an old oak tree.

"Now, Jesse, you were the last man with George Luther Aids," Fitzgerald says. "Now I want you to tell me the whole story, about how long you were with him and what became of him."

Jesse settles back in his seat and with all the ease of Uncle Remus telling the tale of Br'er Rabbit, begins his story.

"On Sunday, October 7th, Luther came by my house and picked me up to take me and my cousin out to Bonaventure Cemetery to visit my mother's grave. After that, we rode around for a while and then we took my cousin home. Then we drove out to the Gold Star Ranch and had a bottle of beer. Luther left to take a girl home, but he came back later to get me. He drove me home and we sat there, talking in the car. Luther pulled out a pocketbook and was looking inside, when I saw a photograph that had been in my pocketbook when it was stolen a few months ago. When I told him that, he said it wasn't my picture; it was his."

Jesse pauses to notice that Detective Perkins has begun taking notes on a pad.

"We got into a little argument," Jesse says, choosing his words more carefully now. "Luther touched me on the back of the neck, and it made me mad. I jumped out of the car and pulled him out and picked up something on the ground and struck him on the head and knocked him down. He revived, and we struggled. I got on top of him and choked him until he was still."

"Then what did you do, Jesse?" Fitzgerald prompts him.

"I don't know what. I jumped up and ran down the street. I didn't know where I was going. I turned around and went back to my house. I listened to Luther's heart and could not hear it beating. I dragged him to the gate and inside our yard. Then I went into the house and got a pillow and laid his head on it. I listened again to his heart and heard nothing. So I dragged him around the side of the house. I didn't know what to do."

Jesse stares blankly at Fitzgerald, as if he expects the detective to fill in the rest of the story. "All of a sudden, I felt very tired," he adds, "and so I dragged Luther under the house, went inside and laid down."

"What did you do with Luther's body?" Fitzgerald asks.

"I didn't know what to do with his body," Jesse says. "The next morning I went to the drug store and bought some detective magazines. I thought I might find an article about how to dispose of a body, but I didn't find anything. I went to work that afternoon and didn't come home again until around 8:30. I went back under the house and when I moved the body, Luther groaned. It scared me. I couldn't stay under there. That's when I got the idea to cut off his head, so that he wouldn't make any more noise. So I went to the back porch and got a hatchet and knife and a flashlight. And I went back under the house and went to work."

The demeanor of the detectives has not changed and no one has moved a muscle since Jesse's story began, and he isn't sure whether he is boring them with details. Fitzgerald urges him to continue.

"Well, I took this knife and cut his head right on around and then took the hatchet and chopped his head off," Jesse continues. "The blood poured so bad that I couldn't stand it. I came out and walked around the block. Then I went back and cut off the arms and legs, cutting the flesh with the knife and using the hatchet to cut the bone. It was around 11:30 when I heard my father come home, so I decided I'd better dispose of the parts. I put the body in a bag that I got from Union Bag that day, and walked out our front gate with it. I hadn't gone but about ten feet when the body fell out of the bag onto the sidewalk. I put the body back into the bag and was going to throw it in the lake in Daffin Park, but I stopped at Thirty-ninth Street. That's as far as I could get. So I left the body there in a shallow ditch in a vacant lot."

Jesse begins to talk so fast at this point that Perkins is having a hard time keeping up with his notes.

"I went back for one of the legs, and went down Thirty-eighth Street and threw it in the middle of a vacant lot," Jesse continues. "I went back and got the other leg and threw it in a lot on Thirty-sixth Street. I went back and got the head and arms and started out for Daffin Park Lake, but when I got there the lake was dry. I saw a police car coming, and I thought they had seen me. So I grabbed the head by the hair and threw it onto the island in the lake, and then I threw the arms after it. I was on my way back home for the last time when I dropped the bags in a lot on Forty-first and Live Oak. I was real tired."

"I think what we better do now is go 'round to all these places and pick up the pieces," Fitzgerald says, over his shoulder. But first, he takes the detectives back to the barracks and instructs Perkins to fetch Dr. Ham, and gives Brennan the sad task of informing Mr. and Mrs. Aids that they will have to come over to Daffin Park to identify their son's remains.

Fitzgerald summons Inspector Raymond Doney to bring his camera, and a uniform to accompany he and

Jesse to retrieve the rest of Luther's body. Photographs are taken and the grim procedure goes strictly by a book that no cop in this city has ever read before, and as Dr. Ham assembles the parts for a coroner's inquest at Henderson Brothers Funeral Home, Fitzgerald finishes the tour of the McKethan house on East 38th Street.

There is perhaps as much as a 3-foot clearance under the house, and Fitzgerald can easily see the place where the body was butchered without having to get down on his hands and knees and slog through the crawl space. Besides, the place reeks of creolin.

"Now, Jesse, where are the clothes?" Fitzgerald asks.

"Right here," he says, pointing to a spot underneath the house.

Jesse crawls underneath the house and digs the dirt three feet down and retrieves a shirt, pants, undershirt and B.V.D.'s soaked with blood. "I used his clothes to keep the blood off mine," Jesse explains. "I can't remember where I put the shoes and stockings."

Jesse then leads Fitzgerald around the premises on a scavenger hunt for the pillow he used under Luther's head and the bloody slipcase that he had hidden under a washtub in the back yard. He retrieves the knife and hatchet from the back porch and hands them over to Fitzgerald, explaining how he made the knife out of band saw steel while working at Southeastern Shipyard and fitted it with a special brass handle. The instruments of destruction were clean as a whistle, prompting Jesse to explain how he fetched a pail of water to wash down Luther's parts and the hatchet and knife when he finished dissecting the body.

Retracing his every step, Jesse finds a leftover bottle of creolin, one of several he purchased to kill the smell of body parts left to rot in open fields. He had gone back to each location and liberally doused each part with the disinfectant, and then washed the soil beneath his house, the stench of which still fills the air.

Fitzgerald mentally runs through a checklist that is rapidly becoming almost impossible to keep up with, and just when he thinks he has everything, Jesse remembers something else. He jumps up and runs back into the house and emerges with the detective magazines that he bought while searching for ways to dispose of a body.

Fitzgerald files the evidence in the trunk of his car, and the uniform cuffs Jesse's hands and places him in the back seat. They drive to Daffin Park, where Detectives McCarthy, Brennan and Perkins have assembled Dr. Ham and Mrs. Aids, who is accompanied by a family friend. A crowd gathers around the pool, the news of the breaking case having quickly spread around town. Newspaper reporters record the scene in print and photograph.

McKethan appears to reporters to be cool and collected as his fiendish handiwork is unearthed. There are no tears, and he obligingly steps from the police car to let a photographer snap his picture. He is dressed in a gray suit and white dress shirt, and does not look at all like the butcher he will be portrayed in the newspaper. He exchanges glances with Mrs. Aids as she views the head of her son rolled out in the sand.

Luther is not recognizable to his mother.

"Is that my son?" she asks McCarthy.

"Yes, ma'am, I'm afraid so," he says.

Dahlia Aids collapses into the arms of her friend, and is led away sobbing uncontrollably. One of the detectives picks up Luther's head and holds it aloft like its some sort of trophy for the gathering crowd standing on the opposite shore to see. A newspaper photographer assembles Police Chief William Hall and Detectives McCarthy, Fitzgerald, Brennan and Perkins for a portrait at the scene of the discovery. They pose standing around the shallow hole that contained the head of Luther Aids, and the photo will be part of a batch sent to *Time* and *Life* magazines and the news wire services clamoring for details of the Savannah Butcher Murder.

"This is the first dismemberment case to have occurred in Savannah that I can remember," Chief Hall says to McCarthy. "I don't believe that another case of this size has been broken so quickly and so thoroughly. You deserve the congratulations of us all."

*   *   *

On Wednesday evening, as the remnants of Luther Aids' body are assembled at Henderson Brothers Funeral Home for Dr. Ham to examine, Jesse McKethan is delivered to the police barracks and formally charged with murder. He is photographed and fingerprinted, and makes a full confession of his crimes in the presence of Detectives Fitzgerald, Brennan, Perkins and Inspector Doney. Sgt. Hallman types the statement.

Jesse takes almost three hours to relate the details that fill up five legal-sized pages. With the second telling of the tale, more details emerge and a few contradictions.

Jesse's memory of the day of the murder is vivid, in spite of having had more than six bottles of beer before the killing. He can remember everywhere he and Luther went, what they ate and drank, who they met and what they talked about. He can remember word for word the argument they had over the photograph in Luther's wallet, and that Luther struck Jesse on the back of the head with his hand.

But then, for the first time, Jesse says "I don't know" when trying to remember what it was that he struck Luther with, and his memories of the struggle are blurry. He freely admits that during the fight he got on top of Luther and choked him to death, and that when he realized his friend was dead Jesse jumped up and ran but he didn't know why and he didn't know where he was headed.

Jesse remembers how he woke up the morning after around nine but didn't get out of bed until eleven. He couldn't figure out what to do with the body of his friend that was hidden under the house, and so he went to a drug store on the corner of 40th and Waters Avenue, and bought three detective magazines to find a solution. He went to work at Union Bag that afternoon where he picked up several large paper bags and returned home after nine p.m. When his father left for work that night, Jesse went to the Dixie Wine Shop on 39th and Waters Avenue, and drank five or six beers until he had summoned enough Dutch courage to crawl under his house and hack up his friend's corpse with a hatchet and homemade knife.

Jesse manages to get through the most horrific parts of his testimony without once mentioning how he felt or what his thought processes were, whether he felt any shock, pain or remorse. He describes going back and forth from a normal life of work at Union Bag and socializing with friends at neighborhood taverns, to butchering his best buddy and scattering his body parts all over Savannah with such dispassion that the detectives can't believe Jesse is telling the entire truth; there's either something missing in the motive or they're not dealing with an ordinary mind.

Jesse goes on to describe how he began the cover-up phase of his crime, first by cleaning the site of the slaughter and masking the stench emanating from the four disposal sites with bottles of creolin, and then repeatedly appearing at the Aids home to inquire of his friend's whereabouts and lend support to the worried parents. Perhaps the only indication to the detectives that they are dealing with a troubled mind comes when Jesse describes his habit of revisiting the site where each part of

Luther's body is hidden every night before going home to bed.

The weirdest part of Jesse's story occurs one week after the murder: "I worked from 3 p.m. until 11 p.m. Saturday, October 13th. When I got off the bus at 40th and Waters Avenue, I met some friends of mine at Pop's place. We drank a few bottles of beer and bought several bottles to carry home with us. We went to my house and sat around drinking until around 3 a.m. Sunday morning, at which time a girl who was in the party with us got drunk and the four of us left the house to walk her sober. I steered them along the same route that I had walked every night in my rounds to the places where the parts of the body were concealed. I left the girl and the other two fellows and went home and got a bottle of creolin and walked back to the spot where the torso was hidden and again poured part of the contents of the bottle over the torso and returned to the house, went under the house to the spot where the clothing was buried and again sprinkled the creolin over the ground to keep down any odor and then went into the house and to bed."

Fitzgerald stares at McKethan like he can't believe what he's hearing. It doesn't make sense that Jesse leaves body parts strewn around his neighborhood and conducts daily tours past the sites, attempting to mask the odor of decomposing flesh with the reek of coal tar, the mixture of which is enough to make a statue want to hold its nose. Had Roger Coursey's dogs not discovered the severed leg in one of the vacant lots the next day, chances are Jesse McKethan would've continued his bizarre ritual indefinitely. It was only when the stranger in Pop's place mentioned the discovery of the bloody bags that Jesse admits for the first time that he was thrown into a dither.

Sgt. Hallman takes the last page of Jesse's confession out of the typewriter and hands it over to him to read and sign. Reporters from the local papers anxiously await its release. Waiting outside the police barracks with them is George Aids and an old friend, Hubert Berne, a deputy sheriff. Earlier in the day, while detectives were waiting for Jesse McKethan to return home from Union Bag, George Aids and Hubert Berne were conducting a little investigation of their own. They went to the McKethan house when no one was home and had a look around. George found a bloody fingerprint on the garage, and it was at that precise moment that he knew conclusively that his son was dead and that the boy's best friend had killed him. George is waiting impatiently for the cops to finish their job, and then he wants the satisfaction of looking Jesse McKethan straight in the eye and asking him one question.

The jailer takes George back to the holding cell where Jesse sits, exhausted from the day's events. "You done me all the harm you can," George says to Jesse. "I want to know why you killed my boy."

And then Jesse McKethan does a very odd thing. Instead of answering George's question, he begins to recite the story of how it happened for the third time that day, as if it's a performance. Unlike earlier versions, Jesse tells George Aids that he and Luther had been arguing about a girl named Faith Floyd, and that led to an argument about a photograph in a pocketbook. George is not satisfied with Jesse's answer; the best he can figure out is that the incident had something to do with drinking too much beer. At least, that's the impression news reporters were left with when they tried to squeeze a statement out of the grieving father when he ran out of the police barracks and disappeared into the night.

Before Jesse's big day is through, he is visited at his cell by Detective Fitzgerald, who will receive most of the credit for cracking the case of the Butcher Murder. Fitzgerald has a few details to go over and a few loose ends to tie up before tying a ribbon around his case file. If it can be said that God is in the details of creation, then it can be said that commendations are in the details of confessions.

"Jesse, how is it that you killed Luther at your house on 38th Street when you said in your statement that you killed him at 40th and Cedar?" Fitzgerald wants to know.

"I don't want to lie to you anymore," Jesse says. "I want to tell you the truth about everything. If you will go back out to my house and look around right in front of the door, you will find my keys I dropped, and that is the spot where I murdered Luther."

Jesse speaks in a different voice than the one used to describe the murder of his best friend to detectives in the Fingerprint Bureau. His tone is softer now and tinged with regret. Fitzgerald had sat through the three hours of the confession and never heard a compelling reason for Jesse's actions, and he figures now is his best chance to dig a little deeper into the mind of a psychopath.

"How long had you known Luther?" Fitzgerald asks.

"Years," Jesse says. "I loved the boy very much. I spent a lot of money on Luther. He was my favorite boy."

Later in the week, sitting around the Fitzgerald dinner table, the detective will be moved to recall the uneasiness that crept over him as he heard for the first time about the killer's unnatural desire for another man.

"Y'know," Jesse continues, "Luther left a few weeks ago and went to Florida. I got mad because he left me, but he came back and we started going together again. Then he started going with a girl."

Fitzgerald keeps silent, nodding his head in interest.

Jesse is not looking at the detective now. His eyes shift to the floor, as if he expects it to fall away like a trap door under a hangman's noose.

"I don't have any passion at all for women. I like to put my arms around boys. Luther was my favorite boy."

"Is that as far as it went?" Fitzgerald presses, sounding like a father asking about his son's date.

"Oh, I never have an erection or anything like that," Jesse explains. "It's just the touch of a boy's body. I don't have any sex desire for man nor woman. But with these young boys, I like to love them. That's all I get any passion from."

"I've known the McKethans maybe fifteen years," Fitzgerald would say later, around his dinner table. "I knew this boy to see him, but never knew him to talk to. I knew his brothers. But I never knew Jesse McKethan was queer. Odd thing was, he found it easier to admit to strangling his best friend and cutting up his corpse like a ghoul, than to admit that he loved the boy. I think Jesse was glad he confessed. I think he was glad to get it off his chest. I think it was making him crazy."

Ed Fitzgerald joined the Savannah police department in 1927. His brother Herbert was also a cop, and when a nigger killed him in 1929, Ed showed no mercy on black perpetrators thereafter. In December 1931, Ed's exploits were splashed across the front page of the local papers in describing his death-defying motorcycle chase of kidnappers while under fire. While in pursuit, the bad guys shot at Ed 20 times. He was awarded a badge of meritorious service, the first of its kind in the department. The medal was engraved, "Officer Fitzgerald evidenced bravery that marks him as a stalwart among men."

Ed was promoted to detective in 1932, and would take charge as captain of detectives upon the retirement of Chief McCarthy, in 1956. Somewhere along the way he saw enough of the evil that men do, and he matured in ways that were surprising to his superiors: when, in 1939, the Tuskegee Institute listed a "Charlie Williams" as having been lynched by whites for insulting a white woman, the Association of Southern Women for the Prevention of Lynching asked for an investigation into the report's accuracy. At a time when no one else in the world seemed to care whether the report was accurate or not, Detective Sergeant Fitzgerald found Williams after a dogged search, and proved the lynching was a fable.

Ed Fitzgerald was the man that the department relied upon like no other. As if he didn't have his hands full in sorting out the criminal element full time, he moonlighted as Captain of Ports along Savannah's riverfront during the war. He had seen just about everything in his career, but Ed Fitzgerald had never seen anything like the Butcher Murder of '45.

Ed Fitzgerald and his wife

PART III:
THE INVESTIGATION

Thursday, October 18, 1945

There's a bit of jailhouse wisdom from olden days that says if you want to know if the right man has been arrested for a crime, all you have to do is check on him in his cell the morning after his arrest: the guilty man will be sleeping soundly because arrest most often is a relief, but the innocent man will still be wide awake after a sleepless night, trying to figure out all the angles and how to get the hell out of there. And when Deputy Sheriff Collie Bruner goes to Jesse McKethan's cell the morning following his arrest, imagine his surprise to find Jesse laying next to his cellmate in the same bunk, reading a magazine.

Meanwhile the morning breakfast tables around town are abuzz with folks digesting the reports of Jesse's arrest along with their bacon and eggs. Several reporters with The Savannah Morning News and Evening Press are assigned to cover every angle of the Butcher Murder, and with the publication of the first article describing Roger Coursey's discovery of the severed leg, the city has erupted in a rash of rumors. The theory is being advanced that if an amputation gone haywire at the hospital isn't the source of the severed leg, then a monster was on the loose. Children were afraid to leave the house to go to school, and as body parts started turning up all over town, it wasn't safe for anyone to be walking around alone. Before the newspaper scribes could get to the bottom of it all, Jesse McKethan was being blamed for the disappearance of every missing person, cat and dog on file.

Of course, by the time Frank Rossiter of The Evening Press had gotten a hold of the story, he had parlayed the shocking nature of the crime and the speed with which McCarthy and his men apprehended the murderer into a glowing review of their brilliant detective work.

"I could have nabbed him Tuesday night as he visited the grass covered lots and the Daffin Park area where parts of the body were located, but it was real dark and I wasn't altogether sure," Detective Fitzgerald was quoted. "I knew he was our man."

Fitzgerald recapped how McKethan had planned to tidy up his rather crude job yesterday when he knocked off from work, how he was going to find a more secure spot to bury the hacked portions of his friend's body. "But detectives had their hands on his shoulder just after he punched the clock and walked through the big gate at the plant," Rossiter wrote. "He was trapped and he knew it."

"Criminals in that position do only one thing," Rossiter quoted Fitzgerald, "they spill their guts." However, the article did not go into the details of the motive. That was left for a second column in which McKethan's entire confession was published.

It was odd how fact ran alongside fiction in the main story and the sidelights that it spawned. The grieving parents were bothered for their reaction to McKethan's arrest, saying that they thought the story about the wallet was bogus and that the murder was planned. Not only did they reveal Jesse's offer to help Dahlia Aids kill her husband for the insurance, George told reporters that he was certain that Jesse's offer to drive her to Port Wentworth to visit a fortune teller was merely a ruse to take her to a remote spot and kill her, too.

"Too Much Beer Was the Cause of the Whole Thing" was the quote from Jesse McKethan that headlined one hurried take that sacrificed accuracy and thoroughness in order to beat a deadline. There was one touching story that made for better reading at the breakfast table that morning, the tale of little Louis Consos, an 11-year-old who had run away from his home on East Charlton Street on Monday, intent on seeing more of the world. His mother had notified police, and the newspaper published an open plea, "Louis, your Mama really misses you." The plea was published on the same page with the story of Coursey's discovery of a severed leg, and when little Louis saw it he became awfully disturbed, thinking his mama might believe he had been killed. So little Louis raced homeward, abandoning his plans to see the world.

In the middle of the stories about the arrest of the murderer was a photograph of the man at the center of it all. It had been taken at Daffin Park, as detectives unearthed the severed head of Luther Aids. Jesse McKethan, in a gray suit and white dress shirt, peers out from the photo, and except for a brief glimpse of the handcuffs linking his hands casually folded in front, this could be the face of a reluctant bridegroom or just a face in the crowd of college students. "Butcher" is the one-word subtitle under the photo, but no one looking into the eyes of Jesse McKethan would be repelled or repulsed by what they see because this is not the face of the monster that has Savannah's children afraid to go to sleep at night.

And, as citizens of Chatham County resume their normal lives on Thursday, Detective Fitzgerald is back on the street clearing up a list of loose ends before attending the coroner's inquest at 11 a.m. At the McKethan's house he finds Jesse's keys in the front yard where he dropped them during the fight, and finds Luther's shoes and stockings hidden in a doghouse in the back yard. Fitzgerald walks up 38th Street to the place where the torso slipped out of the bag and stained the sidewalk with blood, then returns to the McKethan's front gate to check his list.

There are still two pieces of evidence missing, one of which~ Luther's wallet with the photograph~ Jesse says he threw in the Savannah River. The second item is a murder weapon, and its discovery means all the difference in proving whether Jesse acted out of self-defense, as any good defense attorney will contend, or acted on a premeditated plan, as George Aids insists. We are talking degree here, and the difference will decide whether Jesse goes to prison, a psychiatric hospital, or to the electric chair.

It all comes down to which boy struck the first blow. In his initial statement to Fitzgerald, Jesse said that as the argument escalated into a fight, "Luther touched me on the back of the neck and it made me mad." But in his confession at the police barracks, Jesse used a stronger description of the first blow, that "Luther struck me with his hand." However, Jesse said in both statements that it was only after he pulled Luther from the car and they rolled around on the ground that Jesse picked up something and hit Luther in the back of the head, opening a gash which bled all over the pillow Jesse propped under him after Luther was strangled.

So Fitzgerald is searching the McKethan's front yard for that "something," and what does he turn up but an 8-inch length of garden hose with a brass coupling attached, and it looks like someone had made a clean cut of it. If it isn't a weapon, Fitzgerald can think of no other useful purpose. Judging by the amount of blood on the pillowslip, Fitzgerald's hunch is that the blow to Luther's skull had to have been made with a heavier object, say, either the wrench found on the floor of the back seat of the car, or the hatchet Jesse used to butcher the corpse. Fitzgerald decides that he will let Dr. Ham make the final determination at the coroner's inquest, and makes his way to Henderson Brothers Funeral Home for that purpose.

A coroner's jury has been hastily convened, but before viewing the graphic procedure the jurors are advised of the nature of the horror they are about to witness. Under these circumstances, Detective Chief McCarthy is surprised if there are any volunteers.

The inquest is held in the embalming room. Detectives McCarthy, Fitzgerald and Perkins are present, as well as reporters from the newspapers. Jesse McKethan is held in an adjoining room until summoned, if needed.

"It is normally customary to conduct a complete, or radical, autopsy to determine the actual cause of death," Dr. Ham instructs the jury. "To my mind, if the decedent has been choked the actual dismemberment of the body and its decomposition will render it difficult to determine that. The fact that police have already obtained a confession means that I do not think an autopsy is necessary. Of course, it's up to you, the jury, if you think it will help you reach a verdict~"

None of the jurors can move or speak. The stench alone prohibits them from remaining in the room any longer than absolutely necessary. Dr. Ham takes their silence to mean that they have seen enough.

"Dr. Ham, I have a problem that I need your help with," Fitzgerald interjects. "I need to know the extent of the injury to the victim's skull. I'd like your opinion on what kind of instrument caused this fracture."

Dr. Ham rolls the head over on its face. "I won't be able to tell without conducting an autopsy," he says. "Just looking at it in this condition, I can't tell if the decedent was struck with an instrument or if a fracture of the skull was the cause of death. I mean, we can go through all that, if you want me to. The decision is yours. But Reverend Wilder has advised us that the family wants to bury the body today or as soon as *humanely* possible."

"I think if we could hear from the prisoner we might be able to clear this up," the foreman of the jury says. "We'd like for him to make a statement, if he will, and to answer a few questions."

"We can do that," McCarthy says, although he gets the distinct impression that the jurors just want to see the Butcher, that all they really want is to have something to tell their friends and families other than what a body looks like chopped into six pieces.

Jesse is brought into the embalming room by two uniformed officers. His hands are cuffed in front, and he wears the same suit of clothes he had been arrested in. He glances at the body of Luther Aids arranged on the mortician's slab and becomes distraught. If jurors had any questions for Jesse, they have forgotten them.

"Now, Jesse," McCarthy says, trying to steady him, "you are not required to say anything, but you can make a statement of your own free will. You are not under oath. The jury is only trying to determine the cause of Luther's death, and there is some confusion about what happened during the scuffle."

"I strangled him," Jesse begins haltingly. "We got into a fight over a pocketbook. It started in the car, and then we fell out. I hit him with something. Then I got on top of him and choked him."

"Can you remember what you hit him with?" Dr. Ham asks.

Jesse shakes his head. "No, I can't. I was confused. I ran down the street before I realized what had happened. Then I went back and listened to his heart but I couldn't hear it beating. I don't know. I get so confused. When I woke up the next morning, I thought it was all a nightmare. It wasn't until my father asked me about the blood-soaked pillow in the yard that it started coming back to me."

No one from the jury asked Jesse any questions; there didn't seem to be much point. The police had their confession, and, as Dr. Ham pointed out, it didn't necessarily strike him as strange that Jesse couldn't remember what he had hit Luther with, under the circumstances. Based upon Jesse's confession and the decomposition of the body, Dr. Ham did not perform an autopsy. Strangulation was cited as cause of death on the coroner's report.

A crowd began to gather at Henderson Brothers Funeral Home for the brief services conducted by Rev. John Wilder, pastor of the Calvary Baptist Temple. Hundreds of people came from out of nowhere to lend their support to the Aids family. There hadn't been a funeral notice published; yet people from all over Chatham County appeared, a spontaneous outpouring of public grief. They followed the hearse to Bonaventure Cemetery and remained long after George and Dahlia Aids drove away.

Detective Chief McCarthy sought to confer with the Aids' after the funeral but found no one at home. The Morning News was still unopened on their front porch with the account of their son's murder.

Meanwhile in a jail cell at the police barracks, Jesse was slowly changing a few vital particulars to his story of the crime. When Fitzgerald tells Jesse that he found a short section of hose with a brass coupling attached, Jesse changes the scene of the fight from Luther's car and the McKethan's front yard to the back yard, where he jumped Luther from behind.

"I don't know why I did it," Jesse tells Fitzgerald, "but I feel good now that it's off my chest."

Local reporters are still nosing around the station Thursday evening when McCarthy and Fitzgerald find a few moments to brief them on Jesse McKethan. When asked what was the motive for the slaying, McCarthy simply says, "Sex," and lets it go at that. The reporters look quizzically at the grandfatherly cop and can't figure out the angle. With all that he has seen during his 46 years with the department, McCarthy cannot bring himself to go into details on one man's desire for another. He leaves that explanation to Fitzgerald, a younger man with a sweet tooth for the weird things people do and why they do them.

"McKethan loved Aids," Fitzgerald tells newsmen, rolling his eyes, "but he says he don't know why he killed him. Friends knew Jesse as a mama's boy who did not play much with the other boys his age in the neighborhood. He had been in trouble a coupla years ago when the mothers of some of the smaller kids complained that he was tryin' to hypnotize them by massaging their throat nerves, if you can imagine such a thing."

Reporters trying to beat a deadline for the morning paper run back to Bay Street, and when writing up this story will include McCarthy's one-word explanation for motive and highlight the word "love" in quotation marks when citing Fitzgerald. It isn't until Frank Rossiter catches up with George Aids that he gets details about the nature of this "love" of Jesse's for his victim.

George Aids advances two theories for his son's slaying. "Jesse was afraid Luther would leave him...or else Luther had something on Jesse, and Jesse had to shut him up. My boy went regularly with McKethan until Luther went to Florida and spent two years. When he came back they didn't go around very much as Luther had quite a few girlfriends. McKethan didn't like the idea of Luther dating a girl and on occasions when he found Luther skating at the rink with his girlfriend, he would call him aside and make him take off the skates. Luther was really afraid of him."

George Aids looks at Frank Rossiter with reddened eyes. "The night of the murder, Luther dropped McKethan at the Gold Star and went to the skating rink to meet his girl. His girl wasn't there, so he dropped back to the Gold Star to take Jesse and another boy home. Luther called his girl from the Gold Star and made a date to come by her home after dropping off Jesse. My boy didn't get to keep that date. He was enticed into McKethan's house or garage and slain."

George pours himself a "Six O'clock," Jack Daniels straight up, hard, black and even. "Here's somethin' else you can put in your paper," he says to Rossiter. "McKethan knew I was on his trail and wanted to get rid of me. He overheard a remark I made when they found the leg, which was to the effect that the person who put the leg in the vacant lot was the same one who drove the car back to my house and left it parked in the middle of the street. And that's why he suggested to my wife that he kill me, too. When that ploy didn't work, he tried to take my wife out to Port Wentworth under the pretense of going to see a fortuneteller. I made her get outta the car. I was afraid he was just taking her out to the country to kill her. He had my daughter. Hell, he would've killed us all."

Jesse McKethan is given copies of the morning and evening papers and jailers note that he eagerly reads everything that is written about the murder. Fitzgerald is intrigued that Jesse acts like he's reading about people he knows instead of reading about himself. But when he reads that detectives are telling reporters about a sex angle in the motive for the killing, he calls Fitzgerald to vigorously deny it.

"A lot of people have always accused me of being different from other boys," Jesse shouts at Fitzgerald. "It isn't true! I prefer the company of girls. It was a heart ailment that kept me outta the army, the same thing that killed my brothers."

Fitzgerald keeps silent, and allows the prisoner to rave about whatever crosses his mind in this agitated confession.

"I just want to tell the world one thing," Jesse continues. "I would've been in this police department to confess in less than two weeks even if you hadn't found the leg, or if you hadn't caught me. I knew I would be caught and I couldn't live with my conscience."

"Didn't you think you were gettin' away with the perfect crime?" Fitzgerald challenges his prisoner.

"No!" Jesse says, turning his face to the wall. And he will have absolutely nothing further to say to anyone until his court-appointed attorneys interview him in preparation for his defense.

* * *

Since the death of his wife Jessie, some two months before these events and the earlier deaths of his three sons~ all within five months of each other, from June through November 1943~ Peyton McKethan had been residing in the large home at 1101 East 38th Street, with his only remaining son, Jesse. After Jesse's arrest on Wednesday afternoon, Peyton had lived in a nightmare of grief and despair and solitary loneliness.

Neighbors and friends described Peyton as attempting to find solace through prayer. Dreading darkness, he sought the company of others whenever possible, until the lateness of the hour forced his return to the now dreaded house on the corner of busy Waters Avenue. Apparently unable to find sleep in its hollow rooms, he was seen pacing up and down on the front porch and on the sidewalk of 38th Street, alternately praying and sobbing.

When prayer seemed to fail, or didn't work fast enough, Peyton crawled inside a bottle of bourbon. He was drunk when he visited his son Thursday night. When Jesse was called to the visitor's window and took one look at his father, he said, "Dad, do me a favor, will you? Stop drinking!" Then he turned on his heels and went back to his cell.

Peyton was crushed. Nevertheless he returned the next day with a bag of sandwiches, a thermos of coffee and a carton of cigarettes for his son. But after stepping aboard the Daffin Park bus, the sleeplessness and fatigue and whiskey caught up at once and he collapsed. Mumbling incoherently, Peyton was supported down the long row of cellblocks by sympathetic jailers to a cell as far removed from Jesse as possible. They laid him down on a bunk where he immediately fell into a deep slumber, the first rest he had enjoyed since the beginning of this most recent catastrophe.

The jailers kept Peyton's presence in the cellblock a secret from his son. When Jesse asked what all the noise was about, the deputy told him it was an old fellow that they had there all the time.

The jailers felt sorry for Peyton. They shuddered to think what he must be going through. "I don't think you could've gotten me back into that house drunk or sober for the rest of my life," one of the jailers told a news reporter. And another: "I don't know what I would do, but I have some sons of my own and if one of them had done such a thing, I think it would either drive me to drink or make me crazy."

At Police Court on Friday, October 19, there were two McKethans on the docket. Peyton was charged with drunken misconduct, but acting recorder Alderman George Heyward didn't have the heart to come down hard on Jesse the Butcher's father. "Mr. McKethan, I believe you have enough trouble as it is, so I am going to turn you loose," Heyward said to Peyton, swallowing hard. "I want you to straighten yourself out now," and nodded toward the exit.

And then the room filled with witnesses and spectators for the arraignment of Peyton's son. George and Dahlia Aids sat front and center; tears welled in her eyes, while he viewed the defendant with a look of intense hatred and disgust.

Dr. Ham was the first witness. He told of the initial discovery of the severed leg and bloody bags, and how he put detectives on the right path with a description of the victim, which closely matched Luther Aids in the missing persons file. He then related how he accompanied detectives as the slayer led them to various sections of the city where he had hidden parts of the body. The body parts were so badly decomposed, he said, that an examination proved it impossible to tell how the death occurred.

Detective Fitzgerald then gave an outline of the case prior to, and following, the arrest and a summary of McKethan's confession, telling how he killed and dismembered the victim.

Fitzgerald said he had followed McKethan on successive nights before making the arrest. "At first, McKethan claimed he had no knowledge of Aids' whereabouts but after a few minutes of questioning, he blurted out that he wanted to tell the whole thing because it was almost driving him crazy. He said he had developed a strong grip working in the shipyard and, after he struck Aids, he jumped on the youth and choked him for several minutes."

Fitzgerald then described how McKethan secreted the body under the house and had gone to bed. After returning from work the next day, he said, McKethan went under the house and cut off the boy's head. McKethan was then quoted as telling how he disposed of the members, a few at a time, and how on the night that he had carried the head to Daffin Park, a police prowl car had flashed its lights on him, which frightened him so badly that he dropped the arms and fled to his home.

Fitzgerald cleared his throat and then concluded his statement with a comment as to motive. "McKethan has told me that he has known many boys whom he liked very much, but that he really loved Luther. However," Fitzgerald says, turning his glance from Alderman Heyward to Jesse, "McKethan has never admitted any sex angle in connection with the crime."

81

A murmur rippled through the gallery, prompting Heyward to rap his gavel and ask for quiet in the courtroom. Turning to the accused, Heyward asks McKethan if he has any statement to make.

Jesse is direct and to the point. "Detective Fitzgerald has said everything there is to say. All I can add is that I loved Luther and don't know why I killed him."

"If you have nothing else to add," Heyward says to Jesse, "then it is ordered by this court that you be held in the Chatham County Jail without bond on a charge of murder, until your trial before the Superior Court. Will you be represented by an attorney?"

Jesse looks at Alderman Heyward with a mixture of resignation and regret. Again, his response is short and to the point. "What's the use ?"

PART IV:
THE MAN BEHIND THE
MASK

October 19, 1945

Following Jesse McKethan's arraignment in police court that morning, the only visitor he receives at the jail is Rev. Henry Stipe, pastor of Grace Methodist Church. Jesse and his mother had been members of Asbury Methodist, located on East Henry Street, since April 1944. As her medical condition worsened, Mrs. McKethan found God, and her son took her to church regularly until her death, after which Rev. Shearhouse saw Jesse only every third Sunday. Rev. Stipe's church was clear across town, on Park Avenue and Jefferson Street, and although he had been in Savannah for only one year, he had been a pastor almost thirty and considered his flock had no boundary. When he heard about the Butcher Murderer, Rev. Stipe made inquiries of people who knew Jesse yet did not know of his having been in any trouble before this. So Rev. Stipe shows up at the jail— perhaps the only person in this world who wanted to talk to Jesse and didn't have to—in order to find out what in the world had gotten into this boy.

It was the first of many visits for Rev. Stipe, who became visibly moved as Jesse related how the boy he killed had been a good boy, that Jesse loved him, and that he felt sorry for Luther's parents. Rev. Stipe got the quick impression that Jesse was in some sort of denial, that he had not come to fully realize the extent of his actions and therefore not responsible. Following his initial visit with Jesse, Rev. Stipe called Dr. Edward Whelan, the McKethan family physician, and asked him to visit his patient. The reverend was no expert, but he had a strong

83

suspicion that Jesse could use the services of a good psychiatrist.

Dr. Whelan had been practicing medicine in Savannah for twenty years. He was not only the McKethan family doctor but also a member of the Lunacy Commission of Chatham County. He had known Jesse six or seven years, and had treated Jesse's brother for chronic nephritis, Bright's disease and sclerosis of the liver. He had also attended Jesse's mother, who died of a cerebral brain hemorrhage and whose blood pressure shot up over 300 at times. Dr. Whelan knew Jesse to have inherited his mother's constitution, that he had the same congenital heart defect that had wiped out his three brothers at early ages, and that his condition had been made worse from complications due to flu and weakness. Out of all of Jessie Beard McKethan's boys, Jesse, the baby, was closest to her mentally, physically and spiritually; he had been named for her.

Dr. Whelan also knew something else about his patient that no one else knew besides Peyton McKethan: four years earlier, when Jesse was 17, he had been talking to his father when his brother Linwood came up behind him and playfully slapped him on the head. Jesse went into a rage and picked up an end table and smashed it over his brother's head. He had to be restrained, but after he calmed down he wasn't aware of what had just happened. He had gone into some sort of blackout, and Peyton took his son to Dr. Whelan. The doctor examined Jesse's head and noticed a depression in the left posterior Parietal region just above the lambdoidal suture, and Peyton explained that it was an old injury dating back to when Jesse was four years old and fell out of a third-storey window of a house on Taylor Street. Dr. Blake treated him and he was bedridden for months. Jesse never fully recovered, Peyton said, and sometimes suffered blackouts in the same manner as an epileptic. Dr. Whelan deduced that the depression in the skull created pressure that caused these convulsive seizures, and that it spelled trouble in the future of an indeterminate nature.

Now, after reviewing the McKethan family medical records, Dr. Whelan is not surprised to read among Detective Fitzgerald's findings that Jesse related how Luther slapping him on the head had precipitated his murderous rage. In hot pursuit of a medical reason for his abnormal behavior, Dr. Whelan calls Dr. H. H. McGee and orders a Roentgen exam and X-ray of Jesse's cranium, and then calls Dr. Lee Howard for a complete work-up of Jesse's spinal fluid, to be checked for syphilis and other diseases of the central nervous system.

But before calling in a psychiatrist, Dr. Whelan looks into his patient to examine the nature of his sexual deviancy and its possible connections to the bizarre manner in which Jesse disposed of his best friend's body.

Jesse is a willing participant in Dr. Whelan's procedure. He tells Dr. Whelan of his relationships with boys between the ages of 18 and 22, that he would go out with them and have physical contact with them and get the same sensation as a normal person experiences with the opposite sex, except that there was no sex relationship between them. Simply from close contact Jesse got a certain amount of satisfaction.

Jesse speaks with frankness about his lack of any response to women, that he could not directly feel what other men talk about when they mention desire for a woman. He illustrates the point by telling Dr. Whelan a dirty little secret: a friend once took Jesse to Indian Lil's whorehouse on Fahm Street, and treated him to his very own naked lady, just to see what would happen. The girl did every trick in the book to arouse in him some sort of physical desire, from standing on her head to whistling "Dixie," but no matter what the contact, he had no sensation or any incentive toward a sexual act.

"I have never been able to achieve an erection or any sensual feeling from thoughts about the opposite sex," Jesse relates to Dr. Whelan, "or those of my own sex, for that matter."

Wondering if he was a freak, Jesse sought out homosexual men to prove it one way or the other. He was unable to respond, experienced no conscious desire, and told Dr. Whelan he never succeeded with men, either. He had no sensation at all, as if his sexual wiring had been short-circuited.

Jesse responded to all of Dr. Whelan's questions in a relevant and rational manner, but the doctor notes there is little emotional substance here, little ordinary feeling behind his statements. All his reactions convey hollowness, a lack of real vital or intense feeling of any kind. Jesse's failure to experience any erotic sensations toward women or even in a perverse way toward men seems to Dr. Whelan to be indicative of a deep seated disorder and consistent with his emotional shallowness. It was as if Jesse McKethan suffered from a complete lack of participation in his own life.

Jesse makes these statements about his odd bent evidently proud of the fact, and it seems to Dr. Whelan that no normal person would be proud of themselves in this manner. As to his cutting up a corpse and throwing the parts in vacant lots within 60 feet of houses around his neighborhood, Dr. Whelan cannot see how anybody with common sense could do something like that. And on that point, he is certain that a judge and jury—*all of us*— will agree that is abnormal. But in order to convince a judge and jury that Jesse should be institutionalized in a mental hospital instead of a prison, Dr. Whelan figures the defense is going to need the help of an expert in the field of psychiatry and recommends to Solicitor General Andrew Ryan that before he puts the defendant on trial for Murder that he afford this poor soul the privilege of being examined by Dr. Hervey Cleckley, head of the Department of Psychiatry, University of Georgia Medical School, in Augusta.

Dr. Whelan's simple request, made with Rev. Stipe's blessing, is not an easy thing for Solicitor Ryan to grant. He must first consult with Judge David Atkinson, who will preside over the trial, and who must make a request of Georgia Governor Ellis Arnall to dispatch Dr. Cleckley for that purpose. Ryan doesn't have to do it, and the process can break down anywhere in the chain of command for any number of reasons, but Dr. Whelan's request gets a green light at every crossing and his senior colleague is summoned to Savannah to meet Jesse the Butcher.

Dr. Cleckley's examination of the patient begins with a look at Jesse's medical records and the X-ray of his cranium. He then tests Jesse's reflexes and notices that the right knee jerk is very much greater than the left, and the right ankle jerk is slightly greater than the left, which does not prove but strongly suggests some abnormality from the area of the brain to the spinal cord; this is a test always made to determine a person's mental condition.

Jesse talks openly with Dr. Cleckley about his life, stating that he got along fairly well in his work but there had always been a great deal of unhappiness in his home due to the alcoholic abuses of his father and brother. He admits having shifted jobs frequently, and that he had been arrested for forging small checks, which he made good. What particularly impresses Dr. Cleckley is Jesse's lack of ordinary sex feelings toward women and yet denies having any of the ordinary impulses classified as perversion.

The second aspect to Jesse's personality that strikes Dr. Cleckley as exceptional is his claim that he became totally unconscious and had no memory of the struggle after the blow to the head until he awoke and found his friend dead, apparently strangled. Then he spoke of other matters that impressed Dr. Cleckley as being exceptional, such as pulling the body under the house and leaving it there overnight, and the doctor is struck by his patient's calmness and apparent lack of any deep emotion as he relates the most sensitive details of the horrors to follow, so as to give the impression that he was also calm as he went about these sordid affairs.

Further, it strikes Dr. Cleckley that in distributing parts of the body where they could easily be found was not only careless but decidedly abnormal, compounded by his stunning ability to reappear at the home of the victim's family and talk with them without showing any strain or anxiety.

All in all, Dr. Cleckley gets the distinct impression that Jesse McKethan seemed rather content in jail, that he was not going through what a normal person would be experiencing under these circumstances. And here is where only a seasoned professional can glimpse behind the mask: as Jesse speaks reasonably and rationally about regretting his misdeeds, the doctor gets the strong impression that this is only a mask, not a temporarily assumed mask, but that his actual emotions are rather trivial and nowhere near as intense as the doctor would expect from an ordinary person. And that is the conclusion arrived at by Dr. Cleckley in his 9-page report, that Jesse McKethan is abnormal.

When Solicitor General Ryan receives the psychiatric evaluation he impatiently scans the document looking for one thing and one thing only: all he wants to know is whether the defendant is sane and can be held responsible for his actions. And nowhere in Dr. Cleckley's 9-page dissertation does he use the term "insane," which prompts Ryan to call the doctor at his office in Augusta to demand an explanation.

"*Insane* is not a medical term," Dr. Cleckley lectures the Solicitor. "Even if it was a medical term, whether or not Jesse McKethan should be put under that category is debatable. He is not totally responsible for his acts, and at the same time he is not totally irresponsible; that is the impression I have tried to convey."

"Yeah, but I have a heinous crime to prosecute," Ryan argues. "I have to go to trial in three weeks."

"That is your job," Dr. Cleckley reckons. "I have done mine."

* * *

The trial of Jesse McKethan was set to be heard by the Superior Court for the Eastern Judicial Circuit of Georgia on November 21, 1945, in Savannah. Solicitor General Andrew Ryan handled the State's case, guaranteeing that he would put the Butcher's ass in the electric chair and pull the switch personally, a guilty verdict being a foregone conclusion. He convinced Judge Atkinson to make an exception and put the case on the docket in three weeks, reminding him that they would be up for re-election. Nothing like a speedy trial and an execution to let folks know their Superior Court is at work and doing a fine job at that.

Only problem is, Judge Atkinson confides in Ryan, there ain't a lawyer in this entire state dumb enough to take this ass whippin' for the $200 the county can scrape up for putting in an appearance for an indigent madman. The judge thumbs through the list of lawyers on file with the court for such favors and settles on Edwin Feiler, whose main legal practice involves Real Estate transactions. "This shouldn't take long," Judge Atkinson says to Feiler. "The police have a confession, they have all the evidence. Just between me and you and the lamppost, you'll only have to make a brief appearance. It's open and shut, and should be done in a day." And before Feiler can say yea, nay or go to hell, the judge hangs up without so much as a goodbye, adding, "See you in court on the twenty-first."

With only three weeks in which to work, Feiler enlists the cooperation of another attorney, Edward Goodwin, and they set out to throw together some sort of defense for a client who not only confessed but also led police to the body and scavenged for evidence. Five police officers will spell out every detail of the crime, complete with a stack of black and white photographs depicting scenes guaranteed to remain in the memory for a lifetime. Looking around, Feiler and Goodwin cannot find much in the way of help. They have two ministers who will testify that Jesse had always been a good boy, and an elderly neighbor lady who will say that she was a dear friend of his mother and that she always feared he wasn't right in the head. They have the defendant's father, a pitiable man who has lost his wife and other sons to untimely illness, and will try to save his only remaining child from the electric chair by relating how a crack on the head at age four caused him to slaughter his best friend eighteen years later.

If Feiler and Goodwin have half a chance of helping their client, it rests with his family physician and a psychiatrist, and here is where they run into the deepest trouble. Their entire defense distills down to one difficult point to prove: that Jesse suffered a blackout as the result of Luther having struck him first, and not, as the prosecution contends, that he is using an old excuse as the perfect cover for the perfect crime. But the doctors sit on the proverbial fence between Jesse's ability to understand the difference between right and wrong, and the inability to control himself in the event that he goes into convulsive seizures, and that won't help Feiler and Goodwin.

In any event, the defense needs more time to prepare, and Feiler is granted a postponement of two months at the end of which, Judge Atkinson says, ready or not we go to trial.

Sixty days in stir gave Jesse plenty of time with nothing to do but think. He received no visitors other than Reverend Stipe, and reckoned that the court of public opinion had made up its mind in advance of the trial that he was a rat. He got to thinking about his old friends and what they might be thinking and saying about him, and since none of them dared to visit the jail, Jesse decided to jointly address them in a letter. He could think of no better place to mail his regrets than to Mr. Forsythe, the owner of the Daffin Park skating rink, where the gang hung out. Jesse's letter is reproduced here verbatim:

Dear Mr. Forsythe,

I guess you are to read a letter from me but I got to thinking about you and the ring.

I beg your most humbly forgiveness for putting those part out by your ring. I know it must have hurt your business.

Would you tell all my x friends out there I am sorry for what I did. I was out of my head when I did what I did. But it is too late now.

Would you put this letter for me where they can all read it.

(To Whom this may concern.)

You boy x girls that knew me when I had lot of money to spend and show a lots of you big times you know I was alright then but a little crazy in my ways. But I never did do any one of you any harm. I still think the world of a lots of you but I guess you all think I am a first class rat.

Well I guess I am. But I thought I would write you all at one time.

Maby some day I will be free again and show the world I am not a person like the youall thinks. That is if I don't get the chair. I don't know yet what is going to happen. If I do ever get out of this by serving my time they give me if it is 6 months, 6 year, 20 year or 30 year it I live I and coming back to Savannah I try and make my mistakes up to some people that I hurt very much and some people that is helping me get out of this trouble.

Maby some I will see be free.

91

Please those that want to write me here is my address.

You can visit me on Fridays.

Jessie R. McKethan

237 Habersham

When Mr. Forsythe received the letter he posted it on a bulletin board for all to see. After it had hung there long enough, one of the kids took it down and stashed it away for more than fifty years and did not see the light of day until it became part of this story.

* * *

The Superior Court is packed on January 25, 1946. The balcony of the courtroom is opened to spectators for the first time since November 1942, when Polignac Bourquin fired a double-barreled shotgun from the balcony in the general direction of the judge's bench. Since that time the balcony had been locked and no one permitted to sit there during court proceedings. But both the balcony and lower floor is crowded with spectators this day to see the best free show in town.

The jury is composed of citizens from all walks of life, including a bookkeeper, clerk, dairyman, chemist, electrician, insurance underwriter, and two service station attendants. They scarcely have time to settle into their seats in the jury box before Solicitor General Ryan is standing before them nose to nose and warning them in a very loud voice of the shocking story they are about to hear.

Ryan wastes no time in calling Police Inspector Cheatham Hodges, who introduces his garish photograph of a severed leg into evidence. Police Inspector Raymond Doney, who offers seven additional photographs of Luther's body and the crime scenes, follows Hodges. And then Ryan calls Dr. Emerson Ham to the stand to describe his role in the coroner's inquest and the process by which the coroner's jury came to the conclusion that the cause of Luther's death was strangulation.

During Dr. Ham's testimony he tells the court that at the inquest Jesse made a brief statement and answered a few questions. Ham says Jesse admitted to striking his victim with some sort of instrument but couldn't remember what it was, which Ham says did not strike him as strange, under the circumstances. There is a perfect opening here for the prosecutor to explore the blackout defense that he misses, and so Judge Atkinson makes up for the prosecutor's failure by asking questions directly of Dr. Ham.

"I don't remember him saying anything on that particular point," Dr. Ham tells the judge. "I don't remember the word *blackout*. He stated that he ran down the road and realized then what possibly happened and went back and examined the body. I don't know whether that would be termed a blackout, but he did not use that actual term at the inquest. He just said there was considerable confusion, and that he struck the victim with something, he didn't remember what." And that was about as good as the prosecution was going to get out of Dr. Ham short of writing out a response to the question and handing it to him to read.

Detective Sergeant Edward Fitzgerald was sworn in next as the State's star witness, and for the rest of the morning until dinner recess at 2:30 p.m., the man who had recently been awarded an engraved Bulova gold watch for his brilliant work in the case of the Butcher Murder read from his pad about his exploits in tailing the suspect and cracking the case. Fitzgerald was as good a witness as he was a cop, and was careful to preserve the State's case that Jesse McKethan knew exactly what he was doing on the night of the murder and could remember every detail with the exception of what he used to hit Luther.

"I asked him, I said, 'Now, Jesse, were you drunk this night?' and he said, 'No, sir. I do not drink any whisky. I drink beer. I was not out of my mind. I always know what I'm doing.' And I said, 'You remember all this?' and he said, 'Yes, sir. I remember every detail I'm telling you.' Now I'm telling you," Fitzgerald says to the jury, "I've known the McKethans, I imagine, fifteen years. I know this boy to see him, and he knew me to see me. The statements he made to us on Thirty-eighth Street and later before Sergeant Hallman were all made freely and voluntarily. He wanted to do it, and said that he was glad to get it off his chest."

And before handing over Fitzgerald to the defense for cross-examination, Ryan offers into evidence a hatchet, knife, two bloody bags, and a bottle of creolin, Luther's shoes and clothing, a pillow and pillowslip, three detective magazines and a set of keys.

From the moment the trial started, Edwin Feiler found himself in an impossible situation. The train had left the station long ago, leaving Feiler standing alone with nothing in his valise but the insinuation that police had somehow tricked or coerced or threatened Jesse McKethan into a confession in the back seat of a police car parked at the end of a deserted street. It was not a good idea to attack the detective who was being hailed as a local hero, but it was all Feiler had to go on.

"It wasn't necessary to go to the barracks to talk to him," Fitzgerald argues with Feiler. "I can talk to him in a car. That was no departure from ordinary police procedure. It was broad daylight, and the end of Thirty-eighth Street isn't deserted. There are big projects all around there, and there's a house not ten feet from where we were parked. We were with Detectives Brennan and Perkins, and I didn't want to come all the way back to the barracks with him if he was going to show us where the other parts of the body were."

"Had you placed him under arrest before he made this statement to you and the other detectives in the car?" Feiler asks.

"He did not know he was under arrest, but I knew it," Fitzgerald says, drawing smiles of admiration from the spectators. "Y'know, when a person makes a statement sounding strange and abnormal, the natural course is to question him further along certain lines. McKethan's statement, in view of his friendship with Aids, sounded strange because he said he got into an argument with him about this picture. He did not tell me he received this blow on the head. He just said Luther laid his hand back there. According to him, the body was not cut up until twenty-four hours later; that within a few hours of killing him, he took the clothes off in the yard and put them under the house. It sounded to me like a planned murder."

The only other point Feiler can come up with to shoot a hole in the prosecution's case so far is to take up the issue of how Luther's car could've been driven home from the scene of the murder if Jesse does not know how to drive. This fact originally led police to suspect that there was a second person involved in Luther's murder, but Jesse had convinced them that he drove the car in low gear to the Aids' house and left it half way in the middle of the street.

"I asked him half a dozen times how he did it," Fitzgerald testifies. "He'd say, 'I don't know, but I did it.' I've seen lots of them driving who could not drive," provoking a slight but much needed comic relief to the otherwise dismal hearing.

The State's case includes Carroll Hendrix, the 16-year-old boy who had known Luther approximately eight months and who will provide details of events leading up to the murder. He remembers that on the night of the murder that Jesse drank as many as ten beers at the Gold Star—on top of what he drank earlier that day—and that when Luther picked them up to drive them home Jesse was "pretty high." But then, Carroll says, Jesse never stopped at one; he always took three or four bottles of beer.

Carroll is the only friend of Luther and Jesse to appear as a witness for either side. If there is to be any direct testimony about Jesse's freakish ways, it comes from Carroll. The prosecutor delves into Jesse's hypnotic powers, and Carroll admits that Jesse had put him to sleep on three or four occasions by massaging his neck. He says he had seen Jesse do it to other boys, but they always came right back. The idea, as far as Carroll could tell, was to experience what it was like to blackout.

Feiler takes a step further into exploring Jesse's manipulations of young boys and has Carroll describe how on one occasion Jesse held him by the throat and tried to unbutton his pants. "He opened two buttons and mashed my stomach," Carroll says, "but he never made any other advances or improper proposals."

"Were you aware of Jesse having any head injury that he was sensitive about, that other kids may have teased him by trying to touch it?" Feiler probes the witness.

"I knew McKethan had a bad place on his head," Carroll answers. "I saw it and asked him what it was. He said he fell out of a building. I did not know of boys teasing him by trying to touch it."

The Solicitor General then calls George Aids to the stand to describe the events surrounding Luther's disappearance and the odd reappearance of his car at the Aids house the following morning. He recounts how Jesse was always turning up at their door with a new lead or idea on how to find his friend, and the growing suspicions that Jesse knew more than he let on.

There is a new twist in George's testimony, involving the wrench he found on the floor of the back seat of Luther's car. George tells the jury that after Jesse was arrested and made his confession, that he confronted Jesse to find out why he had killed his son. And in describing how a fight broke out over a photograph, "McKethan said he struck Luther with something while sitting in the back seat, Luther in front, and then dragged him out of the car and choked him. He did not tell me that my son struck him in the head."

George's testimony creates all sorts of conflicts with Jesse's confession and the statements he made to police, but the Solicitor General offers the wrench into evidence and which raises an objection from Feiler. It wasn't possible to raise an objection over a hatchet and knife that Jesse willingly turned over to police, but the wrench is circumstantial, has no traces of blood or fingerprints, and is highly suspicious. The coroner's jury having ruled the death to have been caused by strangulation, there is no need for a murder weapon, but to have the wrench thrown out will assist Feiler in his defense that Luther struck the first blow and everything that happened afterwards was the result of Jesse's blackout. Judge Atkinson, however, is way ahead of the defense attorneys and admits the wrench into evidence over their objection.

In winding up the State's case, Ryan puts Roger Coursey on the stand to briefly describe the initial discovery of the severed leg. Coursey is followed to the stand by Detective Perkins, a former licensed embalmer, who will describe the tendency for dead bodies to emit gas sounding like a groan, and then Sgt. Hallman, who takes the jury through the process of Jesse's confession at the police barracks. At the conclusion of Hallman's testimony, Ryan offers Jesse's signed confession into evidence and advises the court that the State rests.

It is late afternoon but not so late as to prevent the defense from calling its first witness; to the casual observer, the speed with which the State presented its case makes it look like they are trying to get this trial over with by the end of the day.

Feiler looks at his short list of witnesses and decides his best chance of turning the tide lies with Peyton McKethan, whose withered appearance makes him look like a ghost. "I am the father of this defendant, who was twenty-one years old the twenty-first of June," Peyton whispers. "Besides him and myself, there are no other members of my immediate family at this time. We had four boys and three of them died by sudden deaths. About two years ago one fell dead on a Sunday night, about twelve o'clock; the other dropped dead four months from that date, five o'clock in the afternoon."

Peyton McKethan looks at his son and begins to cry. The judge and jury and the gallery down to the last man sits stock-still, afraid to so much as breathe. Even Andrew Ryan lowers his eyes to avoid seeing the old man crumble. Edwin Feiler stares at his legal pad and cannot read what he has written as his second question. The witness is excused, and as Peyton limps out of the courtroom all the air seems to have momentarily leaked out of these proceedings.

Feiler calls a man named Wooten to the stand, an employee of Union Bag whose sole purpose is to say that for the seven months he has known Jesse McKethan that he had a good general reputation for peacefulness. From the looks of him, Wooten would rather be in any one of a hundred different places, and the jury regards him with a shrug of the shoulders.

Feiler cuts short Wooten's testimony to get to Mrs. Leila George, an elderly neighbor of the McKethans who was a dear friend of Jesse's mother and had known Jesse all his life. Mrs. George has a tendency to ramble on like a neighborhood gossiper, and hits the ground running in mid-thought. "Last summer Jesse's father had put some tomatoes to ripen on the back porch. I saw Jesse standing there an hour, throwing the tomatoes up and catching them. It did not seem natural for a boy his age. During the illness of his mother I talked with him on several occasions. Sometimes he would act like he knew me and sometimes not. As far as my opinion is concerned, I do not think that he has his full faculties. I only knew about the injury to his head from what his mother told me."

The prosecutor is fully aware that Mrs. George is making an impression upon the jurors. They may not be smart enough to understand everything a psychiatrist may say, but the word of a little old lady in Savannah, Georgia, holds great sway with every mother's son. Mr. Ryan decides he better challenge Leila George's ability to judge a person's sanity before she derails his case.

"Would you know a crazy person if you saw one, Miz George?" Ryan asks the witness, with a smile.

"I never had any dealings with crazy people," she answers, "but I don't think he's right exactly. He is not what I'd call insane, but he is not normal. I don't think he ought to be turned loose on society to run around the streets."

"Well, now, Miz George, how is it that a man who is not mentally right can go to work at the Southeastern Shipyard and be promoted November 2nd, 1942, to ship fitter helper second class; December 7th, 1942, to ship fitter helper first class; January 4th, 1943, to ship fitter worker fourth class; February 1st, 1943, to third class; March 8th, 1943, to second class; May 5th, 1943, to first class; September 13th, 1943, to skilled ship fitter, and finally promoted to lofts man on November 20th, 1944?"

"Well, I don't know," Mrs. George says, drawing herself to her full height. All of a sudden the mother comes out in her, and she scolds Andrew Ryan for his impertinence. "Some people can be smart in some things and dull in others; maybe that's the way he is. I was talking about his behavior as far as I knew; what he did at the shipyard I don't know. Normal people do not throw tomatoes up and catch them for an hour, Mister Ryan."

The Solicitor General had crossed swords with many a legal eagle adversary, but he had never encountered anyone like Leila George. She takes him to school like he's her third-grade pupil, and she will not have him questioning her judgment. Still, Ryan cannot tolerate being shown up by a little old lady, and relentlessly presses on.

"If you felt that way about him, Miz George, why didn't you report him to authorities?" Ryan scores.

"I was a very good friend of his mother. I was not afraid of him," she says, and then pauses to look at Jessie's baby boy. "I am afraid of him now."

Whether or not Mr. Ryan has any further questions of this witness, Mrs. George is exhausted and does not want to entertain any more. The Solicitor General yields the floor.

If nothing else, Leila George's testimony has provided Edwin Feiler with an opening he hadn't planned on. She has cast poor Jesse in a sympathetic light, and no amount of coaching from a lawyer can prompt this kind of response from a kindly old lady unless she is sincere. Feiler asks the judge for a five-minute recess, and then runs out of the courtroom to find Peyton McKethan.

"If I could just have you back on the stand for a moment, sir, I believe we can save your son," Feiler tells him. "Now I want to ask you a few questions about the injury to Jesse's head, and if you think you can bear up under questioning just a little while, your testimony will do a world of good."

Peyton passively submits to Feiler's request, and his reappearance on the stand has the jury and gallery riveted to their seats.

"I will remind you, Mister McKethan, that you are still under oath," Feiler begins. "I'd like for you to tell the jury about Jesse's state of mind at the time of his mother's death in July, 1945, if you could, sir."

"When his mother died Jesse brooded over it badly," Peyton says. "I think he brooded over his brother just as much. I have seen him sit for hours, maybe put on one shoe and sit there and study. He would walk all over the house with one shoe on, and then he would come back and put on the other shoe. Before his mother died, many times she would call him to go to work and he would answer but he would not get up. One day his mother was on the phone to her sister during supper. If there was fifty things on the table he would want some of all on his plate at once. His mother would fuss. As she came from the phone she slapped him on the head. He was out of that house and gone. She said, 'What do you think of that?' and I said, 'He's crazy.' And she got on me for calling the child crazy. He was back in ten or fifteen minutes, and she got after him about it. He said, 'Mother, whatever you do, don't hit me in the head.' When he was four years old he had a fall at a house on Taylor Street, three stories over a basement, and he has never fully recovered from it. His head hit the edge of the curbing, and for four or five days we thought he was going to die."

"Were there any other instances you are aware of when someone slapped Jesse on the head and it provoked a violent reaction?" Feiler continues.

"One night his brother Dick came in drinking and popped him 'side the head with his hand. He did not mean to hurt him, but Jesse grabbed a little table I had made and busted it to pieces over Dick's head, and ran out the front door. Ordinarily he was quiet and peaceful, but when he would get a blow on the head he would go off completely. I think he is unsound mentally. There are so many things we never paid attention to until after this trouble. For instance, I had lots of tools. He would lend people my tools, and I would get after him when he could not think of who got them. I would not get my tools back. I had to watch him."

"And as far back as you can remember, following the accident when he was age four, was Jesse different from his brothers and the other kids in the neighborhood?"

"His head was so much bigger than his body when little that everybody called him 'Jug Head,'" Peyton recalls. "At times he was normal like any other child. At other times he had no sense, due, I think, to lack of coordination between the mind and the body."

On cross-examination, Solicitor General Ryan probes into other instances of Jesse losing control due to a blow to the head.

"I cannot tell all of them," Peyton answers. "I know one day out in the yard in some way he hit his forehead on a pear tree. He had a rock in his hand and he threw the rock as far as he could and out that gate he went. He has spells at times," Peyton says, and then his eyes well with tears and his voice trails away.

"He was the baby boy," Peyton says, his voice cracking. "Sixteen years between him and the next youngest. He was a reg'lar mamma's child, whatever he wanted she let him have it, unless it was something he ought not to have."

There is no point in pursuing a hostile line of questioning with Peyton. Ryan can sense that the jury is solidly on the old man's side.

But before stepping down from the stand, Peyton draws a deep breath and tells the jury something they ought to remember.

"His mother knew the serious injury he had when he fell and yet she slapped him on the head," Peyton says. "When he came back, he said, 'Mamma, whatever you do, don't hit me on the head.'"

As Peyton exits from the courtroom, the lawyers for Jesse McKethan sense a shift in the emotional tide of the trial. The same jurors who had been repulsed by Detective Fitzgerald's detailed account of the murder and looked at the defendant as a monster are taking a second look at Peyton's baby boy. Jesse's fate now rests in the hands of Dr. Whelan and Dr. Cleckley, witnesses for the defendant, who can put a more scientific spin on the nature of the physical and mental problems that plague him.

One word from Dr. Cleckley means the difference between Jesse going to jail, the electric chair, or to a psychiatric facility to receive the help he deserves, and that one word is *Insane*. The only trouble is *Insane* is not a medical term commonly found in Cleckley's vocabulary. How to handle a psychiatrist on the witness stand is Feiler's task; it's enough to drive a man crazy.

Dr. Cleckley

PART V
THE TRIAL

January 25, 1946

As the murder trial of Jesse McKethan enters the second and final day of testimony, defense attorney Edwin Feiler senses that the jury's verdict will be decided on the medical information provided by a family physician and a psychiatrist ordered into the case by Governor Arnall. Feiler sends Dr. Edward Whelan, the McKethan s family doctor, to the stand first. Whelan has been practicing medicine in Savannah for twenty years and is well known. His warm and familiar manner is easier for the jury to relate to than the cold, clinical countenance of Dr. Cleckley.

Feiler takes Dr. Whelan through the tragic medical history of Jesses mother and brothers and how he came to associate Dr. Cleckley in the case through the intervention of Rev. Stipe.

"There arises the all-important question as to this man's sanity, Whelan says, speaking to the heart of the matter. "Is he sane and competent or is he insane and irresponsible. Usually, I believe this issue is determined on the point whether or not a man knows the difference between right and wrong. In the ordinary sense, I have no doubt, Mr. McKethan knows the difference. I am sure that he can speak accurately about the crime involved in the killing of Mr. Aids."

And then the psychiatric report becomes bogged down by hair-splitting definitions that tax the jury's ability to maintain a sympathetic concern for Jesse's state of mind. Dr. Whelan conjugates the verb "to know," and goes into a long-winded explanation of "knowing" the difference between right and wrong and "feeling" adequately towards that difference.

"Often such people can foresee the error of such conduct, but they continue to behave in irrational or anti-social ways," Whelan explains. "Legal and moral responsibility are often complex and profound. A person may know what is wrong in the shallow or verbal sense but may not evaluate emotionally the significance of such an act. In other words, this last statement refers to Jesse McKethan, as having an abnormal mentality."

Feiler is anxious to jump in at this point and help Dr. Whelan fine-tune what he means by "abnormal mentality." Feiler's eyes nervously dart from the doctor to the jury and back, concerned that very good points in the defense's favor are being lost by the rigmarole of medical reasoning.

"If we consider the deviation or abnormality which you are convinced is present, this failure to feel and evaluate life as others do, what can we say as to how this affects the defendant's responsibility or competency?" Feiler directs the doctor.

"Well, as a physician, I would estimate that it makes him less competent than the ordinary man and perhaps less responsible. I do not believe, however, that it makes him totally incompetent or entirely without responsibility for a deed of violence. If one considers the future, one must ask the question: what would such a personality as this be likely to do if he were again free in the community? If my estimate of the case is correct, I feel that on another occasion he would be more likely than the average man to give way again to an act of violence. That does not mean that he would do it out of pure meanness, but he could not help himself."

Dr. Whelan then introduces X-rays of Jesse's cranium, holding them up against the light streaming in the south window of the courtroom where all jurors could see them. He explains the history of the injury Jesse sustained as a child, and points out the depression. "In this area he evidently suffers blackouts in the same manner as an epileptic," Whelan says. "Pressure here causes him to go into convulsive seizures."

Dr. Whelan puts the X-rays on the table in front of Feiler and walks around behind Jesse. And then he does something no one expects: he takes Jesse's head in his hands and shows the jury the indentation, then presses the soft spot. Newspaper reporters would note that Jesse showed no reaction but quietly submitted to the examination; had he jumped or started or reacted in any manner denoting a special sensitivity to the old wound, it would have been better for him. Dr. Whelan returns to the witness stand, and in that fleeting moment, Edwin Feiler's case flew out the window that had shed light on the X-rays.

"Dr. Cleckley and I both consider this boy is homosexual, a man without any apparent love for the opposite sex," Whelan concludes. "I don't mean that he is a pervert, but it is an extremely abnormal condition. Homosexual is not necessarily synonymous with perversion," he explains, and then illustrates Jesse's peculiarities by publicly exposing the dirty little secret of his visit to Indian Lil's whorehouse.

"But to cut up a body, I think we all agree that is abnormal. You don t have to be a doctor," Whelan says to the jury, "but as to whether he should be held criminally responsible for an act committed by him, that all depends: he can differentiate between right and wrong, but if one should hit him on that side of the head and he goes into convulsive seizures, the same as an epileptic, and gets a blackout and does not remember anything that happened...I consider that absolutely abnormal. He would be no more responsible than an epileptic in a state of convulsive seizures. He would not know what he would be doing."

Coming within a breath of using the word *Insane* and then backing away, Whelan has found every other term to describe his patient and before that settles in the jury's mind, the Solicitor General is following up on cross-examination with a few hard questions of his own. Andrew Ryan has an unfair advantage over Edwin Feiler; the Solicitor General is an old hat at trying murder cases. In the next few minutes, all the good that the good doctor had done his patient will be undone.

"My observation and diagnosis are almost entirely subjective, depending on what Jesse has told me," Whelan apologizes. "There was nothing we could put our fingers on except the X-rays. It is possible that brain damage occurring when he was four years of age has contributed to a cerebral dysrhythmia, causing him to have epileptic equivalents. This, however, is far from being established."

Dr. Whelan looks around the courtroom and sees a look of anguish register on Edwin Feiler's face, and makes one more pass at trying to satisfy the question as to Jesse's sanity.

"Frankly, if I may be permitted to say so, I do not think he is a lunatic in so far as we judge lunatics," Whelan says. "He is a menace to society due to a physical defect brought about through no fault of his; it is one of those things that could happen to any of us. My personal view is that he should be under permanent guard and made to work and be of some use to the state."

Feiler seems more satisfied but only for a moment, as Dr. Whelan lays one crucial condition on top of his opinion.

"That is, working upon the assumption that this killing he did was the result of a blackout," Whelan concludes. "If he killed this boy without any blackout, he would be guilty of murder."

Feiler pounces upon Whelan's capitulation, trying to minimize the damage. "Sane or Insane, Doctor?" Feiler shouts at his witness. "Do you really think that after all these X-rays and examinations which you yourself consider to be inconclusive of his condition that this boy should be put in the electric chair?"

Whelan makes every attempt to maintain his professional composure. "There are all forms of insanity," he says. "You don't have to be a raving maniac to be insane. Everyone is not a maniac who is insane. As to whether he should be electrocuted in my opinion...that is not my function."

Feiler excuses Dr. Whelan from the witness stand. Quite frankly, he had expected more compassion from a family doctor and would later tell him so. At his best, Whelan had helped the defense establish Jesse's abnormality even though he had straddled the fence as to his legal responsibility; at his worst, Whelan had congratulated Solicitor General Ryan, Judge Atkinson and Governor Arnall for having used every means in their power to secure adequate attention for Jesse, left-handedly appearing to be on the prosecution's side. At every point in between, wherever Whelan might have taken one last step in declaring Jesse's incompetence, he backed away as if he were afraid of mercy. And that was the same feeling the jury took with them when they went into deliberation.

Feiler hoped to get a measure of mercy from the testimonies of Rev. Stipe and Rev. Shearouse that was lacking in Dr. Whelan, but the rules of evidence prohibited him from pleading the case as if he were standing in front of St. Peter. The most he could get out of the pastors was Jesse's spotty attendance record in church and his reputation for peacefulness. When the religious angle failed to produce, Feiler had no choice but to fall back on science and call Dr. Cleckley to the stand.

After providing his impressive resume, Dr. Cleckley took jurors through his physical examination of the defendant and his general impressions of his psychosexual history. It is when Cleckley turns his attention to the brain injury Jesse suffered as a child that he runs into the same trouble as Dr. Whelan.

"That he had on three different occasions experienced blankness, without being able to recall anything he did, brings up the possibility that there was a skull injury with consequent brain damage. A person subject to epileptic fits may have convulsions, or he may fall into a totally unconscious state and become violently destructive toward anyone present; he would be temporarily unconscious. I am not convinced that this is true in this case," Cleckley says to Feiler, "but I think there is a chance of that."

And before Feiler can maximize the potential benefit of this statement, Cleckley backs away and modifies his position. "I would think, however, to determine that as a very strong probability, he would be more likely to have more of those spells of convulsions. He reports of having them only three times."

Feiler again tries to insert a question of clarification here but is cut off by Cleckley. "On the other hand, there are changes in him which are indisputable. I think any psychiatrist would be impressed by the true personal abnormality, then his lack of capacity for remorse or grief, entirely different from normal. For persons of that sort we usually make the classification of psychopathic personality."

Feiler yields the floor as the psychiatrist establishes an important point only to argue its counterpoint in the next breath.

"Psychopathic personality is a problem on which psychiatrists often argue, and the defendant in this case is not typical of psychopathic personality as it is usually understood. It is generally considered as applying to a person whose emotional or mental state differences from the normal, consisting of incapacity to feel what others feel. I have known people who had definite delusions, would hear voices, and yet have enough judgment left to work and make a living and not harm other people. I feel McKethan can express the difference between right and wrong in words, but not in the full sense."

"Doctor, in your opinion, does Jesse McKethan know the difference between right and wrong?" Feiler asks in plain English.

"I do not get the impression that he wholeheartedly participates, feels the significance in matters of right and wrong or what is desirable or undesirable as the normal or average man does. I will say he is *abnormal*."

"Sane or insane, Doctor Cleckley?"

"*Insane* is not a medical term," Cleckley says, with some satisfaction. "Whether or not he should be put under that category is debatable. He is not totally responsible for his acts, and at the same time he is not totally irresponsible."

While Dr. Cleckley is giving his testimony Jesse sits in the defendant's chair with an expression of seriousness on his face. His hands remain folded throughout the entire proceedings and his features reflect no feeling or emotion or anxiety. Only once or twice does he take his eyes off the witness, and each time they quickly shift back to the witness stand.

It is Andrew Ryan's turn to cross-examine Dr. Cleckley. The last time the two men spoke was on the phone three months before, when the doctor refused to indulge the Solicitor General with a yes or no answer as to the question of Jesse's sanity. There is a leftover animosity that Ryan feels towards Cleckley, and his questions of the witness are designed to shake him up.

"Does a man have a soul, Doctor?" Ryan begins.

"I don't know," Cleckley says, his eyebrows arched.

"Well, a man has a body. Does he have a soul?"

"I do not deny the existence of a man's soul," Cleckley explains. "I do not know whether he has a soul. I would have to have your position more clearly."

"Well, does God tell Man what to do, or does Man have a will power of his own?" Ryan poses.

"I do recognize that Man has some restraint over Nature. Will power is rather a loose term. Whether it is God speaking to you, as you put it, many things make me spend my life as a decent citizen: the pleasure of work, the feeling of its importance. I would not like to use the word conscience."

Whatever prompted Ryan to pursue this bizarre line of questioning comes to an abrupt halt, and he goes off in another tangent designed to trip up Dr. Cleckley. But Cleckley lays enough medical terminology on top of his answers so as to wrestle back control of the situation in a way in which only a psychiatrist can.

"Symptoms are generally referred to as objective or subjective," Cleckley lectures Ryan. "An objective symptom is one largely dependent upon what the patient says. For instance, for objective symptoms you look to the X-rays; for subjective symptoms, the patient may hear voices. Of course, he may be lying. The State maintains in Milledgeville an asylum for the insane. There are also private institutions. So if a person is found insane, he is not turned out upon the streets. It is my understanding that in order for a man to be sent to the asylum at Milledgeville he has to be adjudged insane."

There is a look of complete exasperation on Andrew Ryan's face as he listens to Dr. Cleckley repeatedly use a word which he has repeatedly said he doesn't use: Insane. And here by the psychiatrist's own admission is his awareness of the legal axiom that a defendant may be sent to an asylum only upon a finding of insanity. Even Judge Atkinson is perplexed by this maddening inconsistency, and he interrupts Ryan's cross-examination to get to the bottom of this mess.

"Doctor Cleckley, is the defendant in this case insane?" Atkinson asks.

"We do not use the word *insanity* in this profession," Cleckley answers. "I believe a person may know the difference between right and wrong, and yet there is the question whether he has the will to respond to this sense which enters into the discussion."

The judge looks at the prosecutor with a blank expression, and Edwin Feiler resists a strong urge to throttle the witness. In the next few moments when no one on either side is certain how to solve the conundrum of the psychiatrist who refuses to settle the question only he can answer, a juror speaks up.

"So, if I understand you correctly, Doctor Cleckley, there are a lot of abnormal people running around loose," the juror says, provoking laughter from the gallery.

Cleckley answers with a straight face. "It is possible that a great number of individuals have some slight abnormality," he says, and is excused from the witness stand.

Edwin Feiler glances through his notes and realizes that his star witnesses have failed to deliver what he needs to keep his client out of the electric chair. He is stunned, and he doesn't know what to do next. He has never been in this awkward position, and turns to his client to ask him if he has anything he wants to say to the jury before going to final argument. Jesse rises from his seat and in a quiet voice that barely reaches the last juror, begins an impromptu statement that will run almost thirty minutes.

"Your honor and gentlemen of the jury, I am not guilty of the murder of George Luther Aids," Jesse says. "They say I killed him; if I did I was not mentally responsible at the time. I have a clean conscience, as I did not know what I was doing when I killed him."

It wasn't Blackstone, but then again Jesse was making no less sense than the psychiatrist. He recounts how at age four he had fallen three storeys to the pavement and cracked his head and how he developed a weak heart from remaining in bed for one year. He intersperses the episodes caused by a slap to the head with accounts of the deaths of his three brothers and the alcoholism that had always plagued the family. No one hearing the history of his torment could fail to be deeply moved.

When Jesse speaks of Luther, new aspects of their relationship emerge, as if he wants it known that they were much closer than even Luther's parents would allow.

"I got Luther a job three times," Jesse recounts, "and he was fired all three times. He either laid off or was sick on the job, or for other reasons. I met him at Southeastern Shipyard and we became good friends. We bought a car together and I took him everywhere. I did spend large sums of money on different boys, but that was the only happiness I knew.

"When we would go out together Aids would get highly intoxicated because he was much younger than I and could not hold it. One night he went to Tybee and ran into the tower. He resisted arrest and did not have a driver's permit. I did all I could to help him out. When the trial came up he was fined ten dollars or thirty days on the Brown Farm. Then the Aids' had some trouble in the home: they were arguing and the father attempted to beat the mother, and Luther hit him on the head with something. He was arrested and fined twenty-five dollars or thirty. There are records to verify that. His mother liked for us to go together because I kept him out of trouble and on the job. He did not like to work but liked a big time."

And then Jesse moves into an account of the day of the murder, realizing that his description of how the argument escalated into a fight will be a determining factor in the jury's decision whether the crime was the result of a blackout or cold-blooded murder.

"Sergeant Fitzgerald said he patted me on the head," Jesse argues. "Luther swung at me and I saw he was mad. I had a complete blackout when he struck me in back of the head. The next thing I remember he was lying on the ground. I went into the house and got a pillow and laid it under his head. I don't know how I did it, but I dragged him around to the side of the house."

Jesse's recollections of the days immediately following the murder manage to circumvent a description of how he dissected and disposed of Luther's body. He skips that part to explain why he had confessed to police, that he feared being beat into a confession.

"I heard my brother talking when drinking about how they beat prisoners to make them confess, and I told them what I did because I was scared of them. I knew if they hit me with that rubber hose they would hurt my head and I might have hurt them. I knew their methods," Jesse accuses. "I know how they get statements from other prisoners. I told them and showed them where everything was because I was scared. That's just the way they handle it: they treated me good in the police department because they thought I told them the truth."

And then the statement that had run smoothly and coherently for more than twenty minutes dissolves into a laundry list of minor points Jesse wants to clarify. He begins to ramble, recalling first one event and then another that he had previously mentioned.

"When I went to Southeastern, Mr. Lilly had sympathy for me and that is why he promoted me. Very few people can say that I have caused them harm in any way. I feel very sorry for Luther's mother because I know what she went through. I was not mentally responsible at the time. Everything the detectives have is what I gave them. About the shoes: I did not know how they got there. They told me if I would trail along with them they would be lenient with me. At the time that accident happened we were scuffling, but that was all," Jesse says, and then pauses. "Gentlemen of the jury, that is all I got to say. Thank you."

Jesse returns to his seat and looks at his attorneys. They have no more witnesses to speak on Jesse's behalf, and announce to the court that the defense rests.

The Solicitor General has a laundry list of his own to clean up. He trots out Detective Fitzgerald to straighten out this thing about cops using rubber hoses to beat confessions out of criminals, prompting Edwin Feiler to leap out of his chair and engage the Solicitor General in a heated argument on the appropriateness of taking a suspect into the woods to obtain a confession.

"He knew the case would be a spectacular one," Feiler shouts at Ryan while pointing a finger at Fitzgerald. "He was awarded that watch for his brilliant detective work..."

"All I wanted was the murderer," Fitzgerald interjects, "and I got him."

Judge Atkinson steps between the lawyers before they come to blows and restores order to his courtroom. Fitzgerald is excused, and then Ryan introduces Deputy Sheriff Hubert Berne, who will testify that when he accompanied George Aids to confront Jesse McKethan at the jail that Mr. Aids questioned the suspect without making any inducements or threats.

Ryan also calls Collie Bruner to the stand to relate the odd occurrence of finding Jesse McKethan in the same cot with his cellmate one morning, and Edwin Feiler considers this testimony to be a low blow, obviously intended to inflame the jury.

"So let me ask you, since you brought it up, Mister Bruner, do you find cellmates sharing a bunk to be abnormal?" Feiler shoots at the witness.

Bruner is nonplused. "I am not to judge whether that was the act of a normal person," he says. "I am not going to answer that."

And just to add insult to injury, just to heap another dollop of abuse atop the mounting disgrace, and just because it is within his singular power to do so, the Solicitor General produces George Ennis, Jesse's cellmate, who is currently serving 2 to 4 years for Robbery.

"I remember one morning Mister Bruner came to the cell because we did not get up," Ennis says. "Both of us were in the upper bunk together. Why, I really don't know. McKethan got out of his bunk to come up there."

"Did he ever put his hands on you?" Ryan asks.

"He rubbed his hands over my body, sometimes twice a day. I allowed him to do it because I was scared of him. He said if he ever bumped his head it would cause him to lose his mind. He would not say anything, and it would not last very long. He said if I told on him and he ever got out..." Ennis says, and then stops in mid-sentence. "I was frightened by what he said."

"What did the prosecutor promise you in return for getting up on this witness stand and telling this stuff?" Feiler demands.

"I was tried and convicted in this court back in December," Ennis answers. "I was waiting in jail to be sent up. I pleaded guilty and have no appeal pending."

"And on this all-important day when the jailer finds you and Jesse on the same bunk, what else was going on between you?"

"McKethan was just on my bunk," Ennis says. "He just put his hands on me. He never bothered my private parts."

"One last question," Ryan announces, insisting on having the last word. "Did the defendant ever kiss you, Mister Ennis?"

Ennis looks past the Solicitor General at Jesse McKethan, who knows not what shame is, or if he does he doesn't show it.

"He did not kiss my body," Ennis says. "He would kiss my neck."

* * *

At the conclusion of testimony, Edwin Feiler had had his fill of this proceeding. He had made the mistake of picking a fight with the prosecutor over a detective who was just doing his job, and a fine job at that, according to the unanimous opinion of the public at large. Feiler left the chore of presenting the closing argument to his partner, Edward Goodwin.

Goodwin began his argument by setting forth the laws of insanity, a sound legal principle even if it was not a commonly used medical term, which eventually led to McKethan's principal defense that he was temporarily insane at the time of the murder, as a result of a blow on the head rendered by Aids.

Goodwin recapped how a life starting out was tragically altered by a head injury, complicated by a plague of illnesses that wiped out a family of three young boys, and that, perhaps, Jesse McKethan's odd fascination for other young boys was merely a misguided attempt to replace his dead brothers and not the perversion that the prosecution would have us believe. If Goodwin in his closing argument managed to touch upon the sympathy created by Peyton's testimony and the feisty Leila George, it did not last long with the jury once the Solicitor General took his turn.

After his opening remarks in which he paid tribute to the court-appointed defense attorneys, Ryan castigated Feiler for his remarks about Savannah police officers in which he unfairly depicted them as "would-be gangsters clothed in legal authority."

"Mister Feiler's attack was the most dastardly, unwarranted and unfair attack I have ever heard," Ryan hollers.

Ryan did not stop with Feiler. He still had bullets in the chamber with Dr. Cleckley's name on them. "When Doctor Cleckley said he doesn't know whether a man has a soul or not he is doubting the existence of God," Ryan accuses. "He is the man who comes here and calls Jesse McKethan abnormal. I guess we are all abnormal as far as Doctor Cleckley is concerned."

Although, observers in court are divided between this portion of Ryan's argument and the portion pertaining to McKethan's purported blackout as a main point in swaying the jury. In referring to the alleged blackout, Ryan notes, "He never blacked out, gentlemen, and I'll tell you why he didn't black out: He told the police he struck Aids with an instrument and pulled him out of the car and choked him. How would he know he hit him, choked him, if he blacked out?"

And this is the argument that many believe had great weight with the jury.

Following Ryan's closing argument Judge Atkinson charged the jury, touching on all the law points of determining sanity in a lesson lasting more than thirty minutes. Immediately after the jurors had retired for deliberation, the judge paid tribute to the police officers stating, "I have nothing but the highest respect for those officers who testified here. They are accustomed to criticism and have to learn to take it. They should glory in such criticism."

* * *

There's a bit of old court house wisdom that says you can judge what a jury's verdict will be depending on how long it takes for them to deliberate; the longer they're out, the better it is for the defense.

The jury in the Jesse McKethan case was not out long. Before beginning deliberation in chambers, the foreman offered a prayer for divine guidance and the defendant was found guilty on the first ballot. A second ballot was taken to determine if the jurors should include a recommendation of mercy, which did not pass. And then the jury was back in the courtroom with their verdict while a large number of spectators were still waiting.

Jesse stood quietly and showed no emotion as the clerk of court read the results. The following morning only a handful of spectators were on hand to hear the judge pronounce sentence upon the man who committed Chatham County's most fiendish crime.

Jesse McKethan days before his execution

PART VI
THE EXECUTION

February 26, 1946

"...To the State Penitentiary at Reidsville where he shall, on the eighth day of March, 1946, be put to death by electrocution and may God have mercy on your soul," declared Judge David Atkinson in Superior Court at 10:08 a.m. in passing sentence on Jesse McKethan, convicted slayer of George Luther Aids.

Superior Court jury pronounced the 22-year-old McKethan guilty at 6:03 p.m. last evening after having received the case at 5:15 p.m.

McKethan had been found guilty of murder for the slaying of the 17-year-old Aids on the early morning of October 8, 1945, when it was alleged he struck Aids on the head with an instrument, choked him to death and later dismembered the body and distributed its parts about the southeastern section of the city.

Edwin Feiler and Edward Goodwin, defense council, announced the defense would file a motion for a new trial within the next week.

After reading the charges under which McKethan had been found guilty, Judge Atkinson said this morning "It becomes the unpleasant duty of the court to pass sentence on the defendant." McKethan received the sentence without a sign of emotion, true to form. When he arose from his seat he stood erect and facing Judge Atkinson, blinking his eyes continuously throughout the reading of the sentence. He left the courtroom in the company of a deputy sheriff immediately after sentence was passed.

On March 15, 1946, Judge Atkinson overruled the motion for a new trial. Two weeks later, defense attorneys filed a Bill of Exceptions. On July 3rd, the

121

Georgia Supreme Court affirmed the Superior Court decision in which all justices concurred, and the defense had exhausted all remedies.

On July 31st, only eight days away from Jesse's date with the executioner, a delegation from Savannah appeared before the State Pardons and Paroles Board in Atlanta to ask that the death sentence be commuted to life imprisonment. Peyton McKethan made the journey with Edwin Feiler and Edward Goodwin but was unable to attend the appeal with counsel.

Goodwin addressed the board first, explaining that Jesse was mentally incompetent, that he did not remember committing the crime and that he blacked out during the time at which the crime occurred after receiving a blow on the head.

Solicitor General Andrew Ryan made a brief appearance to advise the board that McKethan was "just playing" on the idea of being blacked out, and that he had told investigating officers all details of the crime and that he was fully aware of having killed his best friend.

The most impassioned plea came from Dr. Edward Whelan, the McKethan family physician, who bore the brunt of the burden of having failed to convince the trial jury that his patient was mentally incompetent. Dr. Whelan went so far as to tell the board he doubted that Jesse was solely responsible for the crime, and suggested that a scientific lie detector test be given to Jesse in an effort to ascertain whether a third party was involved in the killing.

Dr. Whelan described his patient as a "homosexual psychopath" but quickly added that he was not a pervert, which did not seem to help his case.

Even Leila George made the trip in a reprise of the role that had won her the admiration of those spectators in court on the day she bested Mr. Ryan. She, too, believed that a third man was involved in the slaying, but she was far more convincing when she related instances that showed Jesse to be mentally unbalanced.

Mrs. George related that she had visited Jesse since his confinement in jail and that "he had the appearance of a man who was half drunk."

"He's not right," Mrs. George says, in that maternal way which means to persuade without being ugly.

The Rev. Henry Stipe, pastor of Grace Methodist Church, also made an appearance before the board to testify as to the nature of his many visits to the jail to see the prisoner during which he reached the inevitable conclusion that "Jesse is definitely not responsible for his acts. I don't think the boy has ever realized it."

Rev. Stipe repeated that Jesse told him "the boy he killed was a good boy, that he loved him and that he felt sorry for Luther's parents."

Rev. Stipe then read from a letter written by Rev. Ed Fain, pastor of the Wesley Monumental Methodist Church, who came to the same conclusion that Jesse is not normal in his mental condition.

Seemingly from out of nowhere appeared a man named McLamb, a railroad employee from Jesup, who told the board that he had become interested in McKethan's case after he had been imprisoned. "I think he's just as crazy as he could be to be out in a free country," McLamb says. "I know absolutely that the boy did not know what he was doing."

McLamb also testified that McKethan told him there was a third boy mixed up in the crime but that McKethan had told him, "Why ruin his life, too?"

Lastly, Attorney Goodwin introduced a letter from Mrs. J.C. Brewton, a neighbor of the McKethan's, which said that Jesse had suffered a "complete mental collapse" when his mother died.

Solicitor General Ryan patiently sat through the appeal and kept his respectful silence. When everyone else had been heard from, Ryan submitted an affidavit from Deputy Alfred Henry in which the officer declared that McKethan had told him en route to Tattnall prison from Savannah that no one else was involved in the killing of Luther Aids.

Looking at Dr. Whelan, Ryan tells the board, "Just because McKethan is a homosexual is no excuse for commission of a crime. My staff and I did everything possible to give the boy a fair trial. The defense's attempt to say the boy was blacked out during commission of the crime is without justification."

Ryan did not argue too long or too loud; there was no need. He knew that the delegation was fighting a lost battle, and it was unseemly to retry a case he had already won. The board made no response, but indicated that their decision would be made by the end of the day. And when the decision came, Leila George began to cry and did not stop until she returned home.

When news reached Savannah from Atlanta that the execution would not be stayed, George Aids and his brother Ernest filed a formal request with the sheriff to be allowed to witness the execution. It was up to Jesse; under Georgia law the condemned must give signed permission for such requests. Jesse declined, not because he did not want their company but because he was still holding out hope that he would somehow evade his date with the executioner. But when he saw Rev. Stipe and Dr. Whelan coming to say goodbye, he knew he had lost out.

Rev. Stipe led them in prayer, and arranged for a Communion service to be performed by the prison chaplain on the morning of the execution, now moved up from August 8th to the 2nd. And in a brief comment to the newspaper, Rev. Stipe related that the condemned man showed no emotion, true to form, but that he was much more serious now.

The time of the execution was set sometime between 11 a.m. and noon, depending on how long it took the electrician who performed the executions to arrive from Milledgeville. The warden said he would check with the Pardons and Paroles Board prior to the execution to make sure all was clear.

When it finally sunk in that all was lost and his days were numbered, Jesse had only one request to make of the warden: that he be allowed to send a last letter to the person who knew him best and tried hardest to win his reprieve, Leila George. When the request was granted, Jesse slicked back his hair and posed for the prison photographer, who hurriedly developed the film and gave him an 8 x 10 inch black and white print of his smiling face, looking more like a man who'd just found a million dollars than one who was headed for the electric chair.

Jesse put the picture in an envelope with a brief note thanking Mrs. George for all she had done for him. The letter disappeared in time, but the photo of Jesse the Butcher was among Leila George's most personal effects when she died many years later. (Leila's daughter kept the photo as her mother had, and is reproduced here through a minor miracle: the daughter's house had burned down in 1999, and the photo of Jesse McKethan is practically the only thing that survived).

Jesse was moved to the holding cell just a few short paces from the death chamber. He requested that some of his friends in the prison be allowed to visit him but this was denied. He made no other special requests except that he be allowed to pray with an aged Negro preacher who was serving a life sentence in the prison for murder. They spent an hour together discussing sin, forgiveness and death and the old man read from Scriptures the story of the murderer and robber who died on the cross at the side of Jesus Christ.

"When you see the Lord," the old man says to Jesse, "you look Him in the eye and you will be forgiven."

"The boy had a different look about him after the old man left," the guard told reporters afterward. "He seemed to brighten up just a little."

After eating his supper of regular prison fare at 11 p.m., Jesse lay down for a nap, requesting that the death-cell guard awaken him in two hours so they could talk for a while. But when the guard could not awaken him at the appointed hour, he let Jesse sleep until 4 a.m.

"I was dreaming of my mother and my friend Luther," Jesse says to the guard. "I am glad I made a true confession so that I can see them in heaven today. I'm ready to die." And then he asked the guard a lot of questions about the electric chair, its mechanism, and the length of time it takes to electrocute a man.

When the guard was relieved from duty, Jesse thanked him for his kindness. "There was a slight, noticeable change in his demeanor," the guard told reporters, "but he never showed any emotion. After spending an hour with the preacher last night, I believe he has found a complete peace and confidence that he has been forgiven for the crime he committed."

Prison chaplain Paul Lawrence administered Jesse's last Communion, after which the old Negro preacher returned with several inmates to sing hymns at the death cell door. Russell Rhoden, the editor of the Tattnall Journal, watched as Jesse's head was shaved in preparation for the execution, noticing that the condemned man continued to display not the slightest emotion and remained perfectly calm throughout his last moments. It was as if he had disengaged his soul from his body, if he had a soul, as the Solicitor General doubted. He seemed to lack the same participation in death that he had experienced in life.

Perhaps that complete peace which the death cell guard observed was nothing more than the hollow mask observed by the psychiatrist. Either way, the State executed a man who was already in many ways dead.

As Jesse's head was being shaved a telegram was handed him, signed by a girl whose name was not obtainable by Rhoden. The telegram said: "May God be with you, is my prayer."

Jesse handed the telegram back to the deputy without changing his blank expression.

"Anything you want to say?" Rhoden asks Jesse, as the moment of his death draws nearer.

"I've found the Lord, I am ready to go," Jesse says. "I feel I am saved. I am sorry that it had to be so late and this way, but otherwise I might not have been saved."

And then he begins to ramble, telling Rhoden that he wanted to send out a message to young people that they could see by his example that crime does not pay; and odd thing to say, Rhoden thought, since his crime did not involve money. And then he advised people to keep away from roadhouses and juke joints, and spoke out against intoxicants.

Jesse then turned his attention to those who hated him and those who loved him, uttering the hope that George and Dahlia Aids forgive him and that his father's grief might be bearable. He thanked Rev. Stipe and all those who had tried to help him, and as the editor scribbled notes on a pad with a shaky hand he could not help but notice that in his last moments of life on this planet that Jesse McKethan was as devoid of feeling as Dr. Whelan and Dr. Cleckley had advised his judge and jury. So that when Deputy Sheriff Berne told Jesse that it was time, he did not moan or cry or pitch a fit as most men do. He jumped up and fairly ran down the catwalk to the death chamber, not even pausing to take notice of the old Negro preacher and inmates singing hymns or to catch a last glimpse of sunlight that bathed the balcony catwalk, and jumped into the sheltering arms of Ol' Sparky without assistance, confident that he was on his way to heaven to be reunited with his mother and best friend.

As George and Ernest Aids watched from the witness chamber, Jesse settled back in his seat and was strapped in, looking more like a man flying first class on a dream vacation than a condemned man riding a thunderbolt to hell. Wearing prison garb, his right trouser leg was rolled up above the knee, and his feet were covered with comfy brown socks. His shirt was casually open at the neck.

"I have one question to ask you," Berne says to Jesse, being for the benefit of Mr. Feiler and Mr. Goodwin. "Did you tell the truth when you said that nobody else was involved in this crime with you?"

Jesse nods his head affirmatively.

And then as Rev. Lawrence muttered prayers, the electric current was switched on at 11:35 a.m. Ten minutes later Jesse was pronounced dead.

George Aids was the first to speak. "Thank God this is through with. I never wanted to see any man die except for this one. He deserved to die. I had prayed for this and am glad to be through with it."

No one else in the witness chamber had anything to add.

The charred remains of Jesse's body were dumped unceremoniously into a pine box and held at the prison mortuary for pickup. There wasn't a notice published in the newspaper listing the time and date when Peyton McKethan had his son committed to the family plot in Bonaventure Cemetery, at an uncomfortably short distance from the Aids plot. Out of shame and the fear of desecration, Peyton did not erect a marker over Jesse's grave.

The execution of Jesse McKethan drew no further comment or debate in The Savannah Morning News and Evening Press. Some people were glad he was gone because they said he was a monster, and some people were glad because they said he was a nut. Some said he was queer and that was reason enough to end his miserable life. Perhaps in 1946, as the world recovered from a war in which the daily papers recounted the horrors of concentration camps and innocent victims slaughtered by the millions, the death of one deranged faggot in Savannah, Georgia did not warrant much notice nor deserve any more attention than the brief column by Russell Rhoden that was sandwiched between the headlines "Work On Streets Appears Probable" and "Episcopal Home Needs Ice Box."

There were many other things to think about, from the profound to the mundane, but no one who lived in Savannah in 1946 ever forgot the murder of Luther Aids and the execution of Jesse McKethan.

In the days that followed, George Aids sold the Shipyard Inn and opened the Chick-Wee Drive Inn across the street and also ran a barbecue stand until his retirement in 1968. He and Dahlia were blessed with three daughters who married and started families of their own, and the Aids' had the comfort of many brothers and sisters. They did not speak of these matters. They did not write a book or make a movie or start some sort of bogus organization to ban teen violence or launch a campaign to prohibit the selling of beer to minors. They didn't talk about the tragedy and after awhile people stopped asking about it because that's what decent people do.

In the days that followed, Peyton McKethan drank himself to death; it took him ten years to succeed. He was all alone in this world except for two brothers whom he seldom saw. Rather than live alone in a house of horrors on East 38th Street, Peyton tore down the house and leveled the lot. He did not conduct tours of the site for curious tourists. He did not open a gift shop and sell photos of his infamous son or hawk t-shirts emblazoned with "Jesse the Butcher." He did not write a book or make a movie or offer his property for sale for millions of dollars because that's what decent people do.

And when Peyton died in January 1955, his body was placed in an unmarked grave next to his wife and sons as if he was embarrassed to be there. Perhaps when he died there was no one left to care.

* * *

The trial of Jesse McKethan lasted only two days. When it was over, people didn't sit around and debate the pros and cons of the case. There wasn't a Court Channel on TV to broadcast the proceedings with expert commentators to tell viewers the importance of what was going on. But anyone who takes a look at the trial transcripts cannot help but notice where an inexperienced pair of court-appointed lawyers missed a chance here and there to turn the tide of public opinion and perhaps win a different decision. They got no help from Jesse's doctors on the witness stand, as if the rules of decency in that day declared that mercy should not extend to homosexual psychopaths. Certainly if the trial were to be held today, it would last for longer than two days; the appeals might stretch out for years, and the subject of Jesse's sanity would receive far greater circumspection than he was afforded in 1946.

Personally, having read the entire trial transcript, I believe Jesse McKethan was telling the truth when he said he blacked out as a result of Luther having hit him in the head, just as he told the truth at every other point. But there was one aspect of his confession and testimony that defense lawyers failed to pick up on, one element to his behavior which proved he had lost control as if in throes of an epileptic seizure: he ran.

Go back and read what Jesse said to detectives on the day of his arrest. Read the notes of his confession in Detective Fitzgerald's car and his written statement at police barracks. It is a minor detail, but Jesse plainly states that after the fight he ran down 38th Street but did not know where he was going. When he surfaced from the blackout and returned to find his friend sprawled in the front yard he ran inside and fetched a pillow for Luther's head, not realizing he had strangled him. That he was able to provide details of the fight later is not so much the product of memory but deduction. And how is it that he could remember every other gory detail but for the most important: what thing he used as a weapon to strike Luther.

We know this to be true by what Peyton McKethan testified to on the witness stand, that the history of his son's abnormality showed itself in identical episodes on prior occasions. When struck in the head, Peyton said, Jesse would fly into an uncontrollable fit and then take off running like a scalded dog to who knows where. It appears as a minor detail in his testimony and is neither a ploy nor convenient excuse that defense attorneys built into their closing argument. These people lacked the ability, opportunity and sophistication to conjure up the kind of airtight alibi that lawyers dream up these days.

Unfortunately, the "take flight" trial balloon does not fly with my friends who point out that Jesse was not in a convulsive state when he lopped off his best friend's head and littered the neighborhood with body parts. All I can say in response is, if that ain't *insane* I don't know what is. I don't care if it's the result of getting whacked on the head or voices coming from dogs, Jesse's conduct and comportment demanded that Dr. Cleckley finish what tests were begun and never completed: if a psychiatrist on a witness stand cannot conclusively determine a man's sanity, then it is a gross injustice to end the debate in the electric chair, decency be damned.

Of course, it doesn't matter now. Jesse McKethan was exterminated 54 years ago and his charred bones have turned to dust. But it bothers me that I'll never get the chance to stand in front of his jury, cloaked with all the righteous indignation I can muster, and plead a case that is slowly beginning to make even the friends and relatives of Luther Aids change their hardened hearts.

ADDENDUM TO
BEHIND THE
MOSS CURTAIN

Savannah's Butcher Murder of 1945 was not the only time that Dr. Hervey Cleckley's name was in the news of his day. Cleckley, along with Dr. Corbett Thigpen, became famous for writing the book, *The Three Faces of Eve*, which brought the mental disorder of multiple personalities to the public's attention in 1957.

Cleckley and Thigpen first saw the patient "Eve" when she was 25 years old. She suffered frequent and intense headaches, often accompanied by blackouts. After a year of therapy, the psychiatrists diagnosed her with having three different personalities: Eve Black, the flirtatious and outspoken girl; Eve White, the modest and drab housewife; and Jane, the friendly and sophisticated woman. Eve White, her main personality, often experienced memory lapses when the other personalities emerged. In time, Cleckley and Thigpen came to understand that these personalities developed from the early childhood trauma of seeing two murder victims and touching her dead grandmother. They believed Eve was on the road to recovery when she identified herself as Evelyn White, her legal name.

The Three Faces of Eve became a best seller in 1957, and Twentieth Century Fox turned it into the hit movie by the same title. Cleckley and Thigpen were hired to advise fellow Georgian Nunnally Johnson in writing the script and in producing and directing the film. Joanne Woodward, another Georgian, played Eve, which garnered her the Academy and Golden Globe awards for Best Actress. Cleckley and Thigpen were feted at a gala dinner before the world premiere of the movie, and they received the 1957 Literary Achievement Award for Non-Fiction from the Georgia Writers Association.

Chris Costner Sizemore, the real "Eve," finally conquered multiple personality disorder after 46 years and a cast of 22 personalities. In 1977, she wrote her story, *I'm Eve*, which also became a best seller. She toured the country giving speeches and championed mental health programs, receiving the Clifford Beers Award from the National Mental Health Association for her work, in 1982.

Comparing the cases of Evelyn White and Jessie McKethan, one has to wonder why the first was showered with attention for more than a full year by the same psychiatrist who summed up the latter in a handful of days. One has to wonder how it is that Evelyn's case was so fascinating to Dr. Cleckley that it became the subject of a best selling novel and a major motion picture when Jessie McKethan was summed up in a nine-page report and disposed of in the electric chair. Both patients exhibited multiple personalities and both patients experienced blackouts. But Evelyn White became a celebrated champion of mental health while all that was left of Jessie's mortal remains was consigned to an unmarked grave.

Perhaps when Dr. Cleckley examined Eve in 1957, the subject of blackouts received much more attention than it did eleven years before, when Jessie McKethan's lawyers argued that a blow on the head had caused him to blackout and go into a murderous fit. It was the first time in American jurisprudential history that the Blackout defense had been used – the term having only recently been coined to describe what was happening to soldiers in the field during World War II – and the Chatham county jury that was first to hear it wasn't buying.

Such is paying the price of being first.

BUSTER WHITE'S BIG FIGHT NIGHT:

HOW CLOSED CIRCUIT TV CAME TO YOU AND ME

Before the recent advent of pay-per-view at home, fight fans flocked to movie theatres to watch live broadcasts on the big screen. I remember seeing my first closed circuit fight at the Fox Theatre in Atlanta back in 1973, and how funny I felt to pay concert ticket prices for the privilege of watching big screen TV. And you wouldn't think people would yell at fighters on screen but once the fight started the place was on its feet and screaming for Ali to take out Frazier.

I also remember thinking that this remote viewing thing would never go over, but it has. And I was also mistaken in thinking that closed circuit presentations was something new in 1973, but by then television science had been broadcasting the sweet science to auditoriums for more than twenty years.

Savannah's first live broadcast of a title fight was staged at the old City Auditorium on September 21, 1955. Rocky Marciano defended his heavyweight title in a 9th-round knockout of Archie Moore, and it cost locals $3.45 each for a reserved seat or as little as $2.30 for general admission to watch the show. The man responsible for bringing this latest innovation in sports entertainment to town was none other than Buster White.

How Buster White came to bring big screen TV to town is an interesting story, and you won't believe whom he had to do business with in order to bring it here.

* * *

Sports history's first million dollar off-premises fight, the Theater Network Television Company's presentation of the Marciano-Moore title match, owed its existence to a telescope and a former Navy lieutenant. The telescope was located at Cal Tech's observatory in Palomar, California, and from it the TNT people developed the optical doo-dads that retained light long enough to permit its enlargement and illumination. The genius credited with perfecting this process was Nathan Halpern, who left the Navy after World War II and went to work for CBS, where he was given orders to find a way to make television pay.

Halpern looked around the industry at Zenith's phono-vision, where viewers paid the phone company to unscramble the picture on their home TV (the advent of today's cable network), and Paramount's telemeter, whereby users dropped coins in a box on top of sets located in hotels in order to see first-run movies (the advent of today's in-room movie service), and decided that there was a future for closed circuit TV. So Halpern quit CBS and went out on his own in search of it.

Halpern's TNT Company launched its inaugural broadcast with the Joe Louis-Lee Savold fight in 1951, and it was a struggle for technology to keep up with the costs of expansion. Projectors that plucked the electronic image off the wire and splashed it on the big screen were running $25,000 apiece, not to mention the exorbitant AT&T charges. And on top of the technical costs, Halpern had to pay the International Boxing Club a straight fee to be split with the fighters, plus a share of TNT's net profits on an escalating scale.

Actually, Halpern's development of closed circuit television had little to do with broadcasting boxing matches. The original concept was to enable General

134

Motors, Sun Oil and General Electric to introduce new models and products to salesmen and wholesalers through the remote network rather than bring them in to the main office for a look-see. IBM couldn't move its big new electronic brain out of Poughkeepsie to show its salesmen, so Halpern was called in to explain it to them wherever they were.

It wasn't long before political bosses put closed circuit television to their use in addressing state chairmen and local leaders, followed by a civil defense network to allow defense workers to discuss the H-bomb over the open air without alarming the general public. The project that Halpern was most proud of was the broadcast of a coronary clinic sent out from Cleveland to the nation's heart doctors and which President Eisenhower introduced from Washington. And it was Halpern's company that broadcast DeBakey's first heart transplant operations around the country to tens of thousands of medical on-lookers.

TNT had also picked up more than a dozen fights in its first four years of operation, and the Marciano-Moore bout was billed into 126 theatres in 91 cities, a bigger opening than anything even Hollywood had experienced. Halpern was expecting a crowd of as many as 400,000 fight fans, and Buster White wanted a piece of the action for Savannah.

Buster did not know Halpern but he was well acquainted with Nat Fleischer, boxing's historian and columnist, and went to New York to ask for an introduction to TNT. Buster checked into a suite at the Edison Hotel and dropped in on Fleischer, who told him that a Mr. Ed Addis was the contact Buster was looking for at TNT. When Buster appeared at TNT's offices he was made to wait in reception for Mr. Addis, who came out after twenty minutes and seemed to resent the intrusion.

"I want to talk to you about bringing the Marciano fight to Savannah," Buster said to Addis.

"Can't help you, mister," Addis said. "I'm all outta equipment."

"Then I come a mighty long way for nothing," Buster said, nonplussed.

"Looks like," Addis said, then turned on his heels and left Buster standing in reception with his jaw dropping.

Buster returned to his hotel and was hanging around the lobby, figuring to catch a couple of Broadway shows and maybe pick up on a few road dates for Savannah so that his trip is not a complete loss, when he ran into Allie Frank, a fight manager from Philly who had a sideline selling diamonds with a money-back guarantee. Buster and Allie are talking about this and that and who is doing what to whom and whether it is the first or second time when Buster complains about his hard luck with Eddie Addis at TNT.

"I didn't even get in to see this guy Halpern," Buster said. "They gimme the bum's rush."

And then Allie says to Buster like this, "You want the Marciano fight? How long you gonna be here?"

"I got nowhere to go," Buster replies. "Why?"

"There's a guy comes through here about the same time every day named Carbo. He can fix it for ya."

"Point him out to me," Buster says, and it isn't very much longer before a beetle browed gentleman with a prominent nose passes through the lobby of the Edison Hotel with what looks like the starting lineup of the New York Giants done up in spats and slouch hats. Allie wheels around and yells out, "Frankie!" in this gentleman's direction, although one look at this guy and Buster can tell he's no gentleman, in spite of being decked out in a very expensive looking pinstripe suit. But Buster himself is no slouch sartorially speaking, and he presents his card to the gentleman and says like this,

"Excuse me, Mr. Carbo. My name is Charles White and I am a promoter from Savannah, Georgia. I came to town to talk to Nat Halpern at TNT about the Marciano fight but he wouldn't see me. I understand you have some pull with him."

Carbo studies Buster carefully. "You say you're from Savannah?" he asks.

Buster nods, pointing to the address on his card.

"You know Bo Peep?" Carbo asks.

Buster's face brightens. "Why sure I know Bo Peep," he says, surprised that Carbo would bring up Savannah's favorite poolroom proprietor and bookie. "I'm in Bo Peep's place all the time. I put tickets on sale there."

Carbo nods. "Tell you what you do," he says to Buster. "You go back to Halpern's office after three o'clock. He'll see you."

And then Carbo walks away, leaving Buster standing in the lobby of the Edison Hotel, his jaw dropping.

When Buster returns to TNT's offices the second time that day he gets an entirely different reception. Ed Addis is waiting on Buster in the lobby of the building and greets him with a big hello like they're long lost pals. "You're a lucky man, Mr. White. We found you a piece of equipment," Addis says, with a big smile.

And that's how Buster White came to get the rights to broadcast the Marciano-Moore fight at the City Auditorium in Savannah, the 127th theatre in the 92nd town.

Nat Halpern expected the first million-dollar gross with tickets averaging $3.50, one dollar of every ticket going to TNT. A ringside crowd of 50,000 at Yankee Stadium at $40 tops meant a gate of $750,000, and when it was all totaled Marciano's 40 per cent split was estimated at $400,000, and Moore's 20 per cent split at $200,000. Now all Buster White had to do was go back to Savannah and convince people that it was worth their hard-earned money to pay to watch a fight on TV so that Buster could get his piece of the action.

Tom Coffey, the Evening Press Sports Editor, did his part in keeping the fight before his "Coffey-Time" readers. Even though the rest of the civilized world was certain Marciano would beat Moore—no lightweight champion had ever moved up to the heavyweight title although seven had tried—Tom Coffey quoted Buster, calling it an "if fight."

"*If* they were fighting in an alley, no holds barred, Marciano would walk off the winner," Buster said. "*If* the referee enforces all the rules, Moore will have a decided advantage. *If* Moore chops him up early, he will win. *If* beyond ten rounds, Marciano a decided advantage...and *if* Moore should win the title you can bet the return match will be an automatic sellout."

The pre-fight hype and publicity was at an unprecedented high point, prompting a sports writer out of New York to comment, "For the first time since the days of Joe Louis there is a 'big fight' tang in the fall air," and as much print as the match garnered, the press coverage of the closed circuit TV equipment was almost as great. There were entire columns in the local paper devoted to the arrival of the equipment from New York, including details of how the TNT mobile television unit would take the broadcast off the CBS cable through a loop leased from Southern Bell. The machine that reproduced the picture was set up about 20 feet from the screen, and the RCA engineers ran the equipment from two panels and a monitor.

Buster White explained that the showing of the fight onstage would not be on a 24-inch television receiver as rumored, but on a 16-ft. movie screen-sized unit. "This will be better than sitting ringside," Buster was quoted.

And Savannah believed him. Everybody in town ran out to Stubbs Hardware to snatch up tickets to watch TV in the giant living room that was City Auditorium. Buster's gamble paid off when he took a piece of the action of the first million-dollar gate in closed circuit television history. There were two foreseeable problems, however, which posed a threat to the success of the program: one, the tendency for the tubes of this prototype system to blow and two, the threat of Hurricane Ione blowing ashore and filling up Yankee Stadium like a fish bowl.

Buster could do absolutely nothing about the weather, especially New York weather, and when Hurricane Ione blew into the Big Apple on September 20th and kayoed the fight, she forced a one-day postponement. The bad weather only added to Buster's anxiety that something would go wrong with TNT's giant TV and if the picture was lost, so was Buster's money. This wasn't the sort of TV set you could whack with a rolled up newspaper to fix the picture, and seemingly out of nowhere Buster gets a call from a guy with an Italian last name who claims to have a cure for the problem Buster's TV is bound to experience.

"For three-fifty, no, four hundred bucks I can sell you show insurance." the guy says to Buster. "Should somethin' happen to your teevee, which is very likely indeed, you don't wanna drown in your own soup. Am I right about that, Mr. Buster White?"

"I'm not saying you're wrong," Buster replies. "But this insurance, how does it work?"

"This insurance is a beautiful thing," the guy says. "It provides peace of mind in these turbulent times. And the way it works is this: you pay me the premium, and if anything goes wrong, which is very likely indeed, then I step in and see to it you don't lose a cent, what with having to refund all the money and everything. I provide this service for all the theatres. That is how I got your phone number from Eddie Addis."

"Where are you calling me from?" Buster asks with suspicion.

"Sunny California," the guy says.

"Right, and come tomorrow night if my tube blows and I got a thousand people screaming at me for their money back, how does you bein' in sunny California help me in Savannah?"

There is a pause on the other end of Buster's line. "So what you're tellin' me is you don't want this peace of mind, Mr. Buster White?"

"Well, I'll think about it," Buster says, and hangs up the phone. And then he beats a path down to the auditorium to look around and make sure everything is secure.

September 21, 1955, the Marciano-Moore fight goes off without a hitch in Yankee Stadium before 50,000 screaming fans. The champ scrapes himself out of the resin from a second round knockdown to floor the aged Archie Moore four times and knock him out in the ninth round of a furious brawl. A near-capacity crowd at City Auditorium watched via closed circuit TV and from the looks of it, you'd have thought they were ringside in the Bronx. The crowd was mostly for Marciano except for a small contingency of colored patrons cheering for Moore from the section reserved for them in the balcony, and a local scribe reported that they reached such a fevered pitch that one woman almost pulled her own hair out.

Reception for the fight came in loud and clear. Only twice did the picture fog up where it could not be seen and then only briefly. Of all the spectators at City Auditorium clearly none were as pleased as Buster White, the promoter who had ushered in the latest technology for a new generation of sports fans. Who'd a-thunk it: people paying to watch TV.

Buster continued to bring big fights to Savannah by way of closed-circuitry. Sure enough, the picture tube blew during a Basilio fight and Buster had to refund the money to disappointed patrons. And it cost him, too, because he failed to take out "show insurance." There was something about that whole thing that had him worried that he was getting mixed up with guys he'd rather not have to file a claim against. Therefore it came as only a slight surprise to Buster when he picked up the paper to read all about Mr. Carbo, the gentleman he had met at the Edison Hotel and who made it possible for Buster to bring closed circuit TV to Savannah.

In 1958, Frankie Carbo was sentenced to two years on Riker's Island for managing boxers without a license. New York newspapers recalled how he had become the "underworld czar of boxing" in the 1940's, promoting the sport through a bookie operation that included taking action from Savannah bettors at Bo Peep's. Before he became a fight promoter, Carbo's criminal record showed seventeen arrests, five for murder, including the Thanksgiving Eve 1939 gangland slaying of Harry "Big Greenie" Greenberg, who had been talking to police about Carbo. Brooklyn mobsters Abe "Kid Twist" Reles and Allie "Tick Tock" Tannenbaum were all set to testify that Carbo was the killer, but right at the last minute Reles fell through a window of the Half Moon Hotel in Coney Island accidental like, and the case against Carbo collapsed when he threatened to clean Tick Tock's clock.

In the 1930's, Carbo worked for Louis "Lepke" Buchalter in Murder, Inc. He was arrested in 1936, for the shooting deaths of two members of Waxey Gordon's bootleg gang. Carbo was detained six months but the case never went to trial because witnesses developed a case of amnesia.

When in 1960 Carbo was released after serving a two-year stretch for managing boxers without a license, he wasn't loose very long before being hauled back into court to face charges that he had conspired to extort money from welterweight boxing champ Don Jordan, who had won the title in 1958. He also appeared before a Senate investigating committee in 1960 and answered questions about the fight racket with the reply "I cannot be compelled to be a witness against myself" twenty-five times. A year later, he was sentenced to twenty-five years in the Jordan case.

Frankie Carbo was paroled early, due to ill health and died in Miami Beach, in 1976.

If it hadn't been for Frankie Carbo, Savannah would've remained in the dark ages and Buster White would've never brought closed circuit TV to our town.

Thirty-eight years after his death in 1951, the ghost of Shoeless Joe Jackson appeared on a baseball diamond carved out of an Iowa cornfield. His specter has been spotted more recently in a poolroom on Congress Street.

SEARCHING FOR SHOELESS JOE

In 1989 the ghost of Shoeless Joe Jackson stepped out of writer William Kinsella's fertile imagination and onto a diamond carved out of an Iowa cornfield, bringing back to life the infamous Chicago White Sox team that conspired to fix the 1919 World Series. Kinsella's book *Shoeless Joe* and the movie it inspired *Field of Dreams*, starring Kevin Costner, James Earl Jones, and Ray Liotta as "Joe Jackson," have become modern classics. What may interest readers even more is the story of how Jackson came to make his home in Savannah, what he did here, and why he left.

There are so many myths about Jackson—and so many facts that read like fiction—that it's hard to tell exactly where one leaves off and the other begins. But the record books don't lie: in his first full season he batted .408 against a battery of pitchers who ended up in the Hall of Fame, on his way to a lifetime batting average of .356 over 13 seasons; he lead the White Sox to the pennant in 1917 and 1919, and set World Series batting records which lasted for 45 years. Jackson is still ranked

#3 on the list of highest lifetime batting averages, #15 highest single season batting average, #27 in lifetime triples, and #31 in lifetime slugging average. That he had a magic bat is also true, a hickory plank that not only kindled Kinsella's fantasies but provided Bernard Malamud with his epic hero in the book and film *The Natural.*

Yet Joe Jackson is not in the Baseball Hall of Fame. He isn't even a member of the Greater Savannah Athletic Hall of Fame, although he has been elected to the halls of four states that have no greater claim to him than we do. And when his career was wrongfully and prematurely ended by the Black Sox scandal in 1920, Joe Jackson did not simply vanish into thin air only to reappear as a vision in a cornfield some seventy years later. Shoeless Joe never set foot in Iowa, living or dead. No, for when his glory days were over Joe Jackson came home to Savannah, Georgia. And if you want to see the ghost of Shoeless Joe, come with me to a poolroom on Congress Street, where the real field of dreams is covered not by green grass but by green felt.

* * *

Few baseball fans are aware that the great Shoeless Joe Jackson played for the 1909 Savannah Indians semi-pro team three years before his legendary pro career began. Even fewer are aware that we had a team way back then, when Savannah was known throughout the baseball world as the second city in the South—after Charleston—to adopt the "New York game," which was what the forerunner of Baseball was called. Savannah adopted the game in 1866, when a local amateur team played by the rules of Baseball as designed by Alexander Cartwright, in 1845. Before then, the gentlemen's clubs of the South had played by the rules of the "Massachusetts game," which they had picked up from Union soldiers incarcerated during the Civil War.

In 1867 Savannah played Charleston for the "Baseball Championship of the South," and in this period of Reconstruction, when black men were intoxicated with their first heady taste of freedom, a riot broke out at the game when a group of freemen stood on the sidelines and made fun of the white man's sport. The Savannah players, dropping the game, brandished bats and charged the hecklers. It took a company of soldiers to quell the riot and get the Savannah team to its beat alive. So it can be said that Baseball in Savannah was born out of war, its early games fought like skirmishes, and for the first fifty years of its history the box scores read like scorecards in prizefights.

Savannah was a charter member of the South Atlantic (Sally) League when it formed in a meeting at the old DeSoto Hotel, on November 25, 1903. The team's nickname was the Pathfinders, but their fans changed it to the Indians during the first season of play. The rest of the league was comprised of the Charleston Sea Gulls, Jacksonville Jays, Columbia Skyscrapers (later the Palmettos), and Macon Highlanders (aka the Peaches). The Indians played in the meadows of Bolton Park on Henry Street (which was sold in 1913 for residential lots), and the locals chalked up their first championship after only two seasons in the Sally League.

So that by the time that the season of 1909 rolled around and the great Shoeless Joe Jackson made his debut, Savannah already had 40 colorful years of local history in the game. And as things got underway the new president of the league was quoted as saying that there was more interest in baseball in the South than ever before, and that he was confident that the league would enjoy the most prosperous year in its history.

The baseball mood in Savannah reflected the boom in interest around the country in 1909. The New York newspapers had christened baseball as "our national game" and its great prosperity was a conclusive testimony to "its purity, its honesty, its attractiveness and the hold which it has on the national heart." Out of 90 million people living in America at the time, 20 million turned out to watch a game that year. President Taft was photographed at a baseball game throwing out the first pitch, thus giving rise to the practice of politicians campaigning at the ballpark by his example.

The owner of the Savannah Indians, J.F. Sullivan, looked around this bustling town and was convinced locals would support big league ball. Broughton Street was booming from end to end, anchored by Leopold Adler's Department store—Georgia's largest—on the corner of Broughton and Bull. J.T. Cohen also ran a department store at 209 West Broughton, and Savannah families could shop for furniture at Walker-Mulligan or at Haverty's, where a new bed could be had for $19.50. There were several clothing stores on Broughton at the time: Nathan Schultz at No. 19, The Hub at 28 West (Men's suits advertised at $15-$30), Metropolitan Clothiers, Walsh & Meyer at 14 West, Standard Tailor at 220 West, and Baughn, Aspinwall & Ensel at 113 West Broughton. Shoppers had a choice of Regal Shoes at 105 West, or the Hole in the Wall Shoe store, which had been in business at 309 W. Broughton since 1890.

Savannah in 1909 was also experiencing a boom in housing. Woodlawn Park was in development, offering 100 residential lots at $100 each. Take the Isle of Hope trolley to Ferguson Avenue, "the magnificent new boulevard now being built from LaRoche Avenue to Woodlawn." Carl Mendel Real Estate (the author's great uncle) advertised lots along West 38th and 39th streets— "the desirable zone"—for $550 each. Another column announced "To Make of the East Side 'A White City,'" a community of houses all painted alike, white with green shutters, called Collinsville, after Jacob Collins, the builder whose idea it was to market the community to young, single men.

On Park Avenue, between Paulsen and the newly paved Harmon Street, nine new dwellings were planned, and were selling faster than they could be built. The southern boundary of the city in 1909 was 36th Street, and beginner houses could be had for as little as $800, or mansions for as much as $5,000. The west side was also under new construction: Ogeecheeton, comprised of 266 lots, just beyond the terminus of the Battery Park street car line, were selling for $100 and $200 each.

Money flowed in the streets of Savannah in 1909. People had scads of leisure time and when they weren't at the ballpark, they kept the train to Tybee filled to capacity nine times each day, from 6 a.m. until midnight. Access to the island became such a problem that Congressman Edwards came down all the way from Atlanta to tour the site of a proposed road to Tybee, the purpose of which was not only to link the island and Fort Screven with the outside world but to gain easier access to the government quarantine station. The congressman sailed up Turner's Creek to the site of the old oyster canning plant, visited the small fort that had been erected on the northern end of Warsaw Island during the Spanish-American War, and listened to the county engineer's pitch for $200,000 to build the road, including bridges. The congressman said that he didn't care to take any chances, and would ask the State for twice the amount.

Perhaps the most interesting development of the day was the fight that erupted on the editorial pages of The Savannah Press and The Atlanta Journal over which city was the state's commercial center, like it was some sort of contest. In pleading our case, the editor pointed out that Savannah was the third largest cotton port in the United States and the largest naval stores port in the world. In addition, Savannah was one of the largest lumber ports in the South, and the seaport boasted a tonnage equal to that of all other South Atlantic seaports combined. What with the combination of the lowest ocean freight rates and railroad centralization, Savannah was preferable to Atlanta as a strategic point for distribution. Even Atlanta merchants were building warehouses in Savannah, the local paper taunted.

Savannah had direct shipping connections with Liverpool, London and Manchester, in Great Britain; Hamburg and Bremen, in Germany; Rotterdam, in Holland; Antwerp, in Belgium; Barcelona, in Spain; Naples and Genoa, in Italy, and Trieste and Fieuma, in Austria. And, of note regarding the present debate over deepening the harbor, the newspaper reported that for every dollar spent by the government on Savannah's harbor, there was a return tenfold; for every foot of increased depth there had been an increase in commerce of as much as $7 million.

"The Atlanta Journal takes The Savannah Press to task for saying that Savannah is the leading commercial city in the State. Possibly The Press should have said of the South. We do not suppose The Journal is serious in ranking Atlanta with Savannah," the editor of The Press sneered.

But that was Savannah in 1909, when we were young and flush with cash. We were the biggest port in the South, and we bullied the yokels in Atlanta into subservience. We had the best baseball team, too, and if we couldn't find a way to beat your team on the field we'd meet up with them after the game. In the Land of the Crackers, Savannah was the capital.

* * *

Baseball in the Sally League was a mess in 1909. Umpiring was so erratic that most games were interrupted by fights between managers and players of both teams and the lone umpire, several of whom were caught gambling on games that they refereed and had to be replaced.

Gambling on games at the ballparks was open and notorious, and whole sections of the grandstands were reserved for the betting pool. It was from this quadrant of the stadium where the most discouraging words could be heard, followed by a barrage of empty Coke bottles rained down on the losing team. The newspapers called the rowdies and discontent among the rooters "knockers," as in "to knock a player for his poor showing," and the hell the knockers raised kept women and children from enjoying what was supposed to be the national pastime.

Not that the knockers were without justification: some umpires were new to the game and had no concept of a strike zone. "Mr. Gifford is responsible for the small number of hits recently," one sports writer noted. "He puts the batters 'up in the air.' They never know when to let a ball pass, for fear to have it called a strike. The result is that you find the batters striking at everything that comes within reach of the bat, regardless of whether it is over the plate or not. Savannah's best batters go down because of called strikes that are almost wild pitches."

"There is too much rowdyism in the South Atlantic League," complained a colleague in Columbia, S.C. "There is too much wrangling, too much umpire baiting and too little ball playing. The ball playing is all right while it lasts—but it has become so that a spectator who goes out to see a ball game may instead see a long and heated debate between players and umpire, or a wordy passage between spectators and umpire, or he may even see a feeble effort at a fight, or he may see an umpire chased from the lot...in fact, he is apt to see anything but a smooth and uninterrupted ball game—which is what he pays for."

When The Knoxville Sentinel had finally become fed up with press dispatches telling of disturbances at baseball games over decisions of umpires, their sports editor was pushed to suggest a solution: "The one weak feature of the game is the umpire. If some automatic machine could be invented which would obviate the necessity of an umpire the game would be greatly strengthened, but it is very unlikely that such a machine will ever be invented."

Thirteen different umpires passed through Savannah in the first half of the 1909 season, and most were never seen again. Not only did players fight the umpires tooth and nail, it eventually reached the point where team owners forfeited games because they did not want certain men to umpire and unless a solution was found, the umpire problem seriously threatened the continuation of the league.

The umpire skirmishes were but one facet of the diamond wars. Before the season was fully under way, the biggest problem to emerge was the iniquity that was Chattanooga's Chamberlain stadium: the right field fence was a mere 150 feet from home plate, and the Lookouts team was two-thirds lefties who lifted the ball out of the park with the greatest of ease. The hue and cry coming out of the Atlanta newspapers was to the effect that these cheap homers should be ground rule doubles, else there would be no point in playing out a season that Chattanooga was guaranteed to win. And as if that weren't bad enough, it was discovered that during rare occurrences when the Lookouts were losing, their manager would introduce rubber balls when his team was at bat. This was the last straw, as far as Savannah sports writers were concerned, and they called upon Sally league president W.A. Jones to take a flying trip to Chattanooga and straighten out this mess.

As it turned out, President Jones was inept at answering the many emergency calls that swamped his office to settle league business. He was unpopular to start with, having been voted in by the directors who wanted to oust his predecessor, a man deemed to have been the best minor league president in the country by sports editors.

But President Jones had no prior experience in baseball and wasn't even familiar with its rules, which sparked a riot in Savannah when he fined the Indians' star player $15 for missing a tag in a game at Macon. "Cutting a base is not a crime," one critic opined. "President Jones will have to return that money. It would never have been collected had the president taken the trouble to look up the rules."

The 1909 Savannah Indians were judged by regional sports writers to be an A-1 aggregation as the season began. The 13-man squad led by manager Bobby Gilks, who also played first base, knew in advance that pitching was a weakness but what they didn't expect was that hitting would fail them too, from opening day onward. Savannah fans had no patience for ineptitude on the playing field, and the newspaper remarked that many of the 4,000-plus in attendance at each of the first five games of the season were loudly critical of the "town ball" style of the Indians. When the local team lost on opening day—a legal holiday in Savannah—the fans were already suggesting to Manager Gilks that he should waste no time in finding replacements. After dropping four of the first five games, Gilks acquired a new shortstop and a pitcher from New Orleans, and a hitting fielder named Joe Jackson, who was a rookie wash-out from the Philadelphia Athletics in the big show.

"Jackson is a natural batsman," the local paper promised. "Hitting left handed, and a big fellow with it, he can drive hard and often and Gilks was lucky to grab him when Connie Mack decided to season him a year in a 'leetle' bit slower company than the American League."

And that is how Joe Jackson was introduced to the city of Savannah on April 22, 1909, when he took the field for the first time in the sixth game of the season. He was the lone standout in a losing effort, getting three hits and a sacrifice in his first four at-bats, and as an unnamed writer noted, "Gilks has already stamped a big o.k. on Jackson."

Bobby Gilks had played in the big show for Cleveland back in the 1890's, and having hailed from a small town he knew the difficulties that a kid like Joe Jackson experienced in trying to make the jump from his home town in the hills of South Carolina to the daunting bright lights of a big city like Philadelphia. Gilks helped the rookie acclimate to Savannah, first by finding him an apartment in the 100 block of Habersham, and then by preparing him for the unique brand of ball that we played around here. Joe caught on fast, for it took him exactly two games to turn the Savannah Indians around. In the pinch Jackson was there, leading his team to victory over archrival Charleston and battling them to a standstill in a 10-inning tie in game 2.

In describing these contests, local sports writers were pushed to great lengths attempting to capture the color of the action without the aide of photographs— simple line drawing caricatures appeared instead—and there was a list of 100 words interchangeable with the verb "to hit": slugged, smacked, spanked, dinged, plunked, etc. They were pushed even further in coming up with new adjectives for the way in which the ball came off the end of Joe Jackson's bat. He hit the ball so hard that writers took to describing his line drives as 'blue darters,' trailing blue smoke in their wake. After just six games with Savannah, Jackson was collecting rave reviews wherever he played. By game 15, he was already being referred to as "the great Joe Jackson."

As the season wore on, Joe had a love affair going on with the city that the rest of his teammates did not enjoy. In spite of his batting .450 in the first twenty games, his team went 3-18 and won last place by a convincing margin. Savannah fans all the while were having almost as much fun ragging the local team as they would've been to root them on to victory, prompting an editorial to scold, "Does your knocking your jeering, your hooting, your laughter, make that team or player one iota better? If not, then cheer for the opposing team and don't knock the locals."

The near riot-like atmosphere in the bleachers at Bolton Park caused concern for public safety and decency to spill out from the sports pages of the newspaper to the editorial columns. "The average baseball fan never stops to think that if he were to act on the streets as he does at a baseball game that he would be arrested for lunacy. If there is any injustice and narrow mindedness under the skin of a man, let him go to a ball game and it will certainly come to the surface. Tis a pity, though, that a large majority of that class in Georgia happened to settle in Savannah."

Game day in Savannah back in '09 was a singular event even though it was staged on a daily basis for six months of the year. The newspaper reported that Barrett Morrell, "a slavery-time darkey," better known as Happy John, organized a brass band that paraded the streets from Bay to Yamacraw in drumming up support for the Savannah Indians. Dressed in a uniform of blue trimmed in red, with numerous brass buttons, khaki trousers and a "millish" hat, Happy John continued his circuit to the Fort, trailing a long line of newsboys, little girls, delivery boys and citizens of commercial rank as if he were the pied piper of Hamlin, stopping periodically to dance the "pigeon wing." And, by the way, the paper noted parenthetically, Happy John was well known to the local police, mainly because of his publicity stunts. His entire band of one fife, a bass drum and two kettle drummers had been pinched for "internal dissensions and strife," and more than once Happy John was run in because he played his fife too long after midnight from the summit of his stoop, much to the discomfort of his sleep-deprived neighbors.

Frank Manush joined the Indians in May, and local scribes were unable to figure out how we got him. He had been the Cotton States League's 3rd best batter in 1908, when Connie Mack was tipped off that Frank was a find. Mack purchased Manush, who played a total of 23 games with Philadelphia when Mack made the same decision to send Manush down to Savannah, as he had done with Joe Jackson. Only, in the case of Manush, he would not be returning to the bigs with Joe; that honor fell to his younger brother, Henry, also known as "Heinie," who would join Detroit in 1923 and play sixteen years in the majors on his way to the Hall of Fame.

Frank Manush proved to be the addition that the Savannah team needed in taking the heat off of Joe Jackson, their sole star. The team's weakness remained in their pitching, in spite of starting Christy Mathewson's little brother, who was supposed to have learned everything he knew from his sibling. Christy had been the New York Giants ace hurler nine years hence, and won between 22 and 37 games a season for twelve straight years, helping bring a pennant and world championship to New York in 1904 and '05. Between Joe Jackson, the elder Manush and the junior Mathewson, it was a mystery why Savannah was in the cellar with a 4-18 record.

Mathewson would be gone by the first week in June. Labeled a "fair weather" pitcher, who can only pitch well when men are not on base, let him give a couple of bases on balls and the game is gone. He was wild, but Bobby Gilks insisted Mathewson was a comer, and it was that kind of judgment that doomed the team as long as Gilks was boss.

The game of May 18th against Macon was notable not only for Savannah's rare win but for the notice that Joe Jackson's .431 batting average had caught Connie Mack's attention—that, and the fact that Macon's star player was felled by malaria. After only one month with the Indians, Connie Mack notified Indian management that Joe would be called up as soon as the South Atlantic League season was over.

No sooner than Bobby Gilks began to field a team of challengers, the local writers took them to task for "listless, unspirited play, utterly lacking in paprika." Infielders made too many errors, pitchers gave up too many hits. Joe Jackson's average dropped to .350, and one of his teammates ratted out the Indians, saying that no one was trying to score. All they wanted to do, he said, was fatten their batting averages, and whether the team won or lost did not make the slightest difference. On the surface the remarks seemed to be aimed at Joe Jackson and Frank Manush, but the local writers took issue with the team's manager instead.

"The Savannah team is all right," one reporter wrote. "It's true we need a catcher and perhaps two pitchers, but that is all. Make those changes and put in a fighting manager at the head of the team and it will be as good as any team in the league. The team is not outclassed by the other teams. But it is out managed by every one."

The day after the comment ran, May 21, center fielder Ernie Howard replaced Bobby Gilks as manager, as if team president J.F. Sullivan was taking his cue from The Press. The team lost the first game under Howard's stewardship but critics didn't mind. "If the boys play like they did yesterday and the pitchers show half the form they should, we will begin the grand march to the front."

It seemed to fans and knockers alike that the new manager had rejuvenated the team, and their record improved considerably. To inspire and reward performance at the plate, the E&W Laundry paid batters ten dollars as a bonus whenever they hit a ball over their advertisement painted on the fence in center field.

Howard had been at the helm for six games—winning half—when the local press took to calling the

Savannah nine the "Climbers," as an indication of their progress. Nine games later, The Press was calling for Howard's head. He was alternately praised for inspiring the boys to play with ginger and criticized for his failure to teach them something about inside work. Howard was a good player; he was not a good manager. Now the fans wanted someone who could bring the Indians together as a team.

If fans had no other reason to turn out and watch a team still mired in the cellar, Joe Jackson was reason enough. His tenth inning two-run homer to win a game on June 11 was pictured as "a terrific welt...we honestly believe that ball is traveling yet." It may have taken fifty games, but Joe Jackson finally led his team out of the cellar and ahead of seventh place Charleston. Not only did he play outfield and bat in the clean-up position, Joe occasionally came in to pitch relief. In closing out a win against Macon on June 19, a line drawing caricature of Joe was captioned, "Dis ball will beat itself to the plate...and Jackson was right, for he certainly had ten brands of speed."

*   *   *

Midway through the season of 1909 it was apparent that none of the teams were making any money. With the problems in Chattanooga uncorrected, the Lookouts had a 10 game lead over the rest of the league and fans in seven cities had no hope of catching up. There seemed to be no sense in finishing a season where the outcome was never in doubt. Teams were begging fans to turn out, and owners openly solicited interest from other towns to move their franchise. Poor gate receipts not only affected the local club, but it affected the visitors, who got a percentage of the gate; and when the receipts were insufficient to pay railroad fares and hotel bills, the rules provided that the home team had to make up the difference or forfeit the game and pay a penalty. The

Macon club had to go to the hip several times, and the Peaches advised the league that they would be forced to move to greener pastures.

The Charleston club was ready to quit over back salaries. The Sally League was awash in red ink, and the fear was that if Charleston folded the league would follow. President Jones arrived in Charleston to take over the team, in the face of growing criticism that the inability to enforce the salary cap was but one of the causes of insolvency. The club was $1,500 in the hole, and local fans promised to help out through donations, if it meant keeping their Gulls in the Battery. But after raising the money locally to save the team, President Jones reneged on the deal and Okayed a pact that sent the Gulls packing for Knoxville. A Col. James Jackson made an eloquent and impassioned appeal for Charleston, but when the figures were examined and it was found that the league would have to carry the Gulls, the vote to move to Knoxville was unanimous among the eight team owners.

Knoxville, on the other hand, was a bustling city of 85,000 inhabitants—largely white, it was noted—and was a better business rival of Chattanooga. Semi-pro ball had been making money there—and furthermore they had $2,500 cash on hand, enough to pay the players and still have $500 left to start the season. Thus, the Charleston Sea Gulls became the Knoxville Night Riders. Carolina fans were pretty hot over what they considered to be a dirty trick of the president coming to town and making assurances that upon raising the money the franchise would remain in Charleston while at the same time he was secretly planning to deliver the team to Knoxville.

The only sensible way to salvage the season—and the suggestion had to come from sports editors in every city, not the league president—was to divide it in half, award Chatty the pennant for the first half and start a second season. The winner—if it weren't Chatty—would face the Lookouts in a playoff to determine the league champion. There was very little doubt that the season must be divided to maintain a sound financial basis from attendance, for July and August would be fatal if the race was decided in June. Dividing the season put every team back in the running again and fans back in the seats.

The decision to divide the season into halves may have been a sound financial decision for the league, but it wreaked havoc among betting circles. When a line was drawn in the sand on July 4th, ending the first half of the season, Chattanooga was awarded the pennant and the race began again. The question was raised often and loudly: what becomes of the bets made at the start of the season as to the league leader at the end of the season? There were fights over bets at ballparks around the league. Finally a group of gamblers imposed upon the sports editor of The Press to settle the dispute and rather than reject the proposition out of hand for its illegality, the editor instead published his opinion in the paper: "All bets should be declared off," he wrote. "They were made at the beginning of the season upon the assumption that the season would last into September and would be for 130 games. That season has now been cut in half and the bets that were made are void." And this from a newspaper that published impassioned pleas to end gambling at ballparks on a weekly basis!

When the second season began on the 4th of July, Savannah stood a better chance of any of the others to beat Chatty, based on the .800 win streak at the end of the first season. The 4th of July festivities—of which a doubleheader between the Indians and the Jacksonville Jays was the main event—included a full day's fair in Thunderbolt, where folks enjoyed hot air balloon rides, parachute drops, aerial acts, vaudeville performances, an orchestra for dancing, aquatic sports, a swimming contest, and a giant game of Tag, You're It. A program of the fireworks display was published, listing 32 presentations, entitled "The National Colors Wheel," "The Agirandola

Flying Eagle," "The Niagara Falls" and "The Electric Fountains."

Not all of the fireworks were seen in the sky over Thunderbolt. There were plenty of flare-ups at Bolton Park, when the first game erupted into a riot over the umpiring of Mr. Frank Butler. Enraged by his decisions in the eighth inning that allowed two Jacksonville runs to score, the Indians catcher punched the umpire and the knockers in the bleachers took it as their cue to mob onto the field. The police had to come to poor Mr. Butler's rescue. In order to pacify the angry mob, Mayor Tiedeman made a brief speech, in which he assured the fans that Butler would not return for the second game. Only after much pleading from the mayor and pushing by police did the fans return to their seats and the game concluded.

When the game ended, acting on the suggestion of the mayor, a cordon of policemen escorted Mr. Butler to a trolley for his trip home. While waiting for a car at East Broad and Gwinnett streets, Butler was surrounded by a seething mob of frantic fans still complaining about the gift of a win he had presented to the visiting team. Once safely loaded onto the trolley, Butler was followed home by the mob on foot, which shouted curses, threats and insults at him every inch of the way. East Broad Street was literally filled with yelling men and boys, as if a 4th of July parade had run amuck. Near the police barracks Chief Detective Murphy, with detectives Eivers and Umbach, came alongside the trolley in an automobile and persuaded Butler to get in the car with them.

"A short stop was made at the police station," The Press reported, "after which the car made its way up Oglethorpe Avenue to Drayton and down Drayton to the corner of Gordon Street Lane, where Umpire Butler resides. Crowds of boys on wheels and afoot followed the car all the way." Publishing Mr. Butler's address in the paper virtually assured the poor man that his home was to be Savannah's hot spot for the next few days.

When reached for comment, Frank Butler had this to say about Savannah Indians fans: "These people here have just got it in for me, that's all there is about it. They started nagging me earlier in the game. Anybody else might make three or four bad decisions and the crowd would say nothing. But they jump on me whenever a close play comes, no matter how I decide. This is the rottenest place I ever saw about that. These people here are just naturally tough: no doubt about it. I've tried to give them fair play, but they won't let me. They keep nagging at me, just because they've had it in for me for a long time."

Elsewhere in the same edition of The Press, the sports editor published a lengthy piece about Savannah fans, the fracas and a fear of things to follow. "The fans who occupy the bleachers seem to have no regard for the lives and limbs of the ball players," he wrote. "The most vicious practice a fan can be guilty of is throwing empty bottles on the field. A man that is caught in the act should be punished just as severely as if he threw it upon the paved streets to cut automobile tires, for ball players are entitled to as much consideration as automobile tires."

Umpire Butler was not allowed in the park for the second game of the doubleheader with Jacksonville. One of the Jay's pitchers called the game, which J'ville won by a score of 4-2. The pitcher was prepared for hostilities but things remained quiet. Perhaps all the fight had gone out of the crowd.

It came as no surprise when, on July 10, a story came out of Birmingham that an umpire pulled out a pistol to defend a decision he had rendered on the base path. After a close call an argument ensued, and one of the players returned to his bench where he begged his teammates for a knife to change the ump's mind. But the ump was quicker in reaching for a pistol inside his coat pocket, and the police were summoned to prevent bloodshed. There was a question as to whether a policeman could arrest an umpire—umps being considered in the same class of officers of the law—and in the debate that followed, the police, high officials and merchants of Birmingham agreed, without exception, that no less an august body as the supreme court would refuse to allow an umpire to be fined or sentenced for carrying weapons with which to protect himself. (Note: to be ejected from a game in 1909 meant that a uniformed policeman escorted the player off the field and out of the stadium.)

The plight of the umpires was only made worse by the league's president, who attempted to exert his authority on the field by issuing rulings unprecedented in baseball. On one particular occasion President Jones watched from his box seat as an umpire called a balk on the pitcher that prompted players to crowd the ump, shouting epithets. The umpire fined the team's manager ten dollars and told him to take his team back to the bench. But the players marched to the middle of the field and refused to leave. So the umpire pulled out his pocket watch and notified them that they had exactly sixty seconds to clear the field and resume play or risk forfeiting the game. The players stood nose to nose with the ump for a full minute, refusing to budge, and when the minute had expired without the ump carrying through with his threat, the players began to smile. It was more than the ump could bear, and after 72 seconds had expired, the ump walked to the front of the grandstand and announced a winner by default.

The manager climbed into the box seats to appeal directly to President Jones, who wanted to see play resumed. The umpire was not consulted and, after the president had repudiated his decision, refused to officiate. One of the players was chosen to umpire and the game continued, one team thinking it was official; the other team believing it was merely an exhibition for paying patrons and that the forfeiture was theirs, for there was still the small matter of league standings to consider in posting the win and loss.

By the time the dust settled, it had become obvious to all concerned that Mr. W.A. Jones was not up to the task of ruling the Sally League. He was roundly criticized for trumping the ump, and sports editors around the South accused him of having "been weighed in the balance and found wanting."

* * *

The second half of the 1909 season went the way of the first half for the Savannah Indians, who dropped eight of their first ten games. Back in the cellar after just two weeks into the new season, Joe Jackson was the team's lone stand out. Even in losing efforts he gave fans something to shout about, as this dispatch out of Columbus reported on July 17:

"The home run of the brilliant right fielder of the Climbers occurred in the ninth, with one man down. Jackson walked up and in a joking way motioned the outfield to play deep, and he sent one just over shortstop's head. The left fielder was quick to recover the ball, but Jackson touched home plate with ease. He is without a doubt the star of the Savannah team, and his work in right field is nothing short of marvelous."

The following day, the Knoxville paper reported how Joe Jackson stole home while opposing players were arguing a call with the umpire.

And then an odd thing happened: Joe went on a batting tear and the team went on an 11-2 win streak, catapulting the Indians from dead last to third and closing in on second place Augusta. There was heightened interest among fans when the two teams met, on top of the anticipation of watching the highly amusing antics of

Augusta's manager/second baseman, Lou Castro. His exploits on and off the field were colorful if not legendary, and even when his team was permanently camped in fifth place toward the end of the season, eighteen games behind the leader in the loss column, fans continued to pour in to the stands to watch "The Count" at work. Naturally, umpires were Castro's favorite targets.

Castro was Venezuelan and had a dark look. His accent was laced with Spanish salsa, which was poured thicker atop arguments and threats. When a new umpire named Thompson was sent to Savannah to officiate a game with Augusta, Castro approached Thompson and told him, "You'll have to get off the diamond so we can play this game."

"But I'm the umpire," Thompson said.

"You'll have to prove it to me," Castro said. "I'm from Missouri. You don't look like an umpire to me; at least, not like a good one."

"Well, won't you take umpire Van Syckle's word for it?" asked Thompson, seriously.

"Not on your life," said the Count. "I'll take anything else he's got, but I can't take his word. And let's see your authority to umpire this game—something that proves you're an umpire. Hurry up, now."

Thompson, the fall guy, shivered. He trembled. He paled, especially when Castro said, "Show me, or I'll take this dirk here in my shirt and slice your ears off."

And Thompson sent all the way to the DeSoto Hotel to get the telegram from President Jones appointing him an umpire.

When the division of the season had created confusion in the minds of bettors and some of the fans as to what effect it would have on the league champion, Castro milked the debate for all it was worth when he appeared at home plate at the start of a game against Macon and said to umpire Gifford, "If I refuse to play this game, it is forfeited and goes to Macon. And if

Macon refuses to play, it is forfeited and the game goes to us. Now, suppose both of us refuse to play, to whom does the game go?"

Gifford studied the proposition before answering. "Why, to President Jones, of course."

"Well, in that case, we both forfeit," Castro, said, "and President Jones will win the pennant. He will have an average of one win, no losses, and percentage one thousand. Let him play Chattanooga for the title. Let's go back to the hotel, fellas."

During the all-important home stand against Savannah in mid-July, Augusta dropped three games and tied the Indians in an 11-inning match called on account of darkness. When the Count could not bear to watch his lead over the Indians slip away any further, he took an argument over a call too far and was ejected from the game by his old nemesis, Van Syckle. The umpire then called upon a uniformed patrolman to enforce the order, and here was where things got out of hand. The patrolman evidently did not know that rules forbade players to walk the streets outside of ballparks in spiked shoes, for he refused to allow Castro to return to his bench to change styles. The Count insisted on being allowed the privilege, but the patrolman would have none of his infamous antics. The cop brandished his nightstick and pushed Castro toward the exit in front of a thousand protesting fans. Even reporters were amazed at the Count's self control at having been "treated worse than if he had been a Negro criminal."

The actions of the patrolman completely disgusted the fans and for the rest of the afternoon even the Savannah fans applauded the play of Augusta's team, in sympathy with them for the indignity that had been heaped upon their manager.

By mid-August Savannah, Augusta and Chattanooga were in a fight for first place. The Indians were feeling invincible, and as they headed toward a showdown with the Lookouts they tried to put the eekle-peekle on the champions by offering to bet that Joe Jackson would get more hits during the season than their hero, Johnson. Jackson, at this point, had a better average but Johnson had more hits. The wager was refused, and Savannah sent back word that Johnson would not get a hit during the game. Joe hit for a single and a double; Johnson failed to get a hit, in a game won by Savannah.

More importantly, Savannah swept Chattanooga three straight on the Lookouts' own field, something no other team had accomplished that year. The losses knocked Chatty out of first place for the first time all year and into second place, a mere one percentage point ahead of third place Savannah.

So elated were Savannah fans that they suggested to the newspaper that a plea be published to take up a collection for the team, out of appreciation of their incredible comeback. "We remember once this season when Lauzon knocked a home run over the left field fence and a collection was taken up and Lauzon received $67.00 for the lucky hit," the sports editor wrote. "Some friend of the ball players should take up a collection, but let it be for the whole team: let every man go out prepared to give anything from five cents to a dollar and a neat little sum will go to the players. It will serve to make the boys work harder. They will then work to please and not for the salary alone."

In the same issue of The Press that carried a syndicated column entitled "Connie Mack Picks 'em Ripe," in which the writer went on to praise Mack's ability to pick up unknown baseball talent and develop them into major league stuff, came the news that Mack had called up Joe Jackson from Savannah, on September 2. Mack's Philadelphia Athletics were in a race with the league leading Detroit Tigers, and the Sally League's leading batter would be helpful down the stretch of the American League season. Joe said his goodbyes to his

Indian teammates and hopped a steamer for Philadelphia, but not before giving fans one last thrill by lifting "a balloon drive to center field for three bases, a hit that would have gone almost to the sea but for the tall weeds in the center field patch."

Joe Jackson's final review in the local paper included being named to the All-Sally League team of 1909, his nomination reading: "Jackson is a sensation in all departments of the great American game, and that's saying a whole lot."

* * *

Connie Mack's 1909 Philadelphia Athletics team was built around Chief Bender, Eddie Plank, Jack Coombs, Lou Krause, Jack Barry and Eddie Collins, all of who were middle class college men from the Northeast. Joe Jackson was the only illiterate, the only former mill hand (aside from Mack himself), and the only cracker in the barrel. He didn't like Philly, and his play in the field showed it. Following a game with New York, Joe sat the bench for three weeks and watched as his team pulled within 1 ½ games of the Tigers but never got any closer. Teammates told reporters that the rookie had a yellow streak, and Joe's contribution to the Athletics season of '09 was limited to five games.

Big city sports writers pried into Joe Jackson's past for something gossipy to write about. They told their readers that he had been born in Pickens County, South Carolina in either 1888 or '89—nobody was really certain since they didn't keep birth records way back in the hills. They told the story how at age six he went to work in the fields of the Brandon Cotton Mill and never had no learnin'. The work was light but the hours were long, and babies were expected to put in a 70-hour week. And the writers reckoned that's how Joe Jackson developed hands as big as baskets and arms as willowy as buggy whips.

Joe Jackson worked the cotton fields for a dozen years. He began playing ball for the Brandon Mill team at age 13, and five years later he was playing for the Greenville Near Leaguers semi-pro team. Two years after that, at age 20, his reputation as a natural ballplayer was already firmly established when he was first noticed by a pro scout and former big leaguer sent to Greenville to manage the Spinners, a semi-pro team in the Carolina League. Joe quit his job at the mill making $45 a month to play baseball full time for $75.

And it was during these early days of his career that the legend of Joe Jackson began to emerge. He had a magic bat named "Black Betsy," a 36-inch long, 48-oz. slab of hickory that was custom tailored to Joe's grip. The pale white wood had turned black with daily baths of tobacco juice and sweet oil, slept in a cotton cloth between games, and went home with Joe from Philadelphia at the end of the season because, as Joe related, his bats didn't like freezin' any more than he did.

The big city boys got a big laugh at relating how Jackson acquired the nickname "Shoeless Joe" while playing for the Spinners. The country boy who had played barefoot back home in the hills had a hard time breaking in a new pair of spikes. He had such painful blisters that he couldn't get his shoes on, and played the next game in his stocking feet. Nobody seemed to notice until late in the game when he hit a long home run. As he rounded third base, a fan of the opposing team shouted, "Oh, you shoeless sonofabitch!" Scoop Latimer, a baseball writer, was in earshot and used the anecdote in print. The nickname stuck like flypaper (although no Savannah Press reporter used it one time during the season of 1909 in describing the Indians outfielder, out of respect for the best hitter in the league).

Joe Jackson hadn't played twenty games as a Greenville Spinner before the manager was on the line to Connie Mack, owner of the Philadelphia Athletics. Mack wasted no time in buying out Joe's contract for $900 at the end of his only season in semi-pro ball. The only problem was, no one had asked Joe Jackson how he felt about the proposition that would take him away from South Carolina for the first time in his life and ship him north. He reluctantly boarded the train in Greenville bound for Philly, but quickly changed his mind and got off in Charlotte, one hundred and fifty miles away. He came back like a boomerang on a southbound train, where he refused all entreaties and turned back a steady parade of ambassadors from Pennsylvania sent to fetch him.

Connie Mack was used to the erratic ways of ballplayers, but he'd never seen anything like this game of hide and seek—as some writers referred to Joe's indecision— that was so peculiar it warranted notices around the nation. Nobody could remember the last time a rookie failed to report, as playing big-league ball was practically the highest ambition of every American male; that Joe refused to go, as if being drafted into the army to fight on foreign fields, was big news, especially since early reports out of Greenville were that he was "the next Ty Cobb." Finally, after weeks of pushing and pulling, Joe Jackson left Greenville for Philadelphia.

The Philadelphia Athletics of 1908 were in a rebuilding year, having finished sixth out of eight teams in the American League. Joe's teammates included future hall-of-famers Eddie Collins and Frank "Homerun" Baker, but in his first major league game Joe Jackson batted in the vaunted cleanup position. He got a hit with his first at-bat, and Connie Mack critiqued his debut saying, "If nothing happens to him, he should develop rapidly into one of the greatest players the game has ever produced." Not only was he favorably compared with Cobb; the rookie was vying with Honus Wagner for the title of Greatest Ballplayer Ever—after just one game.

One would think that the A's would be happy to have the services of such a talented player, but there were some who resented the incredible attention showered on the new kid and others who were openly contemptuous of his background. Being a rookie, Joe was subject to the good-natured ribbing from the club veterans, but there was a certain meanness to the jokes aimed at his illiteracy and bumpkin background. The night after his first game in the hotel dining room, his teammates tricked him into drinking the water in the finger bowl and then laughed him out of the room. Early the next morning, without so much as a goodbye, he took a train home to Greenville, vowing he wouldn't set foot north of the Mason-Dixon for the rest of his life. Connie Mack ordered him to report at once, under threat of lifetime banishment from the game. Ten days later, Joe returned.

One would think that under such conditions that the team would lighten up and let the boy play ball; they did not. Having bolted for home once, his teammates went out of their way to see what it would take to make him do it again. He went home a third time, and this time he stayed. Connie Mack suspended him, organized ball said he could never play again, and Joe still didn't care. There's only so much a guy should have to put up with, just to play baseball.

The A's were a tough bunch. They were known around the league as cheats, having gone to great new lengths in stealing the signs of opposing teams. Electric wires were run underground from the Philly clubhouse in center field to the coach's box at third base, where a small box with a buzzer was buried. Spies were stationed with binoculars with which to watch the hands of the opposing catchers. They telegraphed the third base coach, who warned his batter. No regular player on the Philadelphia team batted less than .300 while the buzzer was in operation, and several were among the league leading hitters.

No one alive can remember just what was said or done during the winter of '08 that made Joe Jackson change his mind and report to spring training in Atlanta the next year. Maybe it was the prospect of having to go back to picking cotton for a living, but something made Joe move. He toughed it out during practice, and made it all the way back to Philadelphia for the start of the '09 season before he got that old funny feeling again. He told Connie Mack he didn't like the town, and the story goes that one day while standing on a platform waiting for a train that Joe spotted a row of milk cans waiting to be loaded. Each can had a shipping label attached, marked for a southern destination. "I wish I had one of those labels on me," he said, just loud enough for Mack to overhear. Finally reaching the end of his charitable patience, Mack packed Jackson off to play for the Savannah Indians in the South Atlantic League.

Joe Jackson played only one year in Savannah, but he liked the town so much that he made it his permanent home for twenty years. His career would take him to Cleveland, Chicago and New Orleans, but he always made his home in Savannah. He moved his mother and sister here, and he ran two businesses—a poolroom on Congress Street and dry cleaners with locations on East Bay and on Drayton. He drove around town in a new Oldsmobile Pacemaker Eight purchased from G. Bingham Bache on Liberty, with his wife named Katie and a bulldog named Beauty. And when he led his team to the pennant in 1917 and to the world championship in 1919, he came home to Savannah to celebrate. In the land of the Crackers, Joe Jackson was king. He was one of us.

* * *

Joe Jackson's inability to play nice with the other kids on the Philadelphia Athletics baseball team of 1909 created a big headache for team owner Connie Mack: he was afraid that trading "the next Ty Cobb" and "the best player since Honus Wagner" would come home to haunt him, and after a stellar year with the Savannah Indians of the South Atlantic League, Mack moved his prodigy to New Orleans to spend the season of 1910 with the Pelicans of the Southern League. Mack would retain complete control of the Carolina Kid's contract, but the Pelicans were guaranteed Joe would play for New Orleans until the Southern pennant race was decided.

Joe's teammate from the Savannah Indians, Frank Manush, made the move with him. Frank presented Mack with the same dilemma of what to do with raw talent that wasn't aging well in the big leagues. Jackson and Manush liked playing the Southern swing against the Atlanta Crackers, Birmingham Barons, and Nashville Volunteers, and as much as they enjoyed the spicy Creole flavor of N'awlins, they got back to Savannah as often as possible, where their exploits with the Pelicans were closely followed through New Orleans Daily dispatches published in the Savannah Evening Press.

Opening day in New Orleans was April 14, versus the Mobile Sea Gulls. Just about every one of the Crescent City's 350,000 citizens turned out for a parade through the French Quarter before the game as if it were a second Mardi Gras, and 5,000 fans packed the stadium to see Jackson and Manush for the first time. One month later, Joe Jackson was leading the league in total bases, hits and triples. By the end of May, he was leading the league with a .378 batting average. "His triple was a pippin and his two-bagger was a peach," wrote one reporter. The Cajuns did not call him "Shoeless"; they called him "The Candy Kid" and "The Carolina Confection."

After watching his star player perform over the first thirty days of the season, the Pelicans owner/manager Charley Frank told the local sports writers that Joe Jackson was the best all around player he ever knew in the history of the Southern League. As an example of his electrifying play, the article went on to describe how Jackson's peg to home plate from the outfield "almost set the Gull fans crazy, as he deliberately held a hit until the runner passed third base to score and got him at the plate."

The Pelicans had played the Cleveland Naps of the American League a dozen times during spring training. Charlie Somers, owner of the Naps, began cozying up to Joe Jackson with the intention of stealing him away from Connie Mack, but the idea of leaving the South for Ohio was as bad as Pennsylvania, in Joe's opinion, and he wanted nothing to do with the Naps or Athletics. But in a simple twist of fate, Bobby Gilks, the former manager of the Savannah Indians, had become Cleveland's scout, and Somers sent Gilks to New Orleans to tempt Joe into changing his mind. Gilks was successful, promising the rookie that he would not be subject to the same sort of harassment and abuse from Naps teammates as he had suffered at the hands of the Athletics.

The terms made between Cleveland and the New Orleans management seems to indicate that Charley Frank owned Joe Jackson outright, and that Connie Mack had a mighty slender string tied to him. Some observers called this the biggest mistake Mack ever made, and years later he still felt the need to explain his gift of Joe Jackson to the Naps as his appreciation for the way Charlie Somers had helped out Philadelphia in the early days of the league. Truth was, Joe Jackson just didn't fit in with the Athletics.

Trading away Joe Jackson turned out to be the biggest mistake Charley Frank ever made, too. At the beginning of the season the Pelicans were given a slim chance to have a winning season, but New Orleans not only won the pennant they were the only team in the league to show a profit, largely due to Joe as a drawing card. Never again would Frank manage the likes of Joe

Jackson. All Frank got in return for Joe was $10,000 and a player who never amounted to much.

Joe led the league in hits, runs, and with a .354 batting average. In one of his final performances, he hit the ball out of the park three times in setting the unique record of clearing the fences of every stadium in the league. And when the Southern League season was done on September 14, Bobby Gilks was anxiously waiting to take the rookie phenom straightaway to Cleveland for the last twenty games of the American League season, but had just as hard a time getting Joe on the train as Connie Mack had experienced. Joe got off the train in Memphis, true to form, and in need of reassurance from Gilks that Cleveland would be more hospitable than Philly. There was a nasty comment from sports writer Grantland Rice in all the papers, sizing up the chances of recent draftees of making it in the big leagues, in which he singled out Joe as "having the physical stuff, but hardly the mental." Joe wasn't sure that there was anywhere in either league he could play without being dogged as a yokel.

We took a different view of the situation down here. "The purchase of this remarkable player from New Orleans by the Cleveland Club is the most significant negotiation of the season," said an article out of Charlotte published in The Savannah Press. "Jackson is destined to be the shining light of the diamond, a rival of Tyrus Raymond Cobb for the honors and glories of baseball."

Joe reached Cleveland and immediately made a huge impact on the team. They were starved for outfielders, having been forced to use Ted Easterly, a catcher, in right field. They had no chance to win the pennant, but Gilks had been successful in recruiting twenty new players with the intention of becoming contenders in the very next season and he wanted to begin the process of breaking them in quickly. Joe contributed 29 hits in 20 games, for an average of .387. The numbers are even more remarkable for the way in

173

which he hit the ball, for Black Betsy literally knocked cork-centered baseballs out of round. In one game against Boston, Joe smashed a line drive down the first base line so hard that the first baseman could not get his glove up in time. The ball ricocheted off of his wrist high in the air and halfway back to home plate, where the pitcher was able to field it and still beat Joe to the bag.

* * *

1911 was Joe Jackson's first full season in the major leagues. Opposing teams may have had no other weapon in their arsenal to counter his amazing ability than to try to get on his nerves by relentlessly attacking him for a soft-spoken style too often misunderstood as weakness. "I ain't afraid to tell the world that it don't take school stuff to help a fella play ball," he was quoted as saying, and that's as likely to have been the only response the bullies were going to get out of Shoeless Joe.

Fans were quick to take his side in the matter. At his first appearance in New York, fans interrupted the game by walking out on field and presenting the embarrassed ball player with a bunch of roses. For a game that prided itself on fairness, the paying public thought that the rookie was getting a raw deal. Rather than engage in a battle of wits he had no chance of winning, Joe Jackson let Black Betsy do his talking for him. He hit the ball so hard at his detractors that one account records a screaming line drive that hit the center fielder in the stomach and bounced away so far that Joe ended up with a double. On another occasion, a Jackson line drive to Tris Speaker in dead center field hit him in the neck when he failed to get his glove up in time, and Joe was credited with an inside-the-park home run.

"He is a terrific hitter, wielding a bat that would make Samson hesitate," said a feature story in the Savannah paper, which continued to follow Joe's progress as if he were still on the Indians roster.

Joe's friends in Savannah were also interested in keeping abreast of his difficulties in finding acceptance among northern players. For every column that recorded his feats on the field, our local paper caught us up on Joe's social standing, for we were with him in spirit and he was one of us. Never before had one player been so maligned, and no man would again until Jackie Robinson broke the color barrier almost 40 years later.

According to The Cleveland Press, every big league team that the Naps met endeavored to get the goat of young Joe Jackson. "Joe has a curt answer for every jibe," they noted. "So far the score is about even, and, if anything, a little in Joe's favor."

The article went on to reveal how Jimmy Callahan was backed up when Joe told him, "You're another of these fellows after my nerve. Well, keep on after it. I like to have you fellows chase me. I know I'm a good player when the whole pack of you is after me. I didn't know if I would make good before the season started, but I'm certain now."

When a Cleveland reporter caught up with Joe after the game, he confided, "I don't mind them being after me one bit. There's only one way for them to get the Naps uniform off me, and that's to throw me down and cut it off. I heard all these things that are said to me now in the Southern League last season. They had me all sized up the same way down there. I made 'em eat what they said, and Jimmy Callahan, Hugh Jennings, Nig Clark and the other fellows who have been after me will do the same thing."

If Joe's humble beginning and unsophisticated upbringing had been the sort of story that quickly blew over, it would scarcely merit mention now, but it refused to die. Odd how when the opposing players on the field had run out of barbs and one-liners, the press could be counted on to sharpen their pencils on the subject of Shoeless Joe and all things southern. In the middle of the season toward the end of July, with Cleveland 20 games out of first place and stuck in sixth, Joe Jackson was still being scrutinized as a hayseed. "He was a country boy, and what he knew about reading and writing could be put in the left-hand corner of a primary school slate," said one biographical sketch that stretched out over a column and a half of the newspaper.

The writer rehashed the funny stories about Joe and his dislike of northbound trains, and staged an exchange between Joe and a phantom friend:

"What's the matter, Joe, don't you want to be a big leaguer?" the surprised friend of the young star asked.

"No, them big places is too big. Pelzer, Piedmont and Newberry just about suits me," was the gist of his answer.

And, as always, by the end of these columns there was the obligatory reference to Joe's barefoot childhood. "Before the boy got to playing ball for money they say he never wore shoes except in bitter cold weather," it was reported. "Shoes were an abomination to him in the olden days."

But for every time some hotshot sports writer in Philadelphia or New York poked fun at Joe Jackson, calling him "The Barefoot Wonder," there was a retort from the scribes who had followed his progress in the Sally and Southern leagues. And when Connie Mack fired a shot across Joe's bow as being socially unacceptable, the New Orleans Daily responded that "had Jackson been a member of the Mackites this season there isn't the least possible doubt but Connie would have the American League pennant sewed up, as Jackson is clouting the sphere better than any of the Athletics."

At the end of August, with Cleveland in fifth place and playing at a .500 pace, statisticians could hardly believe their eyes when the numbers showed that the Naps rookie was batting over .400 and gaining on league leader Ty Cobb. The Savannah Press featured a daily column reporting on the batting title race between the Georgia Peach and the former Savannah Indian, and even though Cobb won the honors Joe Jackson still earned the distinction of finishing his rookie season with a .408 batting average.

Joe Jackson may have been a poor, dumb country boy but at the end of the season of 1911, even his harshest critics had to admit that his debut outshone any other athlete known to the game, including Cobb, Mathewson and Speaker. "He could neither read nor write before his entry into the upper crust," one story read, "yet he was ripping the cover off the ball...for the poor ignorant cuss is only batting .408 for the year, with a collection of hits that run mostly to three and four bases. For he has already broken two records by driving the pill above the forty-five-foot walls of Cleveland and Washington for the first time on record, and is just getting warmed up. The odds are that he will still hang around for awhile in his chosen profession, and perhaps still have the edge upon a few Shakespearean scholars who can read and write like blazes, but who couldn't bat with a plank."

When the issue of Joe's lack of education began to fall away in the face of his brilliance on the diamond, the only device that the northern establishment, which controlled the game, had to keep him in his place was holding up Ty Cobb as the better player. The press created a rivalry between the two stars which overshadowed any rivalries between teams. Cobb, by virtue of having been in the game years before Jackson, had a distinct advantage. He was baseball's marquee player and no one could argue that he wasn't great. But to elevate Cobb at the expense of a rookie embarrassed by his upbringing was neither fair nor sporting and the folks back in Greenville, S.C. let it be known to reporters sent there to unearth the truth that Joe Jackson was a greater ball player than Cobb or any other player produced so far.

They were forced to admit that the usual stories about Joe's general character were in the main true, including his indisposition to take advantage of educational opportunities, but they defended him as possessed of a much higher than average intelligence, as witnessed by his grasping all the fine points of the game and making the most remarkable record than any player hitherto, and in the face of opposing players and press to "get him."

In preparation for the season of 1912, sports writers around the country were already touting the personal competition between Joe Jackson and Ty Cobb as early as March, as if it were a heavyweight title fight. Batting stances and style of play were critiqued and Joe was always found wanting, as usual. "Joe Jackson, the Cleveland mauler, is probably the most lax of the lot in his batting form," one expert opined. "Long and gaunt, built as if ready to fall apart, hopeless Joe looks to be anything but an alert, concentrated actor at the platter, with his bludgeon swung loosely and aimlessly below the waist line. But when the correct moment comes the coil tightens, the springs flip back into place and Jackson at the second of his swing is the genteel acme of lightness and poise."

The only counter measure to this kind of baiting that the Savannah sports writers could come up with was to turn competition into a regional battle, not a personal one. "Most Diamond Stars Hail From Dixieland," was the headline of one local editorial in which the writer claimed that "the greatest players in the game are boys who like candied yams at meal time and talk with a ragtime dialect," citing Cobb from Georgia, Jackson from South Carolina, and Speaker of Texas as his examples. "The trio is absolutely the greatest outfield combination that could be arranged in baseball," he argued, an attempt to put them on the same side in opposition to northern aggressors.

The Jackson-Cobb debate became such a prominent issue of the day that it was left to an enterprising Broadway impresario to come up with the promotion of the decade. Vaughan Glaser, a producer of stage shows, enticed Ty Cobb and Joe Jackson to join forces onstage as the stars of "The College Widow," a comedy by George Ade. The original play was about a sandlot football player who is induced to come to college to play ball, but his unfamiliarity with society ways gets him in bad with his Ivy League teammates. Glaser had the play made over to a baseball theme; Cobb would play the hero, "Billy Bolton, the Star Half Back," and Jackson would be perfectly cast as "Silent Murphy, Unknown Baseball Star," the player from the sandlots who was "short on talk but long on action: he'll make a couple of great catches, slam out an old-time home run and become the college idol along with Ty."

"Cobb and Jackson Go On Stage" was the syndicated story that circled the country in late September 1911. Glaser, in hyping the production, held a press conference with Joe and Ty and laid out plans to open in Detroit and Cleveland, for the benefit of both men's home team fans, and then proceed to every major league city before finishing up with a tour of the South. "Jackson and Cobb, bitter rivals and enemies in the game, are good friends off the field," Glaser said to the press. And Cobb, as if picking up on his cue, poked Joe in the ribs and said, "We'll show 'em some speed in front of those footlights, Joey, old boy," which got a lot of stage laughs.

Glaser announced that the salaries paid Cobb and Jackson of $2,000 apiece for two months work would set a new record, although there is some evidence to suggest that Glaser entered into a secret deal with Cobb to receive $10,000 for a 3-month run, which was more than he was being paid to play baseball. Shock waves reverberated in every team owner, and fear quickly spread around the major leagues that Broadway and Hollywood

179

would plunder their rosters. Their anxieties were heightened as Christy Mathewson, Mike Donlin, Johnny Evers, Joe Tinker, Meyers, Morgan, Bender and Coombs all followed Jackson and Cobb in attempting a stage career. As "The College Widow" took to the road, August Hermann, chairman of the National Baseball Commission, announced that he was preparing a resolution prohibiting players from performing in vaudeville during the off-season, citing a fear that "late hours and indoor life of stage people would prove injurious."

Little, if anything, was written about "The College Widow" performances. Changes, however, had taken place in the scripting and Glaser reverted to the original football theme once he saw that the team of Cobb & Jackson was having an impossible time remembering their lines. In fact, by the time the production rolled into town in mid-November for two performances at the Savannah Theater, all mention of Joe Jackson had completely vanished from the advert in the newspaper and the write up failed to mention him. If Joe was still with the production perhaps the failure to gain any mention was due to his not having any lines at all.

Ty Cobb quit the play after six weeks. He told his friends and family he was tired of making a damn fool of himself and that he didn't like people laughing at him, even if he was supposed to be starring in a comedy. In January 1912 a story entitled "Ball Players Seldom Make Good On Stage" reported that the rules and regulations passed by organized baseball to curtail the extra-curricular activities of players in the off season were unnecessary, as the boys of summer had bombed on the boards. Hans Wagner, roundly regarded as the greatest player in the game, loomed as the smartest of the bunch by turning down all offers to sing and dance. "Besides," the Flying Dutchman said, "I've got four months a year to spend as I please in automobiling, hunting, fishing, basketball and other pursuits that I really enjoy."

*   *   *

Cleveland finished in third place in 1912, an improvement over the previous year but not what management wanted. Joe Jackson batted .395 behind Cobb, who lead the league again as was his habit for a dozen seasons. They were back to their old selves, their vaudeville venture a thing of the past, and their rivalry continued. The press sided with Cobb, whom they referred to as the Master, in deference to Jackson, whom they took to calling "Sockless Joe, the Carolina Clouter" when they weren't calling him "General Joseph Jackson," in thumbing their nose at his Confederate bloodline.

Jackson was smashing home runs at record lengths, the longest estimated at 460 feet. Ring Lardner, who was a sports columnist in Chicago and New York before publishing his first collection of short stories, remarked "I don't know which is more dangerous~ to ride in a St. Louis taxi cab or play the field against Mr. Jackson because you are bound to get killed sooner or later either way."

The batting honors rivalry between Cobb and Jackson took an ugly turn during the season of 1913 when Ty told reporters that pitchers were favoring Joe. When the Nationals were in Detroit, Cobb approached Walter Johnson, the league's premier hurler, and said: "Say, Walt, is it true that you're pitching 'em over the groove for Jackson and saving all your stuff for me?" Johnson merely laughed at what he thought was a ridiculous accusation and thought it was a joke, until Cobb continued: "Well, it's funny. I know I have to work my head off to get a hit against you, and every once in a while my rival for batting honors cracks one against the fence. And it's the same with the other pitchers. They give me all their stuff and I find it hard to keep going. I know I'm not popular with some of the players, but I'd think the pitchers would think more of their own averages than to dish up easy balls for Jackson to hit."

That this dispute and such unsportsmanlike conduct was bandied about in the newspapers underscored a general dissatisfaction growing among the public with baseball players in general, who were portrayed for the first time as playing not for sport's sake, but for gold. "Organized baseball seems to be on the verge of losing its last vestige of sport for sport's sake," a New York columnist wrote in September 1913. "The commercial end of the enterprise overshadows all else."

Perhaps, then, it was no surprise when Ty Cobb was left off of the All-Star team in 1914. Sam Crawford, Tris Speaker and Joe Jackson made up the American League outfield, and it was the worst knock Cobb had ever received. It was a real affront to Cobb and he felt it keenly, although he laughed with scorn whenever the subject was brought up.

* * *

Following the season of 1914 Joe returned to Greenville, S.C., where he and his five brothers put together a barnstorming team that toured the South during the fall months. He had been a star of the American League for four years and was still only paid $6,000 per year. He had a pal named Joe Phillips who had played for the Mobile Sea Gulls in the Southern League when Joe was with New Orleans, and Phillips introduced Jackson to the bright lights of his vaudeville theater in West Virginia, explaining that a famous name like Joe's could make extra money on the stage without having to learn lines and stage directions. Phillips convinced him that there was a small fortune to be made by assembling a group of young ladies that could perform musical numbers and comedy skits and to be Jackson's props as he took center stage in rendering a monologue about baseball. They had great fun holding auditions in assembling "Joe Jackson's Baseball Girls," billed as a "musical comedy," and raised crowds by blowing into small southern towns and issuing a challenge to play any amateur team, male or female. Joe was his team's pitcher and the only male. Of course, with Joe Jackson in the line-up, they would never be shut out.

The two weeks that the Baseball Girls played Atlanta were standing room only every night even though local critics were not kind. They ridiculed the skits as "tabloid farce" and labeled Joe's halting monologue as a "sob rendition of his rise to fame." Still, people turned out to see them and by the time the tour reached Asheville, N.C. at the end of February 1915, Joe was quoted in the papers saying that he had no intention of breaking up the act just to report to spring training. In fact, it was his plan to report to Cleveland only for the start of the season.

If that piece of news did not go over well with his employers, their eyes bugged out when they read it was Joe's further intention to assemble a show composed entirely of big league players for the winter of 1916. "We have the best quartet of any of the major league teams," Joe announced, in whetting the public's appetite for singing ball players. This kind of foolishness would not have merited so much as a yawn from team owners had it not been for the advent of the Federal League which had been called into play in late 1913 to challenge the American and National leagues and had already siphoned off some of the game's best players. The Federal League came out of Chicago, where moneymen had lured away Joe Tinker and Mordecai Brown from the Cubs and who then turned around and scouted other players for the new league.

The Federal League started with six teams then spread to eight. Men of wealth in Pittsburgh, St. Louis, Brooklyn and other cities were interested in new franchises, and costly ballparks had been built in early 1914. The season ended with all clubs except Chicago heavy financial losers. But Federal team owners were adamant that organized baseball existed in violation of the Sherman Anti-Trust Act, and filed suit in the U.S. District Court in Chicago. Judge Kenesaw Mountain Landis deferred his decision when overtures for peace were made after the chief financial backer of the new league died and his partner refused further assistance.

In three years the only thing Federal promoters managed to do was threaten to disrupt the game through lawsuits, in the name of trying to change a system they said held players in practical peonage. In the final analysis they had succeeded only in proving to the public that players had little conscience and the whole affair disgusted millions of fans. Some observers called the exercise a purifying stage, giving rise to a players union and putting an end to long-term contracts that had only protected the owners' interests. The last thing organized baseball needed now was a challenge from entrepreneurs to turn ballplayers into dancing bears.

Cleveland ordered Joe Jackson to spring training, but he refused, preferring to remain with his show. Besides, he was making more money in show biz than baseball, and told Cleveland that he needed a raise or he'd retire. Mrs. Jackson threatened divorce, when it was perceived that her husband's interest in the Baseball Girls was more than professional. Joe folded up the show tent, bid his girls adieu, and reported for practice only after his wife had him served with papers, just to prove to him that she wasn't kidding.

* * *

The Federal League had so weakened the American and National leagues that the Cleveland Naps were looking to sell off talent when they got into a financial fix. It was the break the Feds were waiting for, and Joe Tinker came after Joe Jackson for Chicago's Federal team in August 1915. Jackson had a contract with Cleveland that specified he was to be paid on the 1st and 15th of each month; August 15th fell on a Sunday, the day that Tinker paid a call on Jackson, and as customary, the club deferred the semi-annual payment until the following day. Tinker told Jackson that technically his contract had been voided by Cleveland's failure to pay him, and Jackson used the ploy to hold up the Naps for more money and a new contract. Instead of caving in to Jackson's demands, Cleveland sold him to the Chicago White Sox, just to spite Joe Tinker and the Chicago Feds.

Cleveland got $15,000 and three players for Joe Jackson. The New York Yankees, who were trying to stave off an assault from the Feds, claimed they had been fouled by the White Sox stealing away the marquee player they had set their sights on. "The whole thing smacks of syndicate baseball," the New York critics howled.

White Sox owner Charlie Comiskey, "The Old Roman," countered the criticism of his shrewd maneuver saying that Joe Jackson was having his worst year ever at the plate—he was only batting .327 at the time of the trade—and if he didn't improve he would sit the bench and be used as a utility player in 1916. Still, Joe Jackson was the only man in sight likely to approach the batting records of Ty Cobb, having amassed a .368 batting average in six seasons.

When the season of 1916 rolled around, Joe Jackson did not sit the Chicago White Sox bench. He showed remarkable speed and agility at spring training, and ran so fast that he spiked himself. He liked his team but he did not like the town and even though he and Katie kept an apartment there, he ran back to Savannah on May 4th and signed a promissory note for $500 with Savannah Realty Management in securing a hideaway at 1802 Habersham, for them to live in between seasons. The owner of Savannah Realty was L. Dawson Wylly, a state legislator and the owner of Savannah Lumber Company. The loan was repaid on June 15th with White Sox funds, and the money was used to buy a house that had been built by Joe's brother-in-law, Richard Ellis.

Richard Ellis was married to Joe's sister, Lula. They had met at a retreat in the hills of South Carolina, fell in love and married. Richard came to Savannah to take a job with Alexander Wholesale Grocers, and his brother Sidney followed him here. The Ellis brothers decided that they stood a better chance of earning a good living as carpenters in a town that was undergoing a building boom, and they were able to lure Lula's brother back to Savannah with favorable terms on the new house they had built on Habersham. And whenever Joe Jackson was in town, he could be found at The Ideal Deli on the corner of Abercorn and Broughton, talking baseball with the owner, Holly Feinberg.

The season of 1916 had become another classic war for the batting title between Joe Jackson, Ty Cobb and Tris Speaker. Throughout much of the summer the trio batted within a few percentage points of each other before Speaker pulled away at the end of the year leaving Cobb in second and Jackson third. Sports writers with nothing better to do studied Joe's odd habits, searching for the secret to his success as a hitter. A reporter noted that "Jackson follows the same plan every day: he indulges in batting practice only a few minutes, leaving long before the other Sox. Then he takes a coaching glove and warms up a few moments with Happy Felsch. Following this Joe takes a handful of small pebbles up into the clubhouse with him and tosses them to the other members of the squad during the afternoon meeting just before the battle. This program is never changed, and as long as Jackson is hitting nobody is going to stop him—that's a lead-pipe cinch."

Joe Jackson was as superstitious as the next guy, and all baseball players are superstitious by nature. The reason for their odd behavior can be explained by the steady, grueling, unchangeable grind of the baseball season, where games are played on a daily basis for sixteen weeks, unlike any other sport. The baseball player gets no rest, and he believes in streaks of good and bad luck. In Joe's case, however, his superstitions were not portrayed in the press as colorful peccadilloes but as belief maintained by ignorance: he collected hairpins, the rustier the luckier, for he believed that bats only had so many hits in them and that they needed luck in addition to the careful attention he showered upon Black Betsy, as if she were as alive as the tree she had been made from. And at the end of the season when Joe finished third in the batting race and behind Ty Cobb for the seventh time, the sports writers explained it as 'Fate."

*   *   *

The Savannah Press of October 12, 1916 announced that Joe Jackson was back in town to spend the winter here with his wife, mother and sister at their new house at 1802 Habersham. He received a royal welcome from a huge crowd of friends and admirers at the train station and was kept busy all morning shaking hands and answering questions. "Just say I am in good health and enjoyed a fine season," he was quoted, and the reporter reminded readers that Joe's slugging and spectacular fielding was the big feature of the Chicago White Sox that year. He spent the winter at home with Katie, having retired from the stage, and getting in no other fights than on the end of a fishing pole.

In February 1917, the president of the National Baseball Commission, Ban Johnson, announced that the war in Europe would not cancel baseball in the coming season. It was un-American to suggest otherwise, as Baseball was considered to be an essential element of our way of life. However, a debate warmed over the concept of healthy, young men being exempted from service just to play a game while their less talented brothers were given guns and told to fight. In warding off criticism, Johnson announced his plan to give all ballplayers military training for two hours each day, from the start of spring training until the end of the season, after which all players and personnel would report to a special army camp. Johnson went even further in petitioning the federal government for drill sergeants for each professional baseball team. Still, his critics would not be silenced.

Baseball was due for the most prosperous season of its history, having just broken loose from the Federal League fiasco, and team owners were looking to recoup the losses of the last four years. Johnson knew that if money were the motive then his harshest critics would have his head on a stick, and so he appealed to their patriotism. In striking a deal to exempt players from the draft in 1917, Johnson agreed that there would be no effort to begin the season of 1918, if the war was still being waged.

When the draft was announced, all able-bodied men between the ages of 18 and 30 were summoned to their local draft board. Joe Jackson was 29 when he appeared before the Greenville examination board and was granted an exemption for two reasons: he was a married man and the sole provider for his family, caring for a wife, mother and sister; and four of his five brothers were already in service, the fifth being too young to serve. The press in Joe's case, however, made an odd distinction as opposed to the way in which they ignored dozens of similar cases involving other ballplayers and the thousands of cases among the general populace. Perhaps it was the old prejudice kicking in, or the collective memory of his former Philadelphia teammates branding him "yellow," or maybe it was a classic case of the most talented man in baseball being singled out for special treatment, but Joe Jackson came to represent what many considered to be the worst kind of slacker.

Part of Joe's problem in the press stemmed from mistakes made in identity. There were seven different men named "Joe Jackson" listed with the Greenville draft board, and a "Joe Jenkins" of the White Sox he was always being confused with. On October 17, 1917, a syndicated story out of New York reported to the sports world that "Joe Jackson Joins Colors," and went on to say that he had foregone playing an exhibition game in Minneola in order to report for military duty at Fort Oglethorpe, GA. It wasn't until a week later upon Joe's return to Savannah after the World Series that he was able to straighten out the mess for the eighth time. There were several notices of "Joe Jackson" being drafted which were followed by a retraction, all of which created in the mind of some detractors that our Joe was repeatedly called up for a draft that he always found a way to dodge. Nowhere did any writer take the time to explain away the confusion and rise to Jackson's defense.

Much of the shine to the coverage of the baseball season in the sports pages was dulled by the horrors of war splashed across front pages. Some newspapers reduced their coverage of arts, entertainments and sports while others dispensed with frivolity altogether. But for those who followed the game of baseball in 1917, there was the thrill of a world series staged between the Chicago White Sox and the New York Giants. As early as April of that year, White Sox owner Charlie Comiskey had promised that only a miracle could keep his team from winning the pennant, and singled out Joe Jackson as "the greatest natural batsman in the game today" as his insurance. Joe barely hit above .300 for the season, but the experts still regarded him as the most dangerous hitter in the series. "There is no pitcher who can successfully outguess Jackson," wrote one observer, "for he bats by natural instinct and is as likely to hit one kind of a ball as another."

When it came to pitching, the Sox had an unfair advantage. Eddie Cicotte had caused much trouble all season with his latest invention, the "shine" ball, which made batters see double. Cicotte polished one side of the ball along the seams then made it dark and heavy by soaking it. The action of the pitch was like a high-powered spitball, the alternating light and dark facets making it appear as if two balls were coming toward the batter, making it impossible to hit either one. Cicotte chalked up 22 victories by early September when Connie Mack prevailed upon Ban Johnson to issue a ruling forbidding Eddie's shine ball.

The Giants manager, John McGraw, thought the shine ball was a gimmick, a cheap stunt and a lot of hype. It was a myth, he told his players. "If you think a pitcher has something on you, he has," McGraw warned his men. "It's all psychological." Unfortunately, the Giants scattered seven hits off of Cicotte in the opener and lost the game.

With a White Sox win in Game 2 of the Series, in which Joe Jackson led his team with three hits, The Savannah Press was quick to jump on the bandwagon in reminding readers that "Jackson made his home in Savannah last winter and made countless new friends besides renewing the old ones made while he was a member of the Savannah South Atlantic team, and every one of them are scanning the box scores each day to see what "Shoeless Joe" is doing." Elsewhere in the same column The Press pointed out that his "multitude of friends here in Savannah are proud of his work in the first two games of the World Series and he is gratifying every wish they had entertained for him." Much was made of his play in the field: once he raced back to the stands and speared a line drive that was labeled for extra bases and on another occasion Joe came in on the dead run and took a low liner out of the grass with one hand. He fell, rolled over and regained his feet in time to prevent a runner from advancing to second.

The Giants came back to beat Eddie Cicotte in Game 3, by a score of 2-0. It wasn't a case of their having gotten any more hits off of him than the first game, but this time they came closer together, while Cicotte got no help from his hitters, including Joe Jackson. The same thing happened in Game 4 when Joe failed to hit and the Giants tied the series at two games apiece. The White Sox won the series by winning Games 4 and 5, and Joe finished with a .304 batting average. However, the victory was tainted when a careful review of the last two games revealed that the Sox had scored all of their runs on errors and rumors circulated among the betting community that the games had been fixed.

One week after winning the World Series, Joe and Katie Jackson returned home to Savannah accompanied by his teammate Lefty Williams and his wife. A huge crowd of well-wishers met them at the train station and followed them to the Hicks Hotel where they stayed until the house on Habersham could be opened.

"We won the title from the Giants because we possessed the better ball club," Joe said, to the cheers of the crowd. "Gameness was our middle name, and we proved it beyond peradventure when, with the Giants on equal terms with us at the conclusion of the fourth game in New York, we came from behind in the fifth contest in Chicago and blazed our way to victory with lusty blows from our trusty war clubs. The game was a heartbreaker for the New Yorkers to lose, but we were not to be denied. "Commy" is a prince to work for," Joe said, referring to Comiskey, "and with the Chicago fans loyal to the core, the winning of baseball's highest honors was a fitting climax to a splendid campaign."

Joe was photographed in a suit, hat and bow tie holding two trophies; one for beating out Ty Cobb in a batting competition, the second for having broken all records for throwing a baseball the farthest, a distance of almost 397 feet. The caption also provided the news that Joe had received a World Series bonus of $3,669.20, and soon after he and Katie were photographed again tooling around Savannah in a brand new Oldsmobile Pacemaker Eight which he had purchased from G. Bingham Bache on Liberty Street.

Savannah honored Joe's World Series victory with several celebrations. The Bijou Theater invited him, as guest of honor, to attend opening night of a new vaudeville show and the first public showing of the latest newsreel, "The Retreat of the Germans at the Battle of Arras." He held court at the Congress Billiard Parlor, and wisely remained at home while the latest version of his Baseball Girls toured the southeast.

Joe behind the wheel of his Pacemaker Eight

On November 17, The Savannah Press ran an article at the top of the sports section to report that Joe Jackson had bought into a poolroom owned by John Sullivan Jr., Buddy Sullivan and Shorty Jenkins, at 17 West Congress Street (where the SunTrust Bank building is now). This was not a new venture for him, as he had previously owned a poolroom back in Greenville five years earlier. Joe also scouted real estate investment opportunities with his brother-in-law, Richard Ellis. Joe's mother and his sister Gertrude lived with him and Katie, and the clan assembled on Sundays for dinner and a ride to Isle of Hope in Joe's new car.

* * *

Five days after announcing Joe's new local business endeavor, the Savannah paper reported a syndicated story out of Chicago that President Johnson of the American League intended to petition the federal government for 288 exemptions—eighteen players from each team—from military service. Johnson said that the high standard of the game would be destroyed if players were indiscriminately drafted and willingly offered to sacrifice the remaining seven players from each team. "Baseball is eager to do its part," Johnson added, "but we would like to be assured of quality players on every club. Otherwise, the pennant races would be very one-sided."

The response out of Washington D.C. that same day indicated that while Johnson's offer was being taken under advisement, nothing would alter the classification of baseball players for military service. "Officials have stated emphatically that no exemptions of workmen as a class except ship yard employees would be made. The classifications are arranged with relation to the value of each individual registrant to the nation in the conduct of the war and of his dependents. Baseball players with dependents thus might be enrolled in classes among the last to be called, but those without dependents and not engaged in business necessary to the conduct of the war would be liable to classification in the first class and thus would be among the first subject to call."

Thus, the debate was joined in the editorial pages of the nation's newspapers, whether baseball players should be exempted from the draft. The first person to publish a well-worded defense of the exemption was John Tener, president of the National League. "When the benefits to be derived from the game of baseball are taken into consideration there is added incentive for its continuation during the coming season," he wrote. "It is to meet this urgent necessity for recreation and relaxation, from time to time, in this crucial period of our national existence that clean wholesome sport is needed and I know of no game that fulfills such requirements better than baseball."

Baseball organizers were certain that the federal government would recognize that certain amusements are necessary during wartime and that baseball would receive the same exemption from the work or fight order as the stage and screen. Secondly, baseball turned over thousands of dollars in war tax and every effort was being made to hold benefit games for the Red Cross and other patriotic enterprises. Thirdly, the majority of ballplayers were engaged in useful and productive occupations outside of baseball, a large number of them being farmers who spent half their time tending to that business when they weren't playing ball.

Provost Marshal General Crowder made a report to congress of the policy formulated to exempt all married men or others with dependents and included a team by team list of how baseball would be affected. The Chicago White Sox stood to lose only two players, as the majority of the veterans came under the married classification, including Joe Jackson. The Chicago Cubs, however, would lose half their team unless the dependency restrictions were relaxed. How the government will interpret "dependents" is still unknown, Crowder stated in his report, but it is certain that a great number of baseball players would qualify.

On the surface, it seemed that Joe Jackson had nothing to worry about: he was married; he supported a wife, mother and sister; four of his brothers were in service, leaving him as male head of the family; and he turned 30 years old in 1918. He qualified for every exemption that was provided by the draft, yet all eyes turned to his case when in May 1918 the government issued a "work or fight" order: all able-bodied men between the ages of twenty-one and thirty had sixty days in which to find "essential work" or be drafted. The owners tried but could not get their players an exemption when Secretary Baker ruled that baseball was a non-essential occupation. A few players were called up and a few enlisted. Joe Jackson was reclassified 1-A up from Class 4 by the Greenville draft board.

No sooner than Joe began preparation to leave the White Sox and report for induction he received a notice from his draft board that the "Joe Jackson" who had been reclassified was one of the other six men who shared the same name. Four days later he received a third notice, this time advising him to appear before the nearest draft board for examination. He reported, as ordered, and was pronounced completely sound by army doctors in Philadelphia, where the White Sox were playing the Athletics. Charlie Comiskey placed Joe on the list of newly drafted men to be called for service between May 25 and June 1.

On May 15, Joe notified the White Sox that he had taken a job with the Harlan & Hollingsworth Shipbuilding Company in Wilmington, Delaware, and that he would begin work the next day. "This comes as a great shock to all Savannah baseball fans," The Press wrote, "because more interest was centered around Joe Jackson than any other player in the big game." However, the story went on to explain that even though Joe was leaving the White Sox he was still eligible to play ball in the Bethlehem Steel League, one of the strongest leagues outside of organized baseball.

And then a very odd thing happened to Joe Jackson: a series of scathing attacks on his patriotism surfaced in the editorial and sports pages of The Chicago Tribune, concluding that by failing to enlist nor submitting to the draft meant that good Americans would not be very enthusiastic over seeing him play baseball after the war is over. Even Charlie Comiskey, his owner, criticized him too. "There is no room on my club for players who wish to evade the army draft by entering the employ of shipbuilders," he said, and followed with threats not to take the "jumpers" back into organized ball.

"Old Savannah Player Quits Baseball Game—Joe Jackson Will Build Ships For Uncle Sam" announced The Savannah Press on May 16. In defense of Joe's opting for essential work, the writer concluded that "From what Savannah knows of Joe Jackson, it is not likely that his friends here will form any such opinion that he is trying to evade the draft law. They will rather think that it is Joe's intentions to do his part in turning out ships for Uncle Sam as speedy as possible."

That sentiment, however, quickly changed when Basil Abrams, sports editor of The Savannah Press, wrote on May 22 that "Joe Jackson very hurriedly a shipbuilder became when they asked him to head toward battlefield fame, and thus he pointed the way for others to tread, if they, too, were afraid to go over there and crack the Hun head." Abrams followed up with another column in which he compared Joe unfavorably with Grover Cleveland Alexander, who had joined the army. "Joe will miss the journey to France in all likelihood; and maybe Grover will not, but Alex has the profound respect of all of his fellow players as well as the kingdom of fandom." And when the exemption board in Greenville received notice from the Emergency Fleet Corporation that Joe Jackson was a necessary employee, he was reclassified 2-B, revoking the order calling him to report for induction but which was announced as "Jackson Gets By With Job" in the Savannah paper.

While the controversy swirled around him, Joe said little and went along doing the best he could for his family. He built ships and took his team to the championship of the league, and he played exhibition games that raised money in support of the Red Cross. And still he was widely regarded as the most famous slacker of the Great War.

Ty Cobb was deferred because he had a wife and three children, but when he saw how the press shellacked Joe Jackson he was moved to issue loud proclamations of his intention to enlist—after the 1918 season was completed. "I feel I must give up baseball at the close of the season and do my duty to my country in the best way possible," Cobb was quoted in the press. "Baseball is good for the entertainment and morale of the people and I love the game, but the close of the coming season will see me out of it until the war is over." On the relative strength of such statements, the same critics who came after Joe Jackson with sharpened pencils turned a blind eye to Ty Cobb.

Even President Wilson was drawn into the debate over the Crowder order. He was quoted as being in support of an exemption for ballplayers, saying that the continuation of healthful sports was an essential factor in wartime and that he could see no reason why sports should be discontinued. But others raised objections in the same article, noting the "telling blow of slackerism, recently exemplified by Joe Jackson and Al Mamaux going into the shipbuilding industry, presumably to escape the draft."

"Why Not Stop Pro Ball Games?" was the typical headline in newspapers around the country at the end of

May 1918. And in answering the question, editors universally agreed that baseball is non-essential and the nation could afford to give it up for a year. "The big thing now is to win the war," said one writer. "It is the only thing that matters supremely. Going to baseball games and spending good money will not help win." But the failure of Secretary of War Newton Baker to act in a timely fashion—until after all of the facts relating to the effect upon the baseball business could be brought out through the hearing of a case appealed from a local board—meant that the debate would continue to rage.

Secretary Baker had not resolved the exemption issue in July when the case of Rube Parnham provided the opportunity to set a legal precedent regarding the status of baseball and the Crowder order. Parnham was a pitcher in the International League and a married man who had been classified 4-A. However, under the Crowder work or fight order he was instructed to find a useful occupation, which he refused to do until a court heard the matter. In this way baseball sought to test the government, to see how far it cared to go with the case. With the minor leagues going out of business and the majors hit hard by enlistments and desertions to shipyards and munitions factories, organized baseball was doomed unless a ruling was made. Actors had been exempted from the Crowder order as workers in essential industries, but the government was having a harder time coming to a decision over athletes. A decision in Parnham's case was delayed while politicians continued to weigh the pros and cons.

Ty Cobb, who was enjoying another great year on the diamond, announced on July 20 that he intended to retire at the end of the season and enlist in the army. He had claimed the same exemptions as Joe Jackson, yet was spared all of the disgrace by making a lot of patriotic speeches to sports writers who feared the game could not spare him. "Baseball will not be baseball without Cobb," wrote Paul Purman, and it is impossible to explain why Cobb was singled out for such treatment in the light of the abuse heaped upon his chief rival whose absence from the game was already being felt.

By the end of July, with the dispute over the Crowder order still hanging in the balance in congress, the major leagues had been decimated by the draft and the even larger number of players engaged in essential occupations such as shipbuilding. "About four old men remain on each team" was the way Jack Cook put it to his readers; "Fans Losing Interest In The Old Game" was the way a writer in Chicago summed up watching a spectacular game devoid of the enthusiasm of its fans. "One wonders what the good of it is," Cook wondered "when there are no resounding cheers, no faces flushed by excitement, no outbursts of fans and fanettes gone insane for the moment."

Sport for whose sake was the question, and the editors of *Stars and Stripes*," the newspaper printed by and for American soldiers, provided the answer when they announced that they had lost their patience with baseball magnates arguing the essential quality of professional baseball. On August 20, 1918, the editors suspended the sports page of their newspaper, vowing a blackout until an allied victory brought back peace. In a brilliant essay in support of the controversial decision, the editors acknowledged the abiding interest most soldiers had in sports, the value of athletic training, and even athlete soldiers themselves, but "they are not to be mentioned today because their job has taken on another hue...ballplayers who have traded the easy glory they knew at home for the bloody heritage of the western front, and their fame here belongs with the mass, not with individual mention."

The column concluded with the larger question at issue: "What is the point of a sporting page printed in France within the sound of the guns?" And in answering their own question, the editors of *Stars and Stripes* decided that such headlines as "Star Players Dive for Shipyards to Escape Work or Fight Order," "Cobb is Thinking of Enlisting This Fall," and "Fulton and Dempsey Haggle Over Purse" did not make a heroic appeal to those grinding away at the job on the front lines or to those living and dying in the mud and dirt of the front three thousand miles from home.

"There is but one big league today for this paper to cover," the editors of *Stars and Stripes*" said, "and that league winds its way among the S.O.S. stations scattered throughout France and ends at the western front. Any work that is part of the big job, either in the lines or back of it, is of utmost value. But entertaining the people back home isn't part of the big job, nor do we believe the bulk of them want to be entertained in any such way."

There was no space left for the Cobbs, the Ruths, the Dempseys and the rest when the Ryans, the Smiths, the Bernsteins and the others were charging machine guns. Spectator sport had been "burnt out by gun fire," and the sole slogan left was "Beat Germany." Anything that pertained to that slogan counted; the rest didn't. And that is why *Stars and Stripes* printed their last sporting page until Allied victory brought peace.

At the end of August, a brief paragraph appeared in The Savannah Press reporting the Shipyard Baseball Championship Series played at the Polo Grounds in New York and in Philadelphia, between the Harlan team of the Bethlehem Steel Corporation and a Brooklyn dry dock company team from the New York District League. Among the pro players appearing in the series was Jackson and Lynn of the Chicago White Sox, and Dumont and Garrity of the Washington Senators. Proceeds of the games were donated to various war funds, it was prominently mentioned, and Jackson led his team to victory. The series received little coverage or notice in the papers.

Organized baseball thought it a wise move to shorten the season by one month so that players could move more quickly toward military service, but no matter what the owners tried they were still criticized. When newspapers announced they would not carry coverage of the 1918 World Series, baseball countered by announcing that 10% of player bonuses would go to the Red Cross. Instead of earning praise for the added contribution, critics assailed them as cheap skates and money-grabbers. In Savannah, the sports editor of The Evening Press, Basil Abrams, fired off a few rounds at slacker athletes and then resigned his post to enlist in the army in September.

The war ended the second week in November, and it is surprising how quickly life in these United States went back to normal, if newspapers of the day were any indication. Ty Cobb, who was given a captain's commission and sent to the rear for all of two months, came home the conquering hero and went right back to his old life without missing a beat. In his opinion piece, "Can Be Ballplayer and a Gentleman," Frank Turner held Cobb out as an example, calling him the "greatest of them all," in citing Cobb's brief stint with the gas and flame division, "only too late to take part in the actual fighting."

Joe Jackson, on the other hand, was deserving of Turner's criticism for having entered the shipyards to avoid service. But Turner went even further, making his attack more personal, by intimating that Jackson was not among the new breed of ballplayer that was also a "gentleman of intelligence and culture." Many ballplayers had taken the same options as Joe, men who had far less at stake than he did in caring for his family, yet whenever writers needed a name to throw around as an example of a first-class slacker, Joe Jackson came to mind first.

*   *   *

Joe Jackson returned home to Savannah in November 1918. He and Katie briefly took up residence at 114 President Street until the second floor apartment of the Ellis's house at 621 West 39th Street was ready. He discovered that during his absence that the City of Savannah had passed new police regulations and amended city ordinances to regulate and shorten the business hours of poolrooms, in order to stamp out loafing places for vagrants, loiterers and slackers during working hours. The measure was originally designed to aide and assist local industries in need of workers, but it must have seemed to Joe Jackson that the measure was, in part, aimed directly at him and his interest in the Congress Billiard Parlor. The owners of six local poolrooms banded together and joined in a lawsuit in superior court to prevent the mayor and police chief from enforcing the ordinance. Joe remained a silent partner, but was seen infrequently in his establishment and began considering other sideline occupations to baseball. He wasn't entirely sure if Charlie Comiskey was going to invite him back to Chicago for the season of 1919.

Fellow owners of major league franchises took Charlie Comiskey at his word when the Old Roman said there would be no room for "jumpers" on the White Sox after the war. Offers came out of the woodwork to buy Joe from Chicago and it was then that Comiskey's puffed up patriotism began to fade. He refused firm offers from the Yankees and the Red Sox and sent Joe a contract for the 1919 season at the same $6,000 salary. And as America looked forward to a return to a normal life of peace and quiet and the prospect of another season of baseball, all references to slackers and heroes, patriots and pacifists faded away.

As if in open defiance of the attacks on their hero by The Chicago Tribune, fans turned out for opening day with banners and signs and a marching band to celebrate the return of Joe Jackson. When he stepped up to the plate for his first at-bat, the game was interrupted by a delegation that presented him with a gold pocket watch. Fans around the league poured out to see him play. Newspapers dropped the slacker stories to resume coverage of a stellar career. Even Charlie Comiskey was forced to put a new spin on his attack of Joe's patriotism by announcing he was glad he had not listened to the critics who wanted him to get rid of Slacker Joe.

As the season rolled around, press coverage of sports was still scant. Most papers restricted sports to two or three columns, but readers of The Savannah Press had new features to pore over: for the first time ever, there were sports page photographs and there was coverage of a new city league. There was also news that another local boy had made good in the big leagues. Arthur Hardy, who had been an amateur phenom over at Park Extension field, moved up to Chicago from the Virginia League and phoned home to tell the newspaper that he was going to be the starting catcher for the White Sox on opening day. "I'm gonna make good or I'm not coming back to Savannah," Arthur told The Press, but on opening day young master Hardy was not in the line-up.

Instead, The Press ran a story how the White Sox swept three of four games in the opening series against St. Louis, chalking up twenty-one hits in the first game alone. Jackson of Chicago starred at bat in the series, with a home run, three doubles and six singles. Elsewhere it was noted that baseball was back to its pre-war basis with all of its players returned from war, and that fans were turning out in record number.

The White Sox were favored to win the American League pennant in 1919. Behind the pitching of Eddie Cicotte and Lefty Williams and the hitting of Joe Jackson and Eddie Collins, the Sox moved into first place by the end of April and held on all year, fending off a late rush by Cleveland.

Jackson batted .351, his highest average in six years. He led the team and was among league leaders in almost every offensive category. But dissension among his teammates and the bitterness they felt toward the miserly Comiskey had taken all of the fun out of the game. Bonuses went unpaid and pay raises were out of the question; an unhappier team never won a pennant.

The 1919 World Series between the Chicago White Sox and Cincinnati Reds was scheduled for nine games. The Sox were heavily favored but lost the series five games to three. Rumors that the fix was in circulated even before the contest began, but such rumors were not uncommon. In fact, gambling had been a perennial problem for baseball ever since its first betting scandal way back in 1877, when the Louisville team of the National League was so far out in front in the standings that they could lose half of their remaining games and still clinch the pennant—which they proceeded to do, to the great financial benefit of the Louisville players. More recently in 1911, when bookmakers were finding it harder to do business at racetracks, they took up residence in the stands at baseball stadiums. They were so open and notorious that the league presidents were afraid the game would be held in bad repute, and instructed club owners that they were in danger of losing their franchises unless some sort of effort was made to curb gambling in the bleachers. By 1918, the problem had not abated and American League president Ban Johnson was still unable to force a higher standard of compliance from club owners. And the season of 1919, ending in the Black Sox Scandal, began with the trial of Reds first baseman Hal Chase for betting on games; that there was a World Series scandal came as no surprise to many who followed the game.

Rumors of scandal began almost as soon as the series was over when Eddie Collins and other members of the White Sox tried to give all kinds of alibis for their defeat. Although it was noted that Joe Jackson had not rushed into print to tell why he lost, Collins, the team's captain, had a litany of excuses that rang hollow. As charges of collusion with gamblers mounted against the Sox, Charlie Comiskey began an investigation that after three months had reportedly failed to find any proof of wrongdoing. But before Comiskey's search for facts was ended, Ray Schalk went public with the announcement that he and seven other teammates would not be returning to the line up in 1920—but wouldn't say why.

A shake-up of the Chicago line-up was certain in the coming season, for one reason or another. Therefore it came as no surprise when in mid-February, Joe Jackson announced from his home in Savannah that he had returned his contract unsigned and would not play baseball for Chicago—or anybody else—unless he received a $3,000 increase in pay, as had his teammates. "You know, I was about the whole show in the last World Series," Joe told The Savannah Press. "If it had not been for me the chances are the White Sox would not have won a single game, and why should I not be given my money?"

And, should he not be paid $10,000 per season, Joe Jackson had made up his mind that he and the Sullivans would franchise their poolroom on Congress Street and move into Birmingham and Charleston. By May, the White Sox reached an agreement with Joe and he was back on track to join the team for spring training in Waco, Texas.

The 1920 White Sox revolved around their great star, Eddie Collins, who was backed up by such leaders as Ray Schalk and Buck Weaver. Joe Jackson's bat was a big feature, but the "Shoeless Wonder" was not a magnetic leader in the same sense that Ruth and Speaker were, in the eyes of the sporting writers. As the slacker scandal faded away, sports coverage moved up to Page 3 of the local paper and afforded a full page of copy, just in time

205

to relate news of a larger scandal brewing, that of the fixed Series of 1919.

In September, as the 1920 World Series was getting underway, a grand jury investigating gambling and baseball convened in Chicago, calling a dozen officials, players and writers to testify. The first and only player to be summoned in the beginning was New York pitcher Rube Benton, who was there to testify about having been offered $750 to throw a game. He then related the story told him by a Cincinnati gambler named Hahn that the 1919 World Series had been fixed by paying off Cicotte, Williams, Gandil and Felsch of the White Sox. The story went that a betting syndicate out of Pittsburgh had promised the four players $100,000, but that the rest of the players had been left out, including Joe Jackson. Benton went on to say that word of the fix filtered throughout organized baseball and that many players took advantage of the tip to rake in a few bucks on bets.

The prosecutor could not find Hahn, the mystery man behind the betting scandal. So powerful was he rumored to be that American League President Ban Johnson had it on good authority that the gamblers had successfully blackmailed the White Sox not to win the pennant in 1920 or run the risk of being exposed for the Series fix of 1919. As fans combed box scores of the waning weeks of the season in search of reasons why the Sox finished second in a close race, indicted players left the team to testify. Vowing to rid baseball of its black sheep, Johnson withheld Chicago's second-place money and reassured the public that the percentage of dishonest ballplayers was very small. By the end of September, four additional White Sox players were indicted and suspended, including Joe Jackson. Even though their suspension would cost Chicago another pennant, Charlie Comiskey vowed to play out the schedule "if we have to get Chinamen to replace the suspended players."

Because grand jury proceedings are kept secret, the only details of player confessions were related to the press by the witnesses themselves. Joe Jackson, who made no formal statement to the grand jury, avoided the press as well. It was left to his teammate Lefty Williams to sketch out Joe's part in the play. Williams explained to the prosecutor how Chick Gandil was the go-between and that he and Joe were promised $20,000 each, but that Williams only received $10,000, half of which he gave Jackson. Once the Williams statement was circulated, Joe was pressed for his side of the story.

"I heard I had been indicted," Joe said to reporters. "I decided these men could not put anything over on me. I called up Judge McDonald, (Chief Justice of the superior court, who directed the grand jury inquiry), and told him I was an honest man. He said, 'I know you are not,' and hung up the receiver.

"I figured somebody had squawked and that the place for me was the ground floor. I went over to tell him what I knew.

"I got in there and said I got $5,000 and they promised me $20,000. Lefty Williams handed it to me in a dirty envelope. I told that to Judge McDonald.

"He said he didn't care what I got, that if I got what I ought to get for crabbing the game of the kids, I wouldn't be telling him my story. I don't think the judge likes me. Before we broke up, I climbed Gandil and McMullin and Risberg about it. They said, 'You poor simp, go ahead and squawk. We'll say you're a liar. Some of the boys were promised more than you and didn't get as much.'

"And I'm giving you a tip," Joe revealed to the newsmen. "A lot of these sporting writers have been saying the third game of the series was on the square (which the Sox won). The eight of us did our best to kick it and little Dick Kerr won the game by his pitching.

Because he won it, these gamblers double-crossed us for double-crossing them.

"They've hung it on me. They ruined me when I went to the shipyards, but I don't care what happens now. I guess I'm through with baseball. I wasn't wise enough like Chick Gandil to beat them to it."

* * *

In covering Joe Jackson's performance during the 1919 World Series, The Savannah Press held out an olive branch. Basil Abrams, the sports editor who had chided Jackson as a slacker during World War I, wrote "If Joe makes good in the world's series, we'll forgive him for that little score we hold against him down here. If he doesn't, we'll be right on him when he comes back here this year to sell Joe's famous sandwiches." And when Joe stroked a ball over the wall in the final game of the series (the only homer hit by either team), he was referred to as "Joe Jackson from Savannah" in the local paper.

Once news of his indictment hit the streets, the paper was cautious in coming down on him. His friends and business partners were quick to report that Joe was innocent of the charges. They stoutly defended his character and branded the proceedings as preposterous. Dennis Sullivan pointed out Joe's stellar work in the series as sufficient evidence to exonerate him, and was confident that he would emerge from the trial with his colors proudly flying.

Purely on the strength of such strong local sentiment, The Press walked a fine line in editorializing the subject of the Series.

"We liked Joe," an unidentified local columnist wrote. "He had an up-hill pull and after getting in the big game he made good. We watched his every forward step with great interest, for we knew Joe. He was one of us.

"And now Joe has confessed.

"He was lured by the lure that takes its toll every year, in some form or another. He is not alone, by no means, no.

"We are sorry that Joe took this step. When the news reached Savannah that he was accused of being in the list his friends said that it was not possible and staunchly stood by him.

"He says that he is through with baseball. That would be a pity. We want Joe to come back. After this one mistake we believe, knowing Joe as we do, that he will come back clean. He has learned his lesson.

"We sympathize with Joe at this time. We cannot overlook the fault. It was a big one. But we want to see Joe come back. He is thoroughly repentant and is sincere. He has learned his lesson."

As soon as he was released from the custody of a deputy sheriff in Chicago, Joe Jackson made his way home to Savannah, where his friends were looking forward to his arrival and the chance to hear his version of the baseball scandal from his own lips. He said that he was in receipt of numerous telegrams from managers who were eager for his services during the coming season, and had been invited to return home to Greenville to play exhibition games. With him here was teammate and fellow co-conspirator Claude Williams.

The probe was temporarily delayed, and the Illinois State's Attorney was quoted as expressing doubt whether the White Sox players committed any serious legal offense in ditching the series. "The only charge under which they might be prosecuted is that of gambling or conspiracy to gamble, which is a misdemeanor in Illinois," he said. "I am uncertain whether any crime has been committed."

There were so many other incidents for the grand jury to delve into that prosecutors intended to go back as far as ten years in rooting out dishonesty. Before the investigation could be concluded, plans were already being discussed to put the game under the control of prominent men not connected with baseball in order to rid baseball of corruption that had completely rotted its integrity.

The investigation reached a high point when prosecutors were finally able to put their hands on John J. "Sport" Sullivan, the gambler who was actively involved in arranging payments to players. Sullivan's revelation that there really was a "great big mastermind" behind the deal to fix the series had the nation wondering who was that devious—and that wealthy.

"It doesn't seem likely, at this writing, that any ball players will go to prison for their part in crooked playing," a Savannah sports scribe wrote in October 1920. "Lawyers disagree as to the chances of sending them over the road for what they've done. The prime object is to get hold of the gamblers who provided the incentive for their crookedness. As long as the dishonest players are driven forever from the game, the fans will be satisfied—provided the gamblers don't go free.

"Prison is no place for the crooked ball players, as they have revealed themselves in the recent confessions of the White Sox. They belong in some nice institution for the feeble-minded, where they can have plenty of hydrotherapy and some bromidium to soothe their tortured brains. They should be taken before some kind-faced old probate judge and tried and found guilty of boobery in the first degree. For, after all, they're just plain, silly boobs."

* * *

In November 1920, Judge Kenesaw Mountain Landis (named for the Civil War battlefield where his father had lost a leg to a Confederate cannonball) became chairman of Baseball and a committee of one as a final court of appeal in all matters in dispute. He had been appointed by President Theodore Roosevelt to a federal judgeship and was paid $7,500 per year, but received $50,000 per year from baseball, a sum lofty enough to ensure he remain out of reach of wealthy club owners who had gotten used to buying their way in and out of everything. When the infamous Black Sox finally went to trial in July 1921, they were found not guilty. Nevertheless, Judge Landis banned them all from organized ball for life in his first official act as commissioner, and he reached his verdict before the criminal trial was over and the jury had delivered its verdict.

The sentence imposed by Landis was an effort to salvage the integrity of the national pastime. The game was clean again, and even though the accused were innocent in the eyes of the law, they were not pure enough for the high moral standards of baseball. As if mentioning the scandal might cause them further harm, none of the participants in the Black Sox Scandal ever spoke publicly on the matter.

While it is certain that there had been a conspiracy to fix the 1919 World Series, much about how it came together is still unknown. Testimony in the trial made it clear that first baseman Chick Gandil and pitcher Eddie Cicotte were ringleaders, but the identities of the gamblers was never made known. Cicotte and Gandil made deals with at least two different groups of gamblers who possibly were being backed by Arnold Rothstein, the man who tradition has it was the brain behind the racket.

The conspiracy, if there was one, was a sad comedy of ineptitude. So many gamblers around the country heard of the fix that the odds on the Sox dropped like a rock before the conspirators could get a bet down. And to this day, no one has ever been able to point out exactly when and where the fix kicked in over the course of eight games. Only the pitchers seemed to have had some sort of idea of what they were supposed to do in making their team lose. The rest of the Sox were so

211

confused by the scheme that they never could agree on which games had been played to lose.

When the story broke, Joe denied the whole thing, then followed his teammates lead and voluntarily appeared before the grand jury to testify. In the comments leaked to the press, Joe appeared to be making a full confession of his misdeeds and named his co-conspirators. Though he later retracted his confession, it was never forgotten.

In a brilliant book published more than twenty years ago, Donald Gropman accessed Joe Jackson's grand jury testimony, the 1,700-page transcript of the 1924 civil suit in which Jackson sued White Sox owner Charlie Comiskey for back wages and assembled everything he could find in an attempt to decide once and for all whether Joe Jackson was a co-conspirator in the scandal, a dupe of city slickers, or truly innocent. Gropman's story is at odds with the traditional version of Jackson's role, and it differs radically from the official version maintained by organized baseball. Gropman's contention is that Joe Jackson was literally innocent of involvement in the scandal.

The facts are these:

Toward the end of the season, Chick Gandil, the team's first baseman, told Joe of a scheme whereby gamblers would pay each player $10,000 to throw the series. Joe said no, and Gandil dropped the subject. Gandil then made a second deal with another gang of gamblers, this time for a flat fee of $100,000. Gandil also told the second group that Joe was in on the fix.

Gandil offered $20,000 to Joe and Joe said no again, but Gandil assured him that the fix was in and that he might as well take part since the Sox were sure to lose. Soon gamblers from coast to coast were privy to the plan. Rumors proliferated and even appeared in print. On the morning of the opening game, Joe bumped into Bill Burns, an American League pitcher, who corroborated the story that the fix was in. Joe went to Charlie Comiskey with what little he knew and asked to be benched for the entire series.

Comiskey refused. He laughed at the rumors, saying the same thing happened every year. So Joe played in the series, and afterward pointed to his record as proof that he had played to win: Joe got more hits than any player on either team and played without error in the field. His .375 average and 12 hits set a World Series record that stood for decades.

When the games were over and the Sox had lost, Lefty Williams tried to push $5,000 on Joe as payment. Joe took the money to Comiskey's office to tell him of the fix but was turned away. Two of the guilty players were already in Comiskey's office and a cover-up was already in the works.

Comiskey, acting on tips from gamblers in the loop, hired private detectives to investigate his own players and publicly offered a $20,000 reward for information of proof of a fix. A few days after Comiskey refused to see him, Joe and Katie Jackson took a train home to Savannah. He still had the $5,000 in his pocket. From his residence at 621 W. 39th Street in Savannah, Joe carried on a brief correspondence with Comiskey, and on October 27th, he wrote to inquire about his Series check. Comiskey responded saying that the money was given to Manager Gleason to divide among the players, and offered Joe the opportunity to return to Chicago to clear his name.

In attempting to clear his name, Joe responded to the charges saying, "I don't see why they make a lot of fuss because we lost as it isn't the first time a series was lost, and I am sure I did all I could to win and I think my record for the series will show, if you look at it."

Comiskey's only response was to invite Joe's participation in the 1920 season, and asked for his terms. Negotiations stretched out over the next four months, during which Comiskey's offer to pay Joe $7,000 for one year was met with Joe's response that he could make more money in the billiard business, and returned the contract unsigned. It rankled him that Comiskey paid Buck Weaver $10,000 and Eddie Collins $15,000 without them having to ask; Joe figured he was worth at least as much. He stuck by his guns, refusing to budge out of his easy chair to play ball for less than ten grand.

In February 1920, Charlie Comiskey dispatched his secretary Harry Grabiner to Savannah to talk to Joe about his contract. Grabiner called Joe from Union Station on West Broad Street and asked him to meet there. Joe had been up all night with his sister who was in the hospital with appendicitis, but agreed to meet Grabiner at the station and take him for a ride around town. They went by the hospital and then to Joe's residence on 39th Street. Grabiner offered Joe $8,000 per year for three years, or $10,000 for one. "Take it," Grabiner told Joe, "or we'll kick you out of baseball."

Joe had Grabiner read the contract to him while they sat in Joe's car parked in front of his house, and then signed it reluctantly.

The 1920 season was poisoned by persistent rumors that all games were fixed. Joe was viewed with suspicion even while batting .390 in mid-season. Babe Ruth, who was on course to hit 54 home runs that year, gave Joe the gift of one of his custom-made 50-ounce bats which Joe promised not to use against the Yankees. By the end of July, Joe, with Ruth's bat, was batting over .400.

1920 was Joe's last season. A new gambling scandal erupted during the pennant race in September, and the resulting investigation re-opened the Black Sox Scandal. Joe's name was published as being one of the infamous eight, and fans booed him in spite of his all-star performances. With the resulting bad publicity, Charlie Comiskey suspended the team until the court settled the matter, pretending he knew nothing of the admissions and investigations of the past year.

Eddie Cicotte was first to crack. He spilled his guts to the grand jury, and said Joe had been in on the plot. When Joe heard the news he went to Comiskey's office but was turned away and told to refer the matter to Alfred Austrian, Comiskey's lawyer.

For Austrian, the question of Joe's guilt or innocence was less important than his potential to expose Comiskey. If believed, Joe's story showed Comiskey had evidence of the fix much earlier than claimed, that Comiskey had lied to the public, and that he had re-signed players he knew to be corrupt. As Comiskey's lawyer, Austrian's task was to convince Jackson that the truth would harm him and that his only chance was in confessing his guilt and acting contrite. If Joe did that, Austrian said the club would stand behind him.

Jackson was forced to admit his part in the scheme, that Gandil had talked him into it but double-crossed him on the money. Joe would play the part of the ignorant yokel taken in by big-city sharpsters, a role which did not need much coaching. As soon as a script had been worked out, Austrian rushed Joe over to the grand jury before it adjourned for the day and had him recite the new set of facts. He signed a waiver of immunity—whatever that was—which of course was in itself a cruel joke because everyone knew Joe couldn't read.

Jackson's testimony before the grand jury is a troubling thing to read: Joe initially admits to being part of the fix, but for the next 27 pages he manages to truthfully recount the succession of events to clearly illustrate that he played no active role in playing to lose. In fact, the grand jury foreman concluded that he never heard Joe's confession.

Of course, Joe's confession—made with the understanding that he could continue to play—was not as troubling to Joe as his concern over how the gamblers were going to take the news that he had double-crossed them by taking the cash and playing to win. Joe didn't know where he'd have to move to hide from that kind of trouble. Newspapers were one thing—he could hide from newspapers because he couldn't read—but gangsters and gamblers posed a bigger threat to his safety.

Walking out of the courthouse on his way from the grand jury room, Joe Jackson was depicted in a syndicated column by Hugh Fullerton as the "ignorant idol of kids who sold his honor."

"It ain't so, Joe, is it?"

"Yes, kid, I'm afraid it is," is the exchange on the courthouse steps that was reported by Fullerton but which never took place; this from the same man who had predicted at the start of Joe's career that he would fail because he was ignorant.

*   *   *

The Black Sox were indicted by the grand jury at the end of September 1920. In mid-November, Judge Landis was named the first Commissioner of Baseball, and his attitude toward the Chicago Eight was that none would be permitted to re-enter the game regardless of the degree to which they participated in the fix. In response to his dictates, Joe and his teammates formed a barnstorming team and called themselves the Black Sox, playing most of their games in Illinois while under order not to leave the state until the trial was over. The power of organized ball prevented them from renting fields on many occasions, and sometimes their appearances were cancelled on what were called "moral grounds."

While waiting for the trial to begin, Joe and Katie lived in their Chicago apartment. Without a salary from the White Sox, Joe opened a poolroom near the university, where he drew most of his customers from the student body.

And then an odd thing happened: the prosecutor to the Black Sox case discovered that most of his case file was missing, including the testimony of the players and their signed waivers of immunity. Scandal on top of scandal brewed when prosecutors received word that a New York gambler had paid $10,000 for the documents soon after they were stolen from the state attorney's office. The grand jury evidence apparently dropped from sight incident to the retirement of State Attorney Hoyne and the taking over of the office by State Attorney Crowe. The original indictments were dismissed and the State had to start all over again with a second grand jury. This time around, Joe Jackson hired a lawyer, and instead of mouthing the script that Comiskey wanted the grand jury to hear, Joe retracted his earlier testimony and told the truth. However, he and six colleagues were still re-indicted. Fred McMullin was cut loose for lack of evidence.

A second arrest warrant was served on Joe Jackson on April 9, 1921, for "obtaining money and goods by means of the confidence game," and his bail was set at $3,000. The trial began in June; seven players and ten gamblers faced a variety of conspiracy charges. Three assistants of the former district attorney—who had helped prepare the original case for the prosecution—now appeared as attorneys for the defense. All of the players showed up in court but a few of the gamblers went on the lam. Hal Chase, who was named as one of the original framers of the fix, simply ignored the indictment and stayed in California. The courtroom was packed, and unindicted teammates—called the "Clean Sox"—visited the courthouse to wish the Black Sox luck.

The district attorney opened the case by announcing that the original confessions, waivers and testimony had been stolen from the files. The court was thrown into confusion about the admissibility of unsigned carbon copies of the confessions, and the State's case was reduced to the testimony of only two confessed fixers who had been granted immunity.

Neither of the two fixers—Billy Maharg and Sleepy Bill Burns—knew the whole story, but their version of the scandal became the best known: Cicotte and Gandil offered to fix the series for $100,000; the other gamblers became involved, including Arnold Rothstein, and Maharg and Burns were double-crossed when the Sox won the third game. Most important to Joe Jackson was that neither fixer mentioned his name in direct connection with the fix.

When Joe Jackson took the stand to testify on July 25th that his original confession had been made only after Judge McDonald promised him that it would never be used against him, he admitted that he had signed something in the grand jury room but didn't know if it was an immunity waiver or what because he was half drunk and couldn't read. He then related how Alfred Austrian had talked him into running to the grand jury in order to "trample the gamblers underfoot," but only after being assured that he wouldn't be prosecuted. From that point, Joe's testimony turned into pure vaudeville, keeping the court in an uproar as he related how he had gotten two court bailiffs drunk. In reviewing his performance on the stand, The New York Herald reported that Joe made a hit before the Chicago jury with "his quaint phraseology and Southern dialect."

"Shoeless Joe asserted that he was drunk when he signed papers waiving immunity after he had confessed before Judge McDonald," The Herald reported. "He said that he would have signed his death warrant at the time if they had told him to do so." Elsewhere in the same article, Joe was quoted from the stand, saying, "Austrian said that after confessing nothing would be done with me and I could go anywhere—to the Portuguese Islands if I wanted. Then they sent two bailiffs with me when I left to protect me, and the bailiffs and I went out and got good and drunk."

At the conclusion of the case, the State asked for jail sentences of five years and $2,000 fines for each defendant. The jury deliberated for less than two hours and found all the defendants innocent of all charges. There was a scene of wild cheering, whistling and yelling from 500 spectators as Judge Friend joined in by congratulating the defendants and telling the jury it had returned a just verdict. Then the Black Sox and their jury went to dinner in an Italian restaurant: that's the Chicago way.

The next day, Judge Landis issued *his* verdict:

"Regardless of the verdict of juries, no player that throws a ball game; no player that undertakes or promises to throw a ball game; no player that sits in a conference with a bunch of crooked players and gamblers where the ways and means of throwing games are planned and discussed and does not promptly tell his club about it, will ever play professional baseball."

The verdict was meant to cover every possible loophole, and served as the basis for Joe's expulsion. Joe Jackson was not banned for anything he did on the diamond; he was banned for not telling his team about the plot—a plot he had tried to warn Comiskey about, but was turned away. When reached for comment, Joe Jackson told newsmen that he was through with baseball and would devote his time to running his billiard parlor. Chick Gandil seemed to sum up the sentiment of the ballplayers best when he chimed in, "I'll give a sailor's farewell to Ban Johnson: Good-bye, good luck, and to hell with you."

* * *

After the trial, Joe and Katie closed up their Chicago apartment and newspapers reported that Joe had gone home in disgrace, back to the hills of South Carolina where he hid away from the world. And if you

219

believe what Kevin Costner's character says in the movie "Field of Dreams," Joe was never heard from again, except by some who said they saw the great Shoeless Joe many years later.

That is not true. Like so many other biographical facts that are destroyed by Hollywood, Joe Jackson did not run for the hills to hide; he came home to Savannah, Georgia, where he bought a new home at 409 East 49th Street, and started the Savannah Valet Service, a dry cleaning establishment—or "pressing club," as they were called—at 1-3 East Broad Street (on the corner of Bay Street, where the Mulberry Inn now stands). And he still owned the billiard parlor at 17 West Congress Street in partnership with the Sullivans. Then the offers came flooding in for Joe to play semipro ball, and he traveled back and forth from Savannah to New York where he played for as much as $200 a game for a promoter who organized a campaign to have Joe reinstated, collecting thousands of signatures on a petition demanding that Judge Landis clear Joe, "in view of his acquittal by jury in a duly constituted court of justice."

Savannah Valet Service. Katie on the left, Joe in center

When the petition was sent to Landis, he duly ignored it. On April 26, 1922, Landis delivered to Joe a letter in which he advised, "in view of the crime in connection with the World Series of 1919, the money cannot be paid you," and further ruled Joe's contract with Chicago null and void.

In June, Joe played a few games with a team in Westwood, New Jersey under the name "Joe Josephs" until he was found out. During the baseball season of 1923, Joe stayed at home in Savannah, journeying no farther than the state line while playing with Americus in the South Georgia League, which also had teams in Albany, Arlington and three other small towns. The South Georgia League was outside the control of organized baseball and couldn't care less about the despotic Judge Landis. But when Landis heard about what was going on down in Georgia, he attempted to reel in the league by announcing that "players who knowingly play with outlawed ball players might subsequently find themselves barred from the minor and major leagues." The owners caved to the pressure and adopted a rule that prohibited players on Landis's blacklist, which had swelled in size to more than fifty names by the mid-1920's.

When the Americus club announced it had signed Joe Jackson anyway, the president of the South Georgia League said it couldn't be done. But the owner, J. Rufus Lane, argued his case by producing a telegram from the National Association of Minor Leagues stating that organized baseball had no link to the South Georgia League. Owners of the other teams protested that Joe's inclusion would give the league a bad name, to which Lane responded that Joe had been found innocent of all charges in a court of law. He appealed to the very same sense of fair play upon which Baseball had been founded, but in the end Lane's most persuasive argument was money: Shoeless Joe was a guaranteed draw for games that heretofore couldn't draw flies.

The rule prohibiting the participation of blacklisted players was thrown in the trash where it belonged and Joe Jackson played ball for Americus.

When news of Joe's return to baseball spread beyond the sports pages of the Savannah newspaper, the same editors who had dogged his pro career sharpened their pencils in making a moral issue out of his participation at any level of the national pastime. And you didn't have to go any further than The Atlanta Journal for disapproval, where one writer attacked Joe as an "ignorant, illiterate fellow" whose very presence would taint baseball in Georgia. He took it upon himself to assure readers that Georgia fans would not turn out to watch a man like Joe play ball.

Like so many other editorial opinions in the Atlanta papers, they were dead wrong about Joe Jackson. Fans turned out in record numbers and cheered him wildly, and at the ripe old age of 36 he took to the game with a renewed vigor and dedication: in his first week playing for Americus, Joe batted .727, and by the end of the season he led his team to victory in the "Little World Series."

Some people said it wasn't fair, that Joe was too good for his company of semi pros who would never make it to the majors where Joe was once the best player in the game, but even his critics had to agree that Joe gave fans their money's worth. Some writers attacked him while others took up his defense; the fans made their own decisions and turned out in droves to see him. The games turned into the biggest events of the social season, preceded by band concerts and barbeques. At the end of the season, a comic article about a fictional pro scout spoke of his newest discovery and the best-looking prospect he'd ever seen: a guy playing for Americus named Jackson.

As soon as the "Little World Series" was history, offers poured in for Joe to play exhibition games. Some promoters wanted the whole Americus team, some only wanted Joe.

* * *

In January 1924, Joe Jackson was back in court over baseball, only this time he was on the prosecuting end. He was trying to recoup payment of back salary and bonuses from the miserly Comiskey. If Comiskey wanted to argue that Judge Landis's decision was cause enough to break Joe's contract and withhold payment for services rendered, then he was going to have to come up with more evidence than that which led the jury in the Black Sox trial to conclude Joe was innocent. He dispatched detectives from Chicago to Savannah to root out any evidence of the 1919 fix and found nothing.

Perhaps the most enlightening element of discovery was Comiskey's attorney Alfred Austrian, who appeared as a witness and related how the infamous gambler Arnold Rothstein had turned up in Austrian's office and laid out plans to pilfer the original Black Sox case files from the Chicago D.A.'s office for ten grand. The stolen files turned up in New York, where Rothstein offered proof of their existence to the local papers. The offer was declined, and the documents disappeared for 65 years following the Comiskey trial.

During the three weeks of the trial the jury heard much conflicting testimony. From the grand jury transcripts they heard Joe alternately testify yes and no to the same questions about his part in fixing the Series. To confuse matters even further, Comiskey admitted under oath that in all the years Joe played for the Sox—from 1915 to 1920—he did not know of one dishonest move committed by Joe on a ball field.

In fact, the strongest evidence to emerge in the trial supported Joe's claim of innocence. The gamblers

Burns and Maharg testified that they never spoke to Joe about the fix and that he never attended any meetings. They testified that they only spoke to Lefty Williams, who said he represented Joe in the scheme. But Williams himself told the jury that he never talked to Joe about the plot.

The problem for the jury to work out was this: if Williams was acting without Joe's knowledge, and if Joe knew nothing of the scheme, then why did Williams pay Joe $5,000 after the Sox lost the Series? Was it a guilty conscience or is Joe guilty of collusion?

The jury reached a special verdict in which the judge asked them a series of questions. When asked, "Did the plaintiff Jackson unlawfully conspire to lose any of the games in the 1919 Series?" the jury answered, "No." The jury also ruled that Joe had been tricked into signing a contract by Grabiner, and that the White Sox owed Joe more than $16,000 as compensation.

But before Joe could celebrate his victory, the judge overturned the jury's verdict for what he termed "misguided sympathy," and put Joe in jail for perjury long enough to force him to accept an out-of-court settlement with Comiskey. Consequently, Joe came to understand that no matter what he did to try to clear his name it would be used against him. He did not make another public statement about the Black Sox for 25 years.

As soon as the trial was over, Joe wasted no time in getting back in the game. In mid-July 1924, he agreed to become manager/player for the Waycross Atlantic Coast Line team, part of an independent City League in South Georgia and North Florida that compared favorably with Class B professional ball. The season was already half over, and Joe had to play his first game for Waycross in his White Sox uniform until a new one could be made. Notices of his first games could be found in one- or two-paragraph recaps at the bottom of the page in The Savannah Press. Two weeks later, a story ran that the president of the City League warned that any player taking part in a game involving Joe Jackson's Waycross team would be fined and suspended from the league, unless and until Jackson was cleared through a pardon from Judge Landis. But in a rather bizarre twist, The Savannah Press was forced to retract the story when the league president wrote a letter explaining that he had no such objections to Jackson playing for Waycross.

However, once news of Joe's participation in an obscure Georgia baseball league reached Judge Landis, he wasted no time in making a federal case out of it. On August 16, Buddy Williamson, a pitcher for the Hattiesburg club of the Cotton States League, was suspended from organized ball by the National Association of Professional Leagues, pending an investigation of his participation in a game at Americus, Georgia, in which Joe Jackson, "outlawed" performer, appeared. Whether Landis's action caused a ripple in the rosters of City League teams is unclear, but there were no other reports of player eligibility conflicts in The Savannah Press for the remainder of the 1924 season, as Joe Jackson finished the most successful season in the history of the Waycross club with a record of 69-31 and a batting average of .475.

In reporting that he would return to play for Waycross in 1925, Joe Jackson was already being described by sports writers as "the greatest natural ball player the game has ever known." And when in October 1924 an entirely new World Series betting scandal blew up over reports that New York Giants players conspired to throw games, Joe Jackson sat on the sidelines and offered his point of view to reporters that such revelations were of no surprise to him. "All I can say is that I am keenly interested in seeing what action Judge Landis, the czar of baseball, is going to take," he said.

Joe was also back in the local news when it was announced that he and Charlie Schwarz had purchased the Grand Billiard Parlor on Congress Street near Drayton and that Joe intended to remain in Savannah as a permanent resident. When his playing days were over in Waycross, Joe bought another new house from his in-laws, the Ellises, at 1411 East 39th Street, where he maintained an earthworm garden for fish bait and kept chickens, cows, ducks and goats. In addition to the poolroom, his Savannah Valet business was kept busy by all of the people who worked at the courthouse, and on Sundays he continued to make it a regular habit of driving out to Isle of Hope in his Nash, stopping by Jenkins Grocery for cokes and Piedmont cigarettes.

In 1932, at age 45, Joe returned home to Greenville, S.C. to play ball as a free lance for any team that would pay him. For several weeks prior to his comeback, Joe had played sandlot ball with the neighborhood kids in Savannah. He took great interest in several of the youngsters who showed some ability and instructed them by the hour in the art of hitting. He still had Black Betsy in tow, and at his age could still hit the ball farther than anybody in three states. Once he got Greenville grass under his feet again, Joe decided that it was time to move back home. He sold his Savannah businesses and quit the scene on 39th Street.

At the same time Joe was going through these changes, *Eagles* magazine published a story that not only preserved Joe's legacy as the greatest natural hitter baseball ever produced, but also perfected the "Say it ain't so, Joe" story. "With the exception of Ruth, no other player was a greater idol of young boys than was Jackson," the story said. And then in telling how a lad broke through the crowd at the courthouse on the day of Joe's grand jury testimony, clutching his hero's hand, pleaded with tears in his eyes, "Say you didn't do it, Joe. Say you didn't do it."

"There were tears in Joe's eyes, too," the story ended. "He patted the boy on the head and walked away—walked out of baseball forever."

* * *

Well, as shown here, the playing career of Shoeless Joe Jackson did not end with the Black Sox Scandal, in spite of maudlin newspaper fables and hackneyed Hollywood movies. Nor did he walk out of baseball forever. He did step away from the game for the final time in 1933, and John Mauldin, Mayor of Greenville, headed up a drive that collected over 5,000 signatures on a petition addressed to Judge Landis in an effort to clear Joe's name so that he might coach the local semi-pro team without prejudice from organized baseball. Even Ed Barrow, the business manager of the New York Yankees, supported the petition, complaining that Joe was "starving down in Georgia, eking out a bare and brutal living pressing pants."

Barrow's comment, obviously intended to elicit some sort of sympathy on Joe's behalf, apparently went too far. At a time when the Savannah Valet Service—two storefronts and a cleaning plant with 20 employees—was making more money for Joe than baseball ever did, newspapers reported that he had failed in life as in baseball, describing him as poor, almost destitute. Westbrook Pegler, one of the most widely read columnists of the era, weighed in on the subject of the petition saying that the appeal should be automatically denied and that Joe be made a horrible example. "Will the citizens condone misconduct in the high places of American life or will they not?" Pegler begged.

The petition to reinstate Joe Jackson was denied by Judge Landis. But he managed a series of teams in Greenville anyway. "The Good Lord knows I am innocent of any wrongdoing," Joe was quoted, and that was good enough for Greenville.

When he wasn't coaching or playing ball in South Carolina, Joe Jackson was running a barbeque joint and a liquor store in Greenville. He returned to Savannah occasionally to visit his old friends at Bo Peep's Billiard Parlor at 17 East Congress Street, and maintained those relationships until the day he died, in 1951.

Soon after Joe's death, several articles appeared calling for his reinstatement, but when nothing happened the pressure died down. From time to time a plea rears up again, for there are still many people who would like to see Joe's name cleared and his banishment lifted so he can take his rightful place in the Baseball Hall of Fame. Until the day he died, Hall of Fame slugger Ted Williams led an effort to clear a spot on the bench for Joe Jackson in Cooperstown. But baseball commissioners are a lot like presidents: they are slow to right past wrongs, and the game has suffered because of it.

I don't know. I suppose it really doesn't matter anymore whether Joe Jackson is in or out of the Hall; his numbers speak for themselves. Scores of books have been written about him and three movies insure that he will not be forgotten anytime soon. Even if I can't stand before his shrine, it is still possible to hang out on the corner where his business used to be, drive by the houses where he used to live, and park in the very same place on 39th Street where Charlie Comiskey's lackey once twisted Joe Jackson's arm in signing a contract to play for the 1920 Chicago White Sox.

One need not wade through an Iowa cornfield in search of Shoeless Joe. One only has to know where to look: Savannah, Georgia.

ADDENDUM TO SEARCHING FOR SHOELESS JOE

With the publication of the first edition of "Behind the Moss Curtain" in November 2002, the author nominated Shoeless Joe Jackson for inclusion to the Greater Savannah Athletic Hall of Fame using the story "Searching for Shoeless Joe" in support of his petition. Founded in 1966, the Hall had overlooked Jackson because they claimed he was neither born in Savannah nor distinguished upon her playing fields, but when the author placed the revelations of his story before the board of directors they were forced to admit the error of their oversight. Embarrassed by an article in the local paper in which its sports editor seconded Silver's motion, the Hall's board of directors was placed in the precarious position of having to admit the long-standing mistake of excluding one of the greatest baseball players who ever lived and an athlete more famous than the Hall's 133 members combined.

Meeting behind closed doors, the Greater Savannah Athletic Hall of Fame hammered out a resolution that recognized Jackson and at the same time saved face. Rather than enshrining Jackson with full honors as an athlete, the Hall meted out a Special Award, as if to say that he still failed in some way to measure up to their requirements.

On May 5, 2003, at the 34th awards banquet, acting on the suggestion of the author, the Hall of Fame presented its plaque to Maggi Hall, Jackson's 88-year-old niece and a lifelong Savannah resident.

THE SAGA OF
SILENT
STAFFORD

Robert Redford rolled into town with his Hollywood circus to make a movie based on the book, *The Legend of Bagger Vance*. The story takes place in Savannah following World War I, and uses the game of golf as a backdrop for a comment on race relations in America. Redford assembled the prettiest cast he could afford: Will Smith, Matt Damon and Charlize Theron. On the surface, the movie looks like *The Sting*, but lurking underneath is a social commentary that pulls fact out of fiction like a bad tooth, glossing over history with glamour.

As the author of an international best-selling biography of a popular figure made into a major motion picture, I am concerned anytime Hollywood attempts to change facts by glamorizing history on the big screen. Whether it's Spike Lee's *Malcolm X* or Oliver Stone's *JFK*, I don't want the principal perception of history coming from Hollywood. It reminds me of high school when I tried to write book reports on titles I hadn't read but saw the movie and figured it was enough to fool the teacher; it wasn't.

Denzel Washington is far more attractive than the real Malcolm X or Ruben "Hurricane" Carter. I don't remember all of these fans, black or white, who rallied around the originals when I was growing up. Whenever Hollywood endeavors to rewrite history, inevitably Denzel Washington and Will Smith are cast in the role of the noble black man, and Laurence Fishburne and Samuel L. Jackson play the bad—but misunderstood—black guys.

Certainly Denzel does for Malcolm X and Hurricane Carter what Ben Kingsley did for Gandhi, what Frank Langella did for Dracula, what Anthony Hopkins did for Hitler's image—but what does that say? That the plain and simple and often ugly truth is rendered more palatable merely by the dramatic interpretation of actors more attractive than their real-life counterparts? Gandhi was a great leader long before Ben Kingsley's prettier face was pasted upon his memory.

If students of history want to know Malcolm X, read his speeches. Don't ask Denzel Washington to recite them to you after Spike Lee has edited them and bathed the scene in a golden light. Those of us who remember Malcolm the first time around, live and in black and white, find it difficult to wax nostalgic for the burning Sixties. The civil rights movement was not a grand Hollywood epic. Race riots were not choreographed like *Lawrence of Arabia*. And this is why Spike Lee chooses to make movies rather than documentaries.

Those who forget history are destined to repeat it. But I say those who glamorize history destroy it entirely.

* * *

If Robert Redford wanted to find a really first-rate story about race relations in Savannah after World War I, he could have done much better than the fictional Bagger Vance with the factual Silent Stafford. We wind the tape back to the '30's, when the City of Savannah was referred to as the "Independent State of Chatham," and the rest of the nation was in the capable hands of Mr. Roosevelt. The local Jewish community centered around the old Agudath Achim synagogue on York and Montgomery streets, and shared its western boundary with the colored section, simply referred to as Brownsville. And it was here that the first tentative steps toward racial equality were made, not on the private golf course of Jekyll Island, where *The Legend of Bagger Vance* (or *Good Will Golfing*, as I like to call it) was filmed.

Buster White, who promoted athletic events and shows of every kind locally for more than fifty years, grew up in the Jewish ghetto on Barnard Street. His partner in boxing promotions was Dick Marcus who fought under the name Dick Leonard, and coached kids on the manly arts in the basement gym of the Jewish Alliance. Boxing was big in those days and every segment of society had its own camp: the Irish, the Italians, the Negroes, the police, the armed services...even Union Bag sponsored a team that was coached by Albert "Monkey" Lodge.

Left to right: Pinkie Masters, Buster White,
Jack Dempsey. Dick Leonard. Savannah, 1944

Marcus came back from a trip to see the 1939 Golden Gloves competition talking about a lightweight prodigy out of Ailey, Georgia, named Walker Smith. He told Buster White to look him up next time he was in the Big Apple.

231

Shortly thereafter, in the fall of 1940, Buster went to New York to buy dates to road companies of Broadway shows and stopped by Stillman's Gym for a look-see. He introduced himself to the owner, Lou Stillman, who kept two rings working at the same time with the best boxing talent in America. And when Buster told Stillman he was interested in seeing the kid from Georgia, Stillman picked up a microphone and summoned Walker Smith to the ring, choosing Dave Castilloux as his sparring partner.

Buster knew Castilloux as Canada's lightweight champ and ranked #4 in the world, and he was surprised that Stillman would allow an 18-year-old amateur in the same ring with a seasoned pro, even if the kid was the Golden Gloves champ of New York and Chicago. Buster was even more surprised when he saw the skinny little black kid, who could not have weighed 130 pounds soaking wet. Walker didn't even have boxing trunks; he wore a skimpy white bathing suit. Buster thought a good wind would blow Walker down.

Stillman rang the bell for round one to commence, and Walker came out of his corner with his hands moving so fast that he looked like he was being paid by the punch. Castilloux stood toe to toe with the kid and at the end of the round pushed Walker against the ropes. As the bell sounded ending the round, Castilloux caught Walker up side the head with a late punch, and Buster White could tell that the kid didn't like it. When the second round began, Walker tried to take Castilloux's head off.

Stillman rang the bell and jumped into the ring between the two fighters. He pushed Walker into a corner and reprimanded him. "You don't fight here!" Stillman yelled at the kid. "You're here to train, not fight!"

Still, Buster White was impressed with Walker Smith, and told Lou Stillman that he wanted to add him to the roster of an upcoming amateur card in Savannah, on October 8th.

"No can do," Stillman told Buster. "The kid turns pro on the fourth. You seen him. There ain't a decent amateur left for him to fight. He's got no choice but to turn pro. And he ain't goin' all the way back to Georgia for free, so if you want him for your card, it's gonna cost you a hundred bucks."

A hundred bucks was a lot of money in 1940, especially for a fighter just turning pro, but money wasn't Buster's problem. His problem was that Walker Smith was black, and the Savannah Boxing Commission would not allow a black man to fight a white man. "There's only one colored boxer I know," Buster told Stillman. "If I can set it up, I'll call you in a few days."

"Why don't you call your man now?" Stillman offered. "I gotta phone here you can use."

"I can't call him," Buster replied. "He's a deaf-mute."

* * *

Sixty years ago, a Mr. James R. Stafford worked at Monroe Funeral Directors on West Broad Street, serving the Brownsville community. His friends called him Sorrowful because he always wore the somber countenance of a mortician, although some said he had looked that way before he went to work for Monroe. They said that on the day the doctor told James Stafford that his infant son was deaf, his face turned down into a permanent frown. And from that day forward, James Stafford was called Sorrowful and his son was referred to as Silent.

The city directory for the years 1938-39 lists the Staffords as residents of the 600 block of 31st and 32nd streets. It's hard to tell exactly where they lived and when because it was the custom of black families to take their address with them when they moved back then. Like

Buckwheat in "Our Gang," Silent Stafford played with the Jewish kids over on Barnard Street. He did not know his place and the Jews didn't care. Silent Stafford could see the difference between his skin and theirs but the differences seemed to end there and at the dinner table. No one ever sat him down and told him he was a nigger. He took a liking to Buster White, and stuck so close to the older white man that Silent Stafford looked like Buster's shadow.

Sorrowful Stafford may not have thought his son was good for much, but one thing Silent could do was box. "He don't need to hear to fight," Dick Marcus said, and allowed Silent to train with his boys at the Jewish Alliance. He learned fast, and in no time at all Tommie Kiene, the Southern Bantamweight Champion, was using Silent Stafford to spar in preparation for his prizefights. When the Lions Club held their amateur boxing competitions, the club's leaders Miller Kaminksy, Bill Kehoe and Eddie Dutton made an exception for Stafford and allowed him to participate with the rest of Dick Marcus's boys.

Silent Stafford turned pro when Buster White heard that the legendary Beau Jack was over in South Carolina, issuing a challenge to pay anyone who could last six rounds with him. Buster brought Silent to answer the call and was so sure of his protégé that he pawned a shotgun to come up with bet money. Silent Stafford had never heard of Beau Jack and did not know he was supposed to be scared of him. He battled Beau Jack to a standstill and the match was called a draw, although Buster raised hell when he thought his fighter had been robbed of a decision.

So when Buster saw Walker Smith in Stillman's Gym, he immediately thought of Silent Stafford. But before he could obligate his protégé, Buster owed a personal visit to Silent's father, as courtesy. "He'll be gettin' in the ring with real talent," Buster told Sorrowful.

"But it's good money, and I think Silent will give a good account of himself."

Sorrowful listened to Buster's proposition and nodded, his forlorn expression never changing. Fifty dollars was a lot of money; there wasn't another place in all of Chatham County where a Negro deaf-mute could earn that kind of cash.

Buster called Lou Stillman and told him that Walker Smith would meet his second professional challenge in Savannah, on October 8th.

* * *

By the time Walker Smith returned home to Georgia for his second professional fight, many things had changed. He had acquired a new name, Ray Robinson, when he borrowed a friend's union boxing card in order to qualify for a match. Having won the match by a knockout, he was too superstitious to apply for a union card under his real name. He also picked up a nickname, "Sugar," which referred to the smooth way he studied the sweet science.

Sugar Ray Robinson dropped by the Jewish Alliance the day before his match with Silent Stafford to meet his opponent. Ray's manager, George Gainford, took one look at Stafford and knew he was no mere amateur, as Lou Stillman had led him to believe. After watching Stafford spar a few rounds with one of Dick Marcus's boys, Gainford thought he spotted the unmistakable style of the great Henry Armstrong's sparring partner. He sent Ray back to his rented room with Gus Hays, who owned a motel and the Downbeat Lounge on West Broad Street. Then Gainford pulled Buster White aside to discuss a few last minute details.

"We wanna use four-ounce gloves," Gainford told Buster.

"Four-ounce gloves?" Buster repeated. "We use eight-ounce gloves. Nobody uses fours. Hell, you might as well fight bare knuckle. There's more than four ounces of padding on ladies' Sunday go-to-meetin' gloves. What are you tryin' to do, kill these kids before they're twenty?"

"No, I ain't tryin' to kill nobody," Gainford spat back. "But I know what you're up to, see. You're tryin' to run a ringer in on me. I recognize your boy, and he's no rank amateur. He fought Henry Armstrong. I'll bet on it. Ask him, if you don't believe me."

"I can't ask him, he's a deaf-mute," Buster replied. "Besides, even if what you're sayin' is true, this kid doesn't know the difference between Henry Armstrong the boxer and Louis Armstrong the trumpeter. It doesn't matter to him who he fights, as long as its fair and the weights are equal."

Gainford stood his ground. "Well, they'll both be wearin' the same gloves, won't they?"

A protective impulse swept over Buster. "Look, I don't want this boy hurt. He's mute, for godsake."

"Four ounces," Gainford repeated. "Four ounces, or forfeit the fight and the purse."

Buster gave in to Gainford's demands. As he made the long, slow walk over to Stubbs Hardware on Congress Street to buy four-ounce gloves, he consoled himself with the memory of Silent Stafford going the distance with the great Beau Jack; the kid knew how to protect himself in the clinches.

The next night, a fine crowd turned out for the amateur boxing exhibition that Buster White assembled in partnership with the Lions Club. The seating arrangements were as segregated as the fight card: the faces that ringed the squared circle were white, and the balcony was set apart for colored. The Jews sat in one section cheering for Dick Marcus's boys, and the Irish were clumped together in a section opposite, to cheer on the entries from Benedictine. Sugar Ray Robinson and Silent Stafford were the main event, and all the kids from the Jewish Alliance crowded around the ring to lend support to their stable mate.

The fight did not last long. In the first round, Silent Stafford seemed to disappear under a barrage of blows from Sugar Ray. He wilted in his corner between rounds; no one had to tell him that Robinson was a rare talent. George Gainford instructed his fighter, "Let's get this over with," and pushed Sugar Ray into the center of the ring for round two.

Sugar Ray threw punches like no one else on this planet. The fight was clearly no contest. Robinson delivered a series of blows to Silent Stafford's midsection that caused him to cry out, and as he sank to the canvas on his knees it was the hometown audience that went silent. He cried out in pain, not a normal moan but an awkward yowl that seemed to come from deep inside a wounded animal. It was the first time Sorrowful Stafford had heard his son's voice, and he jumped to his feet to save him from further punishment. Referee Joe McGhee came between the two fighters and wrapped Silent Stafford in a protective embrace. The fight was over, and the record book recorded Robinson's second knockout in as many professional fights.

* * *

It took Buster White ten years to get a return bout for Sugar Ray Robinson in Savannah. Following the Stafford fight, Robinson continued a campaign of 40 straight victories; including a win over former welterweight champion Fritzie Zivic and future champ Marty Servo. He won his first Fighter of the Year award in 1942, and was on a fast track to the title when he ran across the Raging Bull, Jake LaMotta. Their first fight, a brutal 10-round victory for Robinson, marked the beginning of one of boxing's great rivalries. LaMotta, a middleweight, won their first rematch, Robinson's first defeat in 41 pro fights. Then Robinson avenged the loss three weeks later.

After a stint in the army, Robinson won two more decisions over LaMotta in 1945. No other boxers would fight either man and so they fought each other. As LaMotta later said, "I fought Sugar Ray so often, I almost got diabetes."

Just before Christmas 1946, Robinson won the vacant welterweight championship over Tommy Bell. An eighth-round knockout of Jimmy Doyle the following year proved to be a tragic title defense for Robinson. Doyle suffered brain injuries that eventually cost him his life. When the coroner asked if he figured to get Doyle "in trouble," Robinson said, "Mister, it's my business to get him in trouble."

A reputation of having the hands of a killer helped Robinson dominate the welterweight division, including winning a decision over future champ Kid Gavilan in July 1949. He had no choice but to move up to middleweight, and was looking forward to meeting Mel Bartholomew in Savannah on February 22, 1950, when Buster White received word from New Orleans that the challenger had been shot in some sort of fracas in the French Quarter.

"I had the programs printed already," Buster complained to George Gainford, and then scrambled to find Aaron "Little Tiger" Wade, a journeyman from California, as a last-minute replacement.

It didn't matter to Robinson; he was passing through town and thought he'd pick up some loose change. Although, what was loose change to Sugar Ray was 40 percent of Buster's gate. The auditorium was packed to the rafters with fight fans white and black, still separate, both in and out of the ring. They did not get their money's worth: Robinson kayoed Wade in the third round in what local sports scribe Waldo Spence described as the "biggest disappointment of the year."

"Robinson never during the evening hit Wade with a solid punch," Spence wrote. "But Wade evidently didn't know he wasn't being hit solid, and for some inexplicable reason went down five times...one from a punch on the shoulder...and the fifth time he stayed down with his hand resting in the vicinity of his kidney. It was supposed to have been measured with a right to the jaw. Anyway, that's what the punch looked like to us."

Alongside Waldo's account of the mismatch was a syndicated story out of New York with a headline that read: "Boxing Must Clear House of Crooks and Sharpsters," the juxtaposition of which may or may not have been intentional.

At the end of the night when it came time to settle the score, Buster White invited George Gainford into the box office to divvy up the receipts. They sat on wooden crates using a third for a makeshift table and Buster counted out two for you and three for me. Gainford scooped up Robinson's share, shook Buster's hand and said, "Let's do this again sometime," although it would be another fifteen years before Savannah saw Sugar Ray again.

But before leaving Savannah this night, Sugar Ray Robinson stopped Buster White on the street to ask a personal favor. "I didn't see your boy tonight, Mister White. What happened to your boy?"

"Who you talkin' about, champ?" Buster asked.

"The boy I fought last time, the deaf mute."

"You mean Silent Stafford? Silent Stafford doesn't fight anymore, champ. He'd seen the best when he fought you, and he hung 'em up after that. I got him a job helpin' out as an auto mechanic."

Robinson reached into his pocket and produced a large wad of bills. He took what looked like half and folded it up and put it in Buster's hand. "Do me a favor," Robinson said. "Give this to him next time you see him. Tell him it's from Ray."

Robinson turned and took two steps before he realized his error. "You know what I mean. Show him my picture on tonight's program. He'll know who it's from."

* * *

Sugar Ray Robinson left Savannah in 1950 and resumed his rivalry with Jake LaMotta. At the height of his career, he toured Europe and fought before a crowd of more than 60,000 at the Polo Grounds in 1951. After failing to move up and win the light-heavyweight championship, Robinson announced his retirement to pursue a career in tap dancing. It did not work out.

Returning to the ring in 1955, Robinson would win and lose the middleweight title three more times. He amassed a record of 175 wins in 202 professional fights, the losses coming in a cluster at the end of his career. He retired in 1965, and one of his last fights was staged in Savannah against somebody named Ray Basting, on April 4. Basting fought out of Tampa and trained at Union Bag, and made the fatal mistake of running around town and telling anyone who'd listen that he was going to send the great Sugar Ray Robinson into permanent retirement when word got back to the champ. Ray Basting did not last one round.

Oddly, Buster White passed on the chance to promote the show, and Buster White is such a guy that would've promoted a fight between Jesus Christ and Moses had he the opportunity. But he wasn't interested in swan songs and old pros gone gimpy. It was sad in a way, and it made for idle comments from the crowd of stealing one more payday. Buster didn't understand why a class act wanted to go out like that, but when Ray Robinson rolled into town in a pink Cadillac convertible with his manager, secretary, barber, masseur, voice coach, six trainers, a stable of women and a dwarf mascot in tow, Buster understood Ray's need for greed.

Still, as my father likes to say, not bad for a poor boy from Georgia.

DEM BONES

In 1993, a chunk of the cornice fell off of the Pulaski monument that had been standing in Monterey Square since 1854, and Savannah's city council decided it was high time to repair damage caused by vandalism, neglect, pollution and misguided treatment. Council voted to spend $100,000 on repairs but by the time work began in 1996, the estimate had doubled. Anyone who ever hired a contractor to do a home improvement project knows what I'm talking about: take the original estimate of cost and time to complete the job then double it, and then hold onto your hat—and wallet.

When preservationists began taking the monument apart, 70 pounds of marble broke loose and crashed to the ground, and the realization suddenly dawned upon the workmen that they had bitten off more than they could chew: the sky was falling, and they couldn't put Humpty Dumpty Pulaski back together again. The six-month completion date was vacated and the costs spiraled out of control. The disassembled stones sat like abandoned blocks in a child's play chest for one year while city council looked for money to continue a project they said they could no longer afford, eventually imposing a one-dollar tax on tour buses to get work going again.

After bickering over money, the city and the job's main conservator ended their contract when new cracks developed in the base as the monument was being put back together. Arguments as to the nature of defects in the stone broke out among the conservator and structural engineers and geologists, and the city was forced to hire an independent outside contractor as arbitrator.

241

Matters only got worse. The original Lady Liberty crowning the monument was deemed to be too brittle and fragile to resume her perch, and the company commissioned to fashion a new one out of plaster patched together a monstrosity that just wouldn't do. The iron scaffolding erected around the monument for workmen to climb stood in place so long that it rusted, spreading to the stones and causing a mess that cost another $6,000 to clean up. And then someone got the bright idea that the bones inside the coffin interred in the base of the monument should be tested against the DNA of Pulaski's ancestors to prove it was his remains. Forensic anthropologists from the University of Georgia took possession of the Count, and agents of the Georgia Bureau of Investigation elbowed their way into the case like it was some sort of unsolved crime.

In the end, it took four years and $1 million to complete the restoration project that had originally been estimated to take six months and $190,000. And when the genetic geeks failed to link Pulaski's DNA with his great-great nephew, the federal government refused to pay for a full-fledged burial ceremony of unidentifiable remains. It sort of reminds me of the old schoolyard joke, "Who's buried in Grant's tomb?" Only the sad tale of the restoration of Pulaski monument had long since ceased to be funny.

* * *

General Count Casimir Pulaski died on October 9, 1779 as a result of injuries received in the Siege of Savannah. At a time when British defenses around the city extended from Springhill in the direction of what is now Liberty Street to the Thunderbolt road, the American and French forces were at the same time busily erecting redoubts from which effective fire could be directed and by October 9th both armies were ready for battle. General Prescott was in command of the British,

General Lincoln in command of the allied forces, and Count D'Estaing with the French fleet protecting the line of retreat should any occur. Pulaski was in command of the regular cavalry, held in reserve for the charge if a breach were made in the enemy's works. Watching intently the progress of the siege, Pulaski saw an opening and Lincoln let him take it.

Mounted at the head of his gallant two hundred, Pulaski galloped toward the incessant fire of the British regulars, undaunted, undismayed and mindful of what his plan meant to the events of the day. He came within a few yards of the enemy's battery, when he fell mortally wounded in the leg from grapeshot. Prescott knew Pulaski and respected him, and even in the heat of battle ceased fire to allow Pulaski's comrades to move him to safety. He fell back with the French, who retreated along the Thunderbolt road to Greenwich, rather than go with the Americans along the Augusta road and cross the Savannah River above Zubly's Ferry.

Pulaski was delivered to the Bowen plantation in Greenwich, lingering for two days before dying on October 11th. The burial occurred at night, the procession lighted by torches in the hands of servants. Several hundred yards from the mansion, beneath the shade of a majestic palmetto, all that was mortal of Poland's son was consigned to Georgia soil.

It is important to note that the Bowen's fourteen-year-old daughter attended Pulaski's funeral, for she later married a surgeon in the British army named Beecroft and often related the story to their daughter and a nephew, William Bowen, who was later a member of the Pulaski Monument Commission. When the commission undertook to erect a monument to Pulaski's memory in Monterey Square in 1854, Bowen lead the recovery of Pulaski's remains at Greenwich.

When the bones were disinterred they were placed in the custody of Dr. William Bulloch and Dr.

James Read, both of whom made exhaustive examinations at the Medical College in Augusta to determine that dem bones belonged to the Count. An affidavit was obtained from the overseer of the Bowen estate testifying to the facts, and a second was taken from Mordecai Sheftall, one of Savannah's most prominent citizens, testifying to the story of the funeral as told to him by his father, a guide for the French army. Finally, J.C. Levy weighed in with an affidavit relating how Pulaski's nephew—a captain in the Polish legion—visited the grave in Greenwich in 1803. And with the positive proof of a blue ribbon provenance, Pulaski's remains were placed in a new coffin and interred in the base of a 54-foot high marble monument weighing 120 tons and costing the City of Savannah the royal sum of $20,000 on Dec. 22, 1854.

* * *

That there was some confusion surrounding Pulaski's death and burial is not surprising. Originally, the monument erected to Nathanael Greene in Johnson Square was known as the Greene and Pulaski memorial until the Marquis de Lafayette came to town on March 21, 1825 and laid the cornerstone of two contemplated monuments—one in Johnson Square to Greene and another in Chippewa Square to Pulaski. Ten or twelve years later sufficient money was raised to build one, so the cornerstone was removed from Chippewa to Johnson Square and a joint structure erected. In 1852, twenty thousand dollars accumulated and the cornerstone was removed from the Greene monument and a new one laid in Monterey Square on October 11, 1853, the 74th anniversary of Pulaski's death.

No, what is surprising is that 147 years later, the City of Savannah turned a blind eye to all of these carefully documented facts and cast doubt that the remains which were costing a fortune to preserve and honor were probably not Pulaski's in the first place. City

244

Council had it on the advice of some misguided armchair historian that Pulaski was buried at sea, and not at Greenwich. Whose bones were in the box at the bottom of Pulaski's monument was a matter of conjecture, and by God somebody better get to the bottom of this before, well, before we look like a bunch of dumb crackers. And so forensic specialists and the Georgia Bureau of Investigation were called in, and in the end when tests failed to perfectly match the Count's remains with that of an ancestor, his bones were left to sit in a box in the basement of the GBI, covered by a Polish flag and a crucifix, where they wait until forensic science finds a way to solve the so-called mystery. Rest in peace, hah.

* * *

The Pulaski dilemma isn't the only time Savannah's squares and monuments have been called into question. It's gotten to be some sort of game around here, guessing who's really buried in which tomb. Most people believe that the Yamacraw chief Tomochichi is buried beneath the rough-hewn granite memorial in Wright Square when, in fact, no one is exactly sure where he was buried by colonists. Sometime before 1900, a skeleton was found by diggers in the square that may or may not have been the bones of the chief but were in close proximity to the memorial. And General Oglethorpe, founder of the colony, is not buried under the monument in what is now a median on the Savannah street bearing his name but at home in Cranham, England, where, back in 1923, we tried to kidnap him and bring his bones back to Georgia. It's another dark chapter in our local history that you are not likely to hear on any of the tours:

In October 1923, Dr. Thornwell Jacobs, president of Oglethorpe University in Atlanta, set out for England under full sail with the intention of excavating the bones of General Oglethorpe and removing them to a special shrine to be erected on the campus of his university. He had finessed the rector and council of the Church of All Saints in Cranham to give up the ghost, and the chancellor agreed to conduct a special religious ceremony while the tomb raiding was in progress, "with the utmost reverence," it was stated.

Fishing around in the vault under the church floor expected to take two or three days to find Oglethorpe, and then the government would necessarily have to issue a new passport, the old one having expired one hundred thirty-eight years prior. All of which, incidentally, was subject to the objection of any English citizen whereupon the matter of custody could easily end up in an English court. But Jacobs was undeterred in his disinterment and unafraid of any objections, having it on the authority of the chancellor of the diocese that any such claim would be overruled as without sufficient weight or legality.

Two days later, Oglethorpe was found and objections to his removal began to trickle in once the news spread throughout England and abroad. Jacobs wired home his plea for the continued support of the people and government of Georgia in order to ensure the success of his enterprise when the Society of Colonial Wars in the State of Georgia broadsided him with a protest in Savannah. Meeting at the Stovall home on Estill Avenue, three descendants of Georgia colonists, P.A. Stovall, Harris M. King, and Walter C. Hartridge, adopted a resolution to protest the removal of Oglethorpe's bones on the basis that such a disturbance was a desecration of his grave and secondly, "Oglethorpe, though the father of the colony, was in no sense a Georgian. In every way he was the typical Englishman of his time," which seemed to be a polite way to say, "We don't want him anyhow." And just to make sure that the SoCWitSoG was taken seriously, they zipped off their protest in a hot wire to Washington for good order's sake.

All of a sudden, the bucolic village of Cranham, population 500, came under the harsh glare of notoriety. Although only two or three villagers groused about the inconvenience of it all, the Reverend Leslie Wright, rector of Cranham parish, replied:

"It seems to me it would be very unlike the motherly instinct of old England to refuse to give from the vast treasures of her mighty dead the sacred dust of this one great son who carried across the seas and planted so firmly in far off Georgia the ideals and principles for which England herself stands today.'

Dr. Jacobs emerged from the mortuary chamber—which had been closed to the media—clutching a small fragment that dropped from Oglethorpe's coffin and proclaiming, "Nothing can compare with the solemn reverence I felt in the presence of the sacred dust of Georgia's great hero. I felt that General Oglethorpe was no longer a heap of dust or a group of bones, but was once again the most powerful personality in the Southern states."

Back in the U.S., however, a Harvard professor was taking a different view. Dr. Benjamin Rand, who discovered the missing colonial records of Georgia, complained publicly that Oglethorpe was first and foremost a member of parliament for 32 years following his return from Georgia, died and was buried at home in Cranham where he obviously intended to remain, regardless of the fond wishes of a small college in Atlanta bearing his name. "Blest be the man that spares these stones, and curst be he that moves my bones," Rand admonished Jacobs, quoting Shakespeare, and suggested that if the school wanted to honor the general then they should do something more appropriate, such as commission a copy of a famous painting of Oglethorpe being greeted by Tomochichi.

Disturbed by opposition arising in Georgia to the removal of the bones from their burial place in England,

Representative William Upshaw of Atlanta hurried to Washington to confer with officials of the State Department. He was concerned that when British authorities saw the epistle from the crackpots in Savannah that they would withdraw their permission for transfer of the remains to America. And Georgia Governor Clifford Walker was called on the carpet to explain his support of the protest lodged by the Society of Colonial Wars in the State of Georgia, which had been forwarded by mistake to the chief of Western European affairs instead of to the secretary of state. Nobody in Washington recognized the legitimacy of SoCWitSoG's claim; however, if Governor Walker sent a telegram of his own, there may be a different outcome.

Undaunted by this slap in the face from the State Department, the three members of the SoCWitSoG in Savannah dashed off a copy of their declaration directly to the newspapers in London, thereby circumventing the delicate diplomatic relations between the United States and England and upsetting Mr. Upshaw's apple cart. The same English editorial pages printing the SoCWitSoG protest were deluged with responses from all corners of the British Empire, and every one of them lined up against what amounted to deporting Oglethorpe from his homeland.

"Georgia was founded as an English colony," one of Oglethorpe's countrymen wrote, in response to the Society in Savannah. "Oglethorpe would've never undertaken his great project in the first place had he suspected that some day his colonists would rebel successfully against England."

And when citizens of Cranham thought that the chancellor of their diocese was ignoring their protests, they went over his head to the British Home Office, demanding that the government withhold permission to export Oglethorpe. But Reverend Wright waded right back into the middle of the fray with his assertion that

the government had no say in his jurisdiction and that
the right to transfer the body is entirely up to the
ecclesiastic decision.

Meanwhile, the epistle emanating from the
Stovall home on Estill Avenue in little old Savannah in
the name of the Society of Colonial Wars in the State of
Georgia had so vexed the British press that editors were
bearing their collective weight on the Home Office
secretary to do something anyway. "Body Snatching!" was
the accusation hurled at Dr. Jacobs in newspapers
throughout England. And in the Sunday Express, editor
James Douglas exclaimed "It is an outrage to drag these
honored bones from Essex to Atlanta in order to decorate
an obscure college quadrangle. The American people do
not want them. It is an Atlanta college stunt. The home
secretary ought to veto this sacrilege."

Rather than be labeled a body snatcher, Dr.
Jacobs fired off a few salvos of his own in defense of his
actions. "The exact location of Oglethorpe's bones have
been forgotten in England to begin with," he explained.
"There is no monument to him there. It was my purpose
to make him and his sacred memory an eternal tie of
good will between England and America."

Unfortunately for Dr. Jacobs, he could not
remain ahead of the curve and control the damage of this
huge public relations snafu. The State Department in
Washington was caught off-guard and at a complete loss
as to how to save face, in the same way that their
counterpart in the British Home Office wasn't sure if they
had jurisdiction and if so, how to exert their control. And
in that brilliant way that the English have of making just
about everything into a scandal of epic proportion, a
descendant of Oglethorpe made an appeal directly to
King George V to protect the ashes of his ancestor.

Things got way out of hand the British press
dredged up the forgotten memory of an incident back in
1881, when it was suggested by the State of Pennsylvania

that the remains of William Penn be dug up from their peaceful Quaker burial grounds and shipped to America. At this rate, half of Westminster Abbey would run the risk of being excavated and the bodies of untold numbers of colonists sent back stateside. In the end, Dr. Jacobs decided that the prudent thing to do was withdraw his request to obtain Oglethorpe's remains and quit the scene before he was tarred and feathered by an angry mob.

Dr. Jacobs set sail for New York from London on the Mauritania two weeks after his quest had begun, but not before vowing that pilgrimages of Oglethorpe students would journey to Cranham every year on the date of the general's death to lay laurel wreaths at his tomb. "Cranham will become to Oglethorpe what Mount Vernon is to Washington," he said, and then shoved off for home.

Dr. Thornwell Jacobs

WILLIE
"PIANO RED"
PERRYMAN

*"The Doctor is here, folks. I'm tellin' you, I get it from
the universe and as the Old Man sent it down to me
tonight, I'm gonna send it right out there. And I'm gonna
tell you somethin': music is medicine. I take care of more
people than any doctor in the world. I use music to do it.
And I'm gonna fix you up tonight where you will be feelin'
good for three weeks after I'm gone."*
　　Piano Red
　　Introduction to his live broadcast on
　　WAOK, 1954-68

Editor's Note:　In May 1982, following the publication of
"Great Balls of Fire: The Uncensored Story of Jerry Lee
Lewis," author Murray Silver began compiling notes for a
college text on the history of popular music in America.
Using scores of interviews he had conducted over the past
six years for a variety of magazines as his foundation, he
concentrated on finding the last remaining blues artists to
perfect the record before they got away. Willie "Piano
Red" Perryman was the first name on Silver's list.

　　Perryman had fallen on hard times. His steady gig
as　house　pianist　at　Muhlenbrink's　Saloon　in
Underground Atlanta had ended two years before and he
had a hard time finding work. His health was on the
decline and he worried about finding enough money to
pay the bills on his small house on Winthrop Drive in
Southeast Atlanta that he shared with his son and a

251

parade of homeless kids. He hoped Silver could find merit enough in the story of Piano Red to warrant writing a book and make a few dollars. Silver set about the task only to discover that Perryman's recollections would not amount to a book-length manuscript and the notes from their conversations were set aside.

Perryman died on July 25, 1985. Since then, Arhoolie has reissued the best of his recordings and his brilliant work has stood the test of time. However, biographical notes are sketchy and interviews of Perryman are non-existent. In an effort to preserve his story, Silver has transcribed Piano Red's testimony exactly as it was related to him twenty years ago in the living room of Perryman's residence.

THE FACTS

And now I wanna tell you about the life of Piano Red. I'm gonna tell you from the boyhood days on up through manhood of this guy Piano Red. Now I'm gonna tell you about the whole life of my family and myself.

I remember when we first moved from Hampton, Georgia. In fact, I was six years old (1917). I was born in Hampton. It was about 32 miles from Atlanta.

I wanna get back to the facts: What happened is, we had been farmin' in Hampton. For years my daddy was a farmer and he had a large family. In fact, there was four of us boys, four girls, Mama and Papa. That made around ten people, you see. So we called that a large family.

Like I said, getting to the facts of this thing, my daddy was workin' on halves, supposed to be. He was workin' all night, but the money never did show up. So what had happened this year, we had done a lot of work for other farmers after we had collected our crops, cotton, that type of stuff—they would pay you, and back in them

252

days, why, kids didn't get any money. Didn't nobody get it but the grown people. In fact, they would collect the money for they kids and themselves. So, the family would go out and pick cotton. Of course, I was too small, anyway. I guess I was somewhere in the field there, but I wasn't doin' nothin'. I was, like I said, just six years old.

We lived on a plantation owned by Mr. Davidson. Back in them days, men grabbed tree limbs to whip lazy workers. One day Mr. Davidson come up to my daddy and said, "Henry, where is that gal?"

My daddy said, "If you talkin' 'bout my daughter Sally, she's there in the house. I don't know about that gal you talkin' about."

Mr. Davidson said, "Tell her to come out here. I'm gonna give her the whippin' of her life, then I'm gonna take her home an' make her apologize to Miz Davidson."

My daddy said, "Naw, I don't think you gonna whip that chile o' mine. You may have some Negro chillun, but you ain't got any over here. Nobody whup no chile o' mine but me or they mother."

Mr. Davidson stepped toward the porch. My daddy picked up his six-shooter shotgun that he kept inside the front door—it was a .38 Smith and Wesson long barrel pistol—and cocked it. "Make another step an' I cut you in half." Negroes didn't talk to white folks like that unless they meant it, an' my daddy meant it.

Mr. Davidson told my daddy to bring Sally over to the big house and find out what it's all about. He walked back to his house. My daddy put his pistol in his pants, and took Sally to the big house. The Davidsons told my daddy to leave Sally with them but my daddy said, "I think the best thing to do is take her back with us."

My daddy had made up his mind he wadn't gonna farm anymore, but he didn't say nothin' to nobody. He would take the family to these different plantations and pick cotton or whatever kinda work had to be done. He wouldn't get paid much but over a period of time he come up with some money. He went to Atlanta and found us a house. I never will forget that house. It was number 3 Oliver Street. He came back down and told Mr. Davidson, say, "I'm gonna settle up now." Mr. Davidson say, "All right, Henry." My daddy was named Henry Perryman. So, he took out a lotta papers to get this settlin' up thing together. Finally, he say, "Henry, you didn't make no money this year but you don't owe a dime." My daddy, he was lookin' for them words, anyway. He'd heard 'em so many times. He said, "Well, Mr. Davidson, would you gimme a clear receipt on that?" "Well, sure, Henry, yeah." He gave him a clear receipt and he said, "Thank you, Mr. Davidson."

My daddy had went around to all the other people that he had got little things from. He mostly didn't get nothin' from nothin' but the little country store there. Mr. Davidson owned the store, anyway. But just some other little things where he owed people some few dollars, he paid 'em. He said, "I'm gonna move to Atlanta."

In a small town word travels fast. People'd say, "When you gonna leave, Mr. Perryman?" He say, "Well, I'm movin' tomorrow. We packin' up tonight, done sold my cows." Mules or horses or whatever you call 'em. He wasn't gonna need 'em in Atlanta. He was gonna get a job and go to work.

We had two wagonloads. We didn't have too much furniture, beds, maybe a dresser, things like that. Papa had got some more men who was gonna ride with him and help him when he got to Atlanta. But before we got away from Hampton, Mr. Davidson went all over town wantin' to know if Henry Perryman owe anybody anything, he was runnin' off. But Papa wasn't runnin' off, he was just tired of workin' for nothin'.

So, that mornin' come. I remember. They say you can't remember things over a long time ago, but I

254

remember, 'cause we had water on the wagon, be drinkin', and Mama always had plenty of food. In fact, they had killed hogs. We had meat loaded on one wagon. We had plenty of food to last us a long time, more than a month, 'cause my daddy had raised all this stuff. So we got started that mornin' ridin' in a horse and wagon. We'd stop, drink water, eat some food. See, 32 miles was a long ways in just a horse and wagon. You couldn't make any time, just ride along. But I tell you what we did: we just kept movin' along and just before dark we got into Atlanta.

We didn't know about streets 'n' things. In the country people just go by certain houses. So, soon as we got in to where the sign say Atlanta City Limits, I remember my daddy stop the wagon and ask where was number 3 Oliver Street. We was lucky. We came into Atlanta right through on Ashby Street and people would tell us—they knew we didn't understand—to go straight on in and after you get further in, somebody'll tell you where Oliver Street is, and then you look for number 3.

So we came on down Ashby Street, ridin' along. Everybody was happy 'cause we was movin' to Atlanta, one of the big moments in all our lives.

FATLANTA 1917

I had a brother named Rufus who was old enough to work. Him and daddy found a job at a place called the Miracle Machine Shop. Rufus was an albino like m'self and couldn't do nothin' but certain types of work because he was nearsighted like me, but they had some work for him. So my daddy and Rufus went to work at the same place.

My grandparents had moved to Atlanta two years before. They lived on Sunset Avenue, three blocks away. They helped us find a house. I hadn't never been to school. I was gonna get the chance. Monday mornin' my Mama was gonna take me and Dora and Henry and John to school. Come Monday mornin' she did, and what about this: the school was on Ashby Street. We didn't have to walk too far. I'd never been in a school. One of the greatest moments in my life, goin' to school. Look like luck was in our favor.

Ora found a job at a laundry. Sally didn't care to work, she stayed around home. My Mama didn't care if she worked, she never made us.

There were streetcars in them days. People were real friendly to us 'cause we had just moved to town. Back in them days there weren't many places to go. So whenever you went any place, the whole community would be there. But they enjoyed theyself. There was one place you could find just about everybody, and that was the church.

We'd been in Atlanta about a year when my Mama said one day, "I wish I could get a piano for all you kids. Some way y'all might learn to play like your brother Rufus." Rufus turned out to be Speckled Red. He was playin' the piano when I was a little boy. Rufus learned to play on a church pump pedal organ. He had left his job at the machine shop and was playin' around house parties and Saturday night fish fries. Lucius Pullen sponsored these shows. I don't know whether they was payin' him or payin' him much or not. He had a place to stay and that's all that mattered to him. He'd be gone two, three days. Sometimes we didn't see him for a week.

Mama said, "The first time somebody come by here talkin' about a piano I'm gonna see if I can't buy one for you kids." The man come through there one day, he tol' her, says, "You only pay a dollar down and a dollar a week." Mama cooked and washed and ironed for people and she got that piano. The man tol' her, "If things get tough for you, pay just fifty cents a week." Mama thanked him to the highest.

WILLIE "PIANO RED" PERRYMAN

I never will forget that piano. It was a Gainesborough upright, probably not a new one but it was a good 'un. Had a good sound and looked good. That was the greatest thing that ever happened, we had a piano in the house.

Rufus decided he was gonna go up North. He left Atlanta in 1921 for Detroit, and the next I heard of him he had recorded "Dirty Dozen." He never did come back until 1960. He wouldn't have come back then if I hadn't reached him through the Musician's Union. They told him I was lookin' for him and he called me that night. 'Course, Rufus always called collect. A month from then he come down and stayed one month. He was in St. Louis then.

They had somethin' that we call Community Clubs. That was to give the people somewhere to go. What they did, they would meet at different ones' houses and what made it so good—the reason I wanted to grow up so fast—when they'd get through discussin' whatever they was talkin' about they would serve 'em punch and samwiches and ice cream. Boy, I wanted to grow up. I had started ping-pongin' around on the piano, just bangin'. Mama didn't care how much we banged on the piano. It was perfectly all right. I was playin' 'cause I said, "I'm gonna learn, I'm gonna learn." It was in my mind and I said, "I'm gonna learn." And I learned just a little bit every time. Next thing you know, I'm beginnin' to learn different songs.

I started out playin' for a dollar at daytime parties. I was still goin' to school. We'd get a three-room shotgun style house and take the furniture out of the livin' room, put it on the back porch. There'd be just empty rooms and a piano. Slide and dance. Play the blues and let 'em hug around each other and drag across the floor. Too many people for fast numbers. Back in them days the troubadour guitarists were popular in Atlanta. Willie McTell, Barbecue Bob, Charlie Hicks, Buddy

Moss, Curly Weaver. They played street corners until someone invited them inside. I played with 'em for nickels and dimes.

Big John's parties were house dances that started Sunday night and went til five Monday morning. White lightnin', fish, cold drinks. People came from all over. Got a permit, as long as it wasn't on Sunday. Started one minute after midnight. Then we moved to the cafes. It was nice to know I was getting to people.

Went up on Peachtree Street, an' that meant I was gonna go play for white people. This was before integration. Got an invitation from a white man in a bread truck who worked for the city. He told people we had "a diff'rent atmosphere on 'em, a unique style that nobody could copy." We were playin' intermissions for a country band. Made more money in ten minutes than I had three or four nights where I'd been playin'. Ten dollars. Tipped me every time I played. Ten was like a hundred to me. That was some big money, believe me. It was then I knew I was on my way to success.

NEW SHOES

I started playin' schools and storefronts in Jefferson, Georgia (northeast of Atlanta, near Athens). I had a friend in Gainesville named Willie. I stayed with his sister over in Chicopee. There was a café on main street of the black community with a piano in back where I played on late afternoons and evenin's.

I never drank my whole life. I was walkin' home from Gainesville to Chicopee, passed by a fillin' station country store. Six or seven white fellas drinkin'. One of 'em looked up, says, "Here come a nigger." Other one says, "He's a white neeger." First one says, "Yep, that's what he is, but he can dance like the rest of 'em. We gonna have some fun offa him."

258

I said, "I can't dance. I'm goin' home."

He say, "Oh yeah, all niggers can dance." Another say, "Hey, nigger."

I made like I couldn't hear. "You talkin' to me?"

He say, "Ain't no mo' niggers out there."

I say, "Yeah." No, I prob'ly said, "Yessir."

He say, "How 'bout dancin' for us?"

I say, "It's jus' like I tol' this fella here, I can't dance."

He say, "All niggers can dance, an' you gonna dance too."

I went to walk on. The man scratched a pistol out, a .38, and shot right down to the ground by my feet. He say, "Dance." I didn't know, I really didn't know I had that much dancin' in me. You talk about dancin', I done some dancin'. I don't know if it was dancin' or junkin', but I had two dollars and eleven cents when I left there.

They passed the hat around and took me up some money. They gimme that money. Y'know, the shoes I had on, I kept 'em shined so people wouldn't look at 'em so hard. But I didn't have no bottoms in them shoes. I could get a pair at the second hand store for a dollar, dollar an' a half. Them people gimme about two dollars an' some change. So I turn around back towards the second hand store an' they call after me, "Hey, ain't you goin' this a-way?"

I say, "Not now. I'm goin' back up here an' get me a pair o' shoes."

They say, "It didn't sound like you needed shoes."

I say, "It might'na sound like it, but that was m' feet hittin' the pavement." My foots sounded like taps.

So I bought them shoes, a $50 pair from the pawnshop. And I walked home along the railroad. I danced more that day than I ever had in my life.

RESPECT

"You can demand respect if you give respect. I wanna tell you something, my friends: There ain't but the one way and that's the right way. I came up in the church. My Mama and daddy and all of us went to church. I never been a guy to drink liquor. Don't misunderstand me: Anybody can drink it that wants it and I think it's great. I bought a lot of whiskey for my friends. I had parties at my house, but from a li'l boy on up I didn't drink liquor. I think it was good for me throughout my career, in more than one way. A lotta people, when they find out you don't drink, if they don't know anything about you right then they start havin' respect for you. I got friends. I got thousands and thousands of friends I don't even know because they like my music and if they talk to me, they like my personality."

I stayed in Thomaston, Georgia (west of Macon) for a while back in the early Thirties. Played the Cotton Mill Ball. Back in Atlanta, I played Saturday night fish fries in Buckhead (an Atlanta neighborhood) for Mr. Brown. We'd start at 3 p.m. and go all night. One day I was walkin' around Buckhead and a police stopped me and asked me where I work. I said, "Nowhere." Police say, "What you doin' down here?" And I say, "I come with Mr. Brown." Police ask Mr. Brown who I was and he said, "He's a piano player, he don't need no job."

The police say, "He walkin' around here with a nice clean shirt on. We don't have that around here from you people. If he gonna stay out here, he gonna have to work." Police didn't like to see blacks walkin' around in the daytime while everyone else was workin'. I had a trio with Jack and Tom. The police questioned us about a break-in in Decatur. They told us to go home, stay off Decatur streets. I went to North Carolina, to Forest City and Henrietta (60 miles west of Charlotte). Run into Sonny Terry up there.

THE THREE COURSES

The first music I remember is the old banjo stuff, like "O, Susannah." That's what they played at those frolics, Saturday Night Frolics they called 'em. It's them type of songs where they used to flail those banjos. We were poor, but my mother used to find the money to buy me Fats Waller records 'cause she knew how much I liked 'em.

I don't care what kind of music anybody likes; I can make 'em pat their feet 'cause I can get through to 'em. I've got three different courses I can take. The first one is the blues and rhythm, that rhythm thing. I hit that first, and that usually goes through. And then I got this thing, I can do things in the pop style, but it's got the rhythm feel. And the next thing, if I'm in the right section and the people want it, I fall into blues. I dreamed a church song while I was comin' back from Europe once, "Jesus is Coming Back One Day."

In 1931, I played three nights a week at this country music club. Danceland, and at the White Café on Howell Mill Road in Atlanta. Clyde Ramey was lookin' for somebody to play his rest camp in Tulula Falls in the north Georgia mountains during summer. Up around Clayton, Lakemont, Lake Burton. P.C. Terrell was my drummer and James played sax. I'm satisfied they would charge 'em a li'l somethin' at the door.

In 1933, Blind Willie McTell and I recorded together in Augusta, Georgia, for a man named Calloway. He was with Bocallion Records, or Cotillion or somethin' like that. Vocalion. We laid down some tracks but they were never released. Taped it on wax disc direct. Warped.

We were paid ten dollars per song and we recorded ten songs.

That was around the time Jack Hemphill joined me on guitar. We hitchhiked to Athens, Georgia, and stopped in Lawrenceville to play. People came as far as Monroe, chipped in with some pretty nice money. Run into somethin' pretty good there. Caught a truck goin' to Athens. Well, we was goin' to Winder. Got another set-up for the weekend. Stayed around there two, three weeks. In Athens, we started walkin' through the colored community. Lady sittin' on her porch asked us to play a tune. Lady named "Chicken."

We called our band the Dixie Jazz Hounds. We went to Brevard, North Carolina, and played Greasy Corner every Friday night. Hawkinsville, Thomasville, Griffin, Macon, Savannah, Eastman—all small Georgia towns. We ran into a fella with a car who carried us around. He liked music so much he didn't care if he only had gas money, and that hit our pocketbooks exactly right. I played with Abel Collins, CowCow Dempo, and Ernest Cox on saxophone. Played Fat George's Café in Jefferson, Georgia. People came from miles around to hear Red's un-usual sound. Run into Curly Weaver and Buddy Moss.

John Mullins was a bootlegger who had a café on Sunset and Magnolia in Atlanta. Beer wasn't existin' too much at that time. He had these daytime parties. I played; Blind Willie McTell played his 12-string guitar. Over in Athens, a pianist named Jerome Bell sponsored a contest over the radio with $25 to the winner. I won the contest, five-to-one.

DR. FEELGOOD

This is my story and I ain't gonna hand it to ya except exactly the way it was. I got married in 1940, to

Carrie. My son Junior was born in 1951. I had a studio at
home so I could broadcast live over the air from my living
room. God give me this special talent.

I seen this town (Atlanta) grow along with me.
No clubs when I started in the Twenties. People enjoyed
themselves, though, even if they had no place to go. Blind
Willie McTell played a big part in my life. He wanted to
see me make it. Took me to make my first record back in
'36. It wasn't released, but Willie say, "One day you
gonna come out with a record."

I was playin' down on Decatur Street, Auburn
Avenue, at the Hole in the Wall Club. Mr. Young at
Central Record Shop heard me playin' at the Hole. He
said, "Y'know, you sounds good, and I buy thousands of
dollars of records from record companies, especially
RCA. I b'lieve you sound better than most of them what
I'm sellin'. I know a lotta these record people. I'm gonna
get in touch with Sam Wallace, RCA's distributor here,
and see if he'll contact New York about you."

Sam Wallace came to hear me. "I don't know
much about your music, but I like what I hear." New
York sent Steve Sholes to Atlanta to see me two weeks
later. I had an audition at WGST. I did "Rockin' with
Red" and "Red's Boogie." Steve Sholes said, "I'm a
country man. I don't know nothin' about this type of
music either. But when it sounds clear to you and it don't
sound extorted when we play it back and you say take this
tape, that's what we'll do. They told me to record you and
that's what I'm gonna do."

The record was released in October 1950. They
tested it in Atlanta, New Orleans and Memphis. It went
so fast, got to sellin' so many records, they released it all
over. Sold like wildfire. Zenas Sears was a deejay at
WAOK in Atlanta. He played Red all the time. When
Zenas became president of the station, he offered me my
own show. An hour-long show live every afternoon. My

job was makin' people happy. Makes me feel good all over when I know peoples really enjoyin' themselves.

My second record was "You Got the Right String, Baby (But the Wrong Yo-Yo)" and "My Gal Jo." Followed it up with "Diggin' the Boogie" and "Let's Have a Good Time Tonight," then "She's Dynamite" and "I'm Gonna Tell Everybody," then "Bouncin' with Red" and "Count the Days I'm Gone." RCA also released "Your Mouth's Got a Hole In It" and "Decatur Street Boogie," and "Just Right Bounce" with "Jumpin' the Boogie."

In 1961, the Okeh Record label released a remake of "Wrong Yo-Yo." Followed that up about a year later with "Dr. Feel-Good," which is a song about a doctor of love who only likes big womens. When the record come out it said the song was by "Dr. Feelgood and the Interns," and the name stuck from then on.

At the Toledo Club during intermission one night a lady got up and told the crowd, "This man, Dr. Feelgood, is the cause for me bein' alive today. The doctor told me I had cancer. My daughter tol' me to get my mind on Dr. Feelgood. I started listenin' to his radio show, and I heard him say, 'I'm workin' on cancer. I want all you people jus' to concentrate on my music and when I go offa this air, jus' forget you ever had a cancer.' And I said I'm gonna do jus' that. That day I prayed to God, 'Lord, make this cancer be gone.' Three days later I went back to the doctor and there was no sign of cancer. The doctor said, "I don't know if it was Dr. Feelgood—it might be the Lord—so you thank Him."

After that, I'd go on the air and say, 'Dr. Feelgood workin' on strokes today...high blood pressure tomorrow, heart attacks."

Before you know it, I was playin' all the colleges in the Sixties—Princeton, Harvard, Yale, Miami, Georgia Tech, Emory, Georgia—and was playin' Europe. I played the Montress Festival. Montrex (Montreux). Opened the show on Sunday. Supposed to do twenty minutes, did thirty-five, closer to forty. In 1977, Norbert Hess booked me all over Europe on a six-weeks tour. I was workin' out of three agencies: Best Band Attractions, Universal Attractions, and Ted Hall Attractions. No contracts. Nine years. People always liked my music.

Anything you gonna do, if you don't put God in the front, you ain't gonna do nuthin' to start with. And that's what I do. I be's prayin' when I'm drivin' in my car. I be's prayin' at the intermission of my show. God let me know a while back when I was makin' records it wasn't me, but Him, and I never forgot that. I been a good fella ever since. From then on I put God in front of me and I been doin' good ever since.

NOTE: The best of Piano Red is presently available on CD 379 from Arhoolie, a collection of solo performances recorded in 1972 plus previously unissued songs and live recordings from 1956.

T.S. Chu Family, early 1940's

THE CASE OF THE SNAKEHEAD SMUGGLERS

AUGUST 1999

A hectic Wednesday morning, and local lawyer Amy Copeland is on her way to Claxton for an initial consultation with a client appointed to her by U.S. Magistrate G. R. Smith. The client's name is Zhi Zhong Zhang, captain of the 40,000-ton freighter that made its way up the Savannah River with a human cargo of 132 illegal Chinese immigrants stashed below deck. With Mrs. Copeland is Dr. George Wang, Ph.D., a Chinese-American immigration lawyer who will serve as interpreter in what has become known as the Case of the Snakehead Smugglers.

If it's said fast enough, the captain's name sounds like the ricochet of a bullet in a comic book. Mrs. Copeland isn't sure whether his first name is Zhi or Zhang, and Dr. Wang loses her in a ten-minute dissertation on the workings of Asian nomenclature. It then dawns on Mrs. Copeland that if it takes this much effort merely to decipher her client's name, she may be in for a tedious time representing him before the federal courts.

"I was thinking," Mrs. Copeland says, "how difficult it must be for these men to be locked up in an American jail without anyone to talk to or explain things. I don't think they even know what they're charged with. After two weeks, they probably think they've been

267

forgotten, and will spend the rest of their natural lives behind bars in Claxton, Georgia. It must be terrible."

"Yes," Dr. Wang agrees.

The remainder of the hour-long drive is spent in silence, the quiet ride of the Copeland's mini-van lulling Dr. Wang into a mid-morning catnap.

CLAXTON JAIL

The Evans County Jail in Claxton may be Sheriff Eddie Bradley's turf, but for the past eighteen years Ms. Dana Brown has run the show. Perched in a glass booth like a ticket taker at a movie theater, she greets visitors while keeping an eye on what goes on in the common areas of the lock-up through a bank of video monitors. Anybody wanting in or out of the jail has to get past Ms. Brown first.

When asked about her newest boarders, Ms. Brown seems unimpressed that they are involved in the biggest illegal alien smuggling operation in U.S. history. In fact, Ms. Brown is surprised that a reporter would come all the way over from Savannah just to inquire as to their welfare.

"After eighteen years, you learn to treat this as just a job," Ms. Brown explains. "There ain't any crime man can commit that I ain't seen, and I learned a long time ago not to be too surprised at what folks will come up with next."

Talk to Ms. Brown longer than five minutes and she'll say she's been blessed in her life—even though she's had to raise three kids on her own and is grandma to three more. To make ends meet she works weekends as security over to the mall, and spends her evenings counseling troubled teens because one of her sons was "in the system" once.

"He was drinkin' and actin' wild and gettin' into trouble," Ms. Brown continues. "It used to just kill me havin' to sit here and watch him back there on the monitor. I told him I was prayin' for him—I pray about everything—and it kinda made him mad. He said, 'Mama, I ain't gonna be locked up here forever.' And I said, 'Well, son, looks like you're doin' a pretty fair job of it to me."

But before the listener can come to any conclusions on the fate of Ms. Brown's son, she provides the happy ending. "It's like what the Bible says about the prayers of righteous men can work wonders. I went to three or four righteous men in the community and asked them to pray for my son. That was four years ago, and it's been that long since he's been in trouble."

"This is a place of correction," Ms. Brown says, as if conducting a tour of the facility. "It's meant to correct those who will learn by their mistakes and return them to society. And it's a place of incarceration for those who can't be corrected and are a threat to society. It's like the Serenity Prayer: God grant me the serenity to accept the things I cannot change..."

"Do you think Zhi Zhong Zhang understands that principle, Miz Brown?"

"Who?" she asks, with a quizzical look.

"The captain of the ship that tried to smuggle all those Chinamen into the country, the prisoner you've got back there."

"Oh," she says, "I don't know. It all depends on what he believes, don't it? Do you think he believes in the Bible?"

NEW ARRIVALS

A large map of the area hanging in the lobby meets visitors to the Evans County Courthouse and Jail

269

in Claxton. The map was drawn in 1915, when the county was so sparsely populated that the cartographer identified every plot of land by its owner and staked out even the smallest landmarks, including the still on the Sands property. For most of the past hour, Mrs. Copeland and Dr. Wang have driven through mostly undeveloped land that looks like it hasn't changed in 84 years.

A probationer wanders around the courthouse grounds, a one-man work detail in charge of cutting the grass and trimming the bushes. He wears an oversized coverall with "County Probationer" stenciled on the back like a scarlet letter, obviously meant to embarrass the wearer and insure its safe return to the county. The sheriff must trust him, though, because he's also been outfitted with a ferocious pair of hedge clippers and the kind of power trimmer frequently used as a prop in slasher movies.

The probationer is hesitant to speak to passersby, and anyone can tell he's starved for a polite word from someone on the outside. With the least encouragement, he'll tell you he's got six months to go on his sentence, but he won't say what he's in for. Ask him about the newest arrivals at the jail, and he doesn't have much to tell.

"One of 'em's scared and one of 'em's mad," the probationer says, "but it's hard to tell 'cause they don't speak no English. One of 'em seems like he's crazy. He sings the same Chinese song all day long, over and over. It goes somethin' like, 'Wang Dang Doodle, Wang Dang Doodle.' The marshal come and took him away, but I don't know where."

""Wang Dang Doodle" isn't a Chinese song. It was written and recorded many years ago by a Chicago bluesman named Willie Dixon."

The probationer mulls it over, wondering how its possible for a Chinese cabin boy caught up in the Case of the Snakehead Smugglers to have run across the music of an old bluesman the probationer hasn't even heard of.

"I can tell you one thing," the probationer says, as if he's offering valuable insider information, "those Chinamen don't like the food here none."

"Who does?"

The probationer thinks about it a minute. "Yeah, you got a point there."

BACK IN SAVANNAH

The day before, as a sudden downpour erases plans to walk the beach in late afternoon, Dr. Wang makes his way over to the federal courthouse that faces Wright Square in Savannah, in search of U.S. Magistrate G. R. Smith. He is an unexpected visitor, and wanders the three floors only to encounter a maze of locked doors guarded by linebackers in blue blazers.

He encounters the judge's deputy, Sherri Bouchillon, in the hallway. She's loaded down with legal files and has no time to spare, but Dr. Wang persuades her to advise the judge that he's here to help the court in the Case of the Snakehead Smugglers. Bouchillon disappears into the judge's chambers, and it's a full five minutes before she ushers Dr. Wang before Judge Smith.

"I realize this is highly unusual, Judge," Dr. Wang apologizes, "but when I read in the newspaper that the court was having difficulty finding an interpreter who could speak various Chinese dialects, I wanted to offer my services to you free of charge."

Dr. Wang places his impressive resume on the judge's desk. "For many years I studied comparative law between China and the United States," he points out. "The primary difference is that in China everybody is guilty unless proven innocent. The police can arrest anyone without cause or proof, and interrogate them

271

until they confess. Here, everybody is innocent until proven guilty."

Judge Smith reads the resume, taking note that Dr. Wang has specialized in Immigration law for more than 32 years, that he has lectured at dozens of Asian universities, and is legal adviser to the governor of Yunnan province. Qualifications aside, Smith is concerned that Dr. Wang might be a representative of the Chinese government, or of any other foreign concern with an interest in the case before his court.

"I am an American citizen," Dr. Wang says. "I served eight months in a Taiwanese prison for pro-democracy activities. This was in 1969."

Judge Smith listens intently, as if he is hearing testimony in his courtroom.

"For many years I represented American servicemen before Chinese courts. Many of them were black, and many of them had been accused of abusing Chinese women. And because I was very successful representing them, the Taiwanese government tried to stop me. There was a case of a black officer who was driving under the influence and ran over a group of children that fled the scene. I took his case all the way to the Supreme Court, and won on appeal. The government was so infuriated that they threw me in jail. They accused me of bribing the lower courts with American dollars.

"Upon my release from prison, I was a hero to the U.S. military," Dr. Wang continues. "A black colonel and a black major general invited me to become a member of their Masonic lodge. I am their only fraternal lodge brother in the world who is not black."

Judge Smith appears to be convinced of Dr. Wang's political leanings, and after examining his personal documents feels more comfortable of his allegiances. On a personal note, however, the judge is interested to know why this particular case has caused

272

George Wang to come out of retirement and travel a great distance at his own expense just to lend a hand.

"I know what it's like to be a poor immigrant trying to reach America," Dr. Wang admits. "I know the kinds of oppression these people are fleeing, that they have risked their lives and all they possess just to come here for the chance of earning a living. I have a fiancée in Yunnan who is forbidden to travel outside China. If I am to marry her, I am forced to return. But I cannot go back. It is not safe."

Judge Smith reaches his decision. "I see no reason why you can't offer your services as interpreter to defense counsel in this case," he says.

COURT-APPOINTED LAWYERS

With a list of lawyers appointed by the court to represent the seven defendants in the Case of the Snakehead Smugglers, Dr. Wang repairs to his room at the Comfort Inn to call each and offer his assistance. Of the seven lawyers, he reaches only one, T. Mills Fleming. The others are either busy or out to lunch, and Mr. Fleming asks Dr. Wang to meet him right away. And with an evidentiary hearing in seven days, Mr. Fleming puts in a call to the Effingham County Jail and arranges with the sheriff to meet with his client, Cheng Sun, in one hour.

The rain is coming down in torrents, a waterspout has been spotted off the coast of Tybee, and power is out all along the trail between Fleming's office on St. Julian Street and the jail in Springfield. Fleming and Wang dodge raindrops and present themselves to the sheriff, who leads them to the interrogation room to meet Cheng Sun. Cheng Sun, however, is not present. The jail has two of the seven defendants, and neither is Cheng Sun. Mr. Fleming's client has been transferred to another jail by federal marshals in an effort to keep the defendants from talking to one another. If Mr. Fleming wants to meet his client, he's going to have to drive another hour to Claxton.

Mr. Fleming is trying to maintain his professional composure. "I don't think the sheriff of Effingham County knows who's in his jail," he says. "I don't think he can tell one name from another. There's two named Zheng, one Zhang, and two Shi's."

Dr. Wang loses Mr. Fleming in a ten-minute dissertation on the workings of Asian nomenclature. And it dawns on Mr. Fleming, as it had on Mrs. Copeland, that if it takes this much effort just to find his client, he may be in for a tedious time representing him before the federal courts.

It's late in the day, too late for the Evans County Jail to straighten up for company, and Mr. Fleming is advised to try again tomorrow. As it turns out, a scheduling conflict will prevent him from making the trip to Claxton the next day.

Dr. Wang retires to his room at the Comfort Inn to find five urgent messages from Savannah lawyers in desperate need of his services.

TAIWANESE SCAM

The day before, Monday, finds Dr. George Wang in Atlanta, having flown in from California late the previous evening. He has a ten o'clock appointment with U.S. Senator Max Cleland's chief of staff, Wayne Howell, and the senator's state director, Bill Chapman, at the senator's office in the Russell Federal Building.

Dr. Wang is on urgent business on behalf of the American taxpayer. He believes he has uncovered a scam whereby officials of the government of Taiwan have pocketed more than $3 billion in U.S. aide due to Taiwanese World War II veterans, whom Dr. Wang represents. It amounts to one of the largest reserves of dollars outside the United States. Because Senator Cleland is on the Armed Services committee and has special interest in veterans' affairs, Dr. Wang is certain that he will be instrumental in demanding an accounting from Taiwan through proper channels.

"Taiwan is not the democracy that it wants Washington to believe it is," Dr. Wang asserts to the senator's staff. "The escalating missile crisis with China will cause the U.S. to reevaluate the situation, and we could go a long way in gaining the cooperation of Taiwanese people by forcing the government to pay pensions that are long overdue. Many of these veterans are disabled, and they live in poverty. For the sake of humanity, Taiwan should be compelled to release these funds."

Mr. Howell and Mr. Chapman make independent notes on legal pads. carefully recording the details of Dr. Wang's findings. Turning to another matter, Dr. Wang wants the senator to be aware that American business interests in China are not protected.

"Three years ago I invested in a patent to manufacture Chinese herbal medicine. The government-owned Yunnan Biological and Medical Company infringed upon my patent and marketed their own product. I filed suit in Kumming, but the court postponed judgment for eighteen months. During that time, my patent was revoked. I was followed by agents of the secret police who told me that unless I dropped the suit and left the country, I would be murdered. I fled, leaving behind my fiancée, who was denied a visa."

The senator's staffers continue to make careful notes of Dr. Wang's complaint. On the surface, there seems to be no quick and easy solution to these delicate matters. Dr. Wang tries to put his conflict with China into perspective.

"The Chinese have infringed upon copyrights to books, movies and music for many years, even though they say they have cracked down on piracy. If they can steal my patent and put me out of business, what's to keep them from doing the same thing to Coca-Cola?"

His business with Senator Cleland completed, Dr. Wang returns to his hotel. Scanning a local newspaper he spots a story from Savannah about a boatload of illegal Chinese immigrants who have been taken into custody. It's the largest case of its kind in U.S. history and confusion abounds. There is a shortage of qualified lawyers to represent the captain and six crewmen who are charged with federal crimes. Worse yet is that no one can be found to translate three different Chinese dialects into English.

"Drop everything," Dr. Wang says to his assistant. "Take me to Savannah."

In less than twenty minutes, he is packed and headed south on I-75.

TYBEE HOMECOMING

A stormy August Sunday, and there's an end-of-summer sale in progress at Chu's department store on Tybee. A dignified Chinese gentleman enters, perhaps seventy years of age, and draws the attention of shoppers guessing at sandal sizes. He's no typical tourist, clad in black shirt and trousers and dress shoes. He files down the aisle to the office where he surprises Mola and Joan, owners of the store and daughters of the original proprietor, T.S. Chu.

"Well, George Wang, I haven't seen you in ages," Joan says, giving her old friend a hug.

"What are you doing with yourself, George?" Mola asks, after pleasantries are exchanged.

"I have just returned from Taiwan," he replies. "I was in Atlanta visiting Senator Cleland on an urgent matter when I read about those poor people who were caught in the smuggling operation. I came here immediately, to offer my help."

"I thought you retired," Mola says.

"Semi-retired," he says smiling, "but this is an important case. So many people, and none speak English. I can help."

He pauses and looks around the store that has changed imperceptibly over the last sixty years.

"You know, I remember the case of a Chinese who wanted to immigrate to America twenty-five years ago. The commissioner of immigration and naturalization in Atlanta told him that he would need a sponsor in the U.S., but the immigrant didn't know anyone. The commissioner knew only one person he could call for help, and that person was T.S. Chu."

Mola and Joan smile and nod in agreement.

"T.S. Chu brought him to America, gave him a place to live, even sold him the Sundowner Oceanfront Inn at a meager profit to give that immigrant an income. And that immigrant later became a highly respected lawyer. That immigrant, of course, is me.

"It's all about freedom," George Wang says. "Whether it's my case, or the Case of the Snakehead Smugglers, whether it's the poor veterans of Taiwan or my fiancée back in Yunnan. I know what it's like to be a poor immigrant from China, and I have never forgotten your father's many kindnesses toward me. And that is why I'm here to help these poor people. Only in this way can I repay T.S. Chu."

GREAT SAVANNAH STORIES

SO DEEP,
SO WIDE

Recently I have discovered the joy of walking the Rails to Trails path that runs along the road to Tybee near Fort Pulaski. I avoided it for the longest time, thinking that the six-mile stretch of abandoned railroad track cutting through the marsh was a haven for mosquitoes and rabid raccoons. And then one wintry day when I wasn't up for a drive all the way to the beach I decided to give the trail a try. I was pleasantly surprised to find its flat, smooth, firm surface was easier than a sandy beach to walk on and just as pleasant, maybe even better: the tree-lined route provides plenty of shade and, maybe best of all, there are no parking meters ticking away like time bombs.

Granted, there are gnats, but where besides the mall can you stretch your legs in this part of the world without dousing yourself in Skin So Soft?

Truth be known, the real reason I had been avoiding the Rails to Trails path was out of fear of running into the Monkey People. If it's one thing I'm afraid of more than gnats and rabid raccoons, it's Monkey People. And it's surprising the number of people I've met on the path who have never heard of the Monkey People.

Back in the '30's, my grandfather owned several tracts of land across the Savannah River, near Beaufort. The federal government bought one of these parcels and erected a laboratory where they conducted secret experiments during World War II. Chemicals used in warfare were tested on monkeys, and out of these experiments came the first tentative steps toward genetic engineering. Somewhere along the line these nutty professors mixed and matched monkey genes with

279

human, and when the project ran out of funding these pathetic creatures were let loose in the Low Country rather than put to sleep.

Some of the Monkey People learned to fish and some learned to farm. I do not know if they married into the local populace, but sometimes I wonder: there has to be an explanation for professional wrestling. All I know is back when I was a kid my father refused to take us across the river to Hilton Head, and when I demanded to know why, he said it was because of the Monkey People. And that's the sort of thing one never forgets.

It took a long time for me to work up enough nerve to set foot on the Rails to Trails path, and then only in broad daylight. Every so many feet you run across a small plaque with a picture of a hawk or turtle that tells what kind it is, but there aren't any plaques identifying Monkey People. There are, however, signs clearly stating that Rails to Trails closes at dark, and now you know the reason why.

Another feature of the Rails to Trails path that has the beach at Tybee beat is the benches and picnic tables along every step of the way. Some of these picnic tables offer a lovely view of the water and some of these benches are close enough to provide a perfect place to sit and fish right by the roadside. And one day last week while I was perched at my favorite spot, imagine my surprise when the ground gave way beneath my feet like a Ferris wheel taking flight, and I realized then that the path was never intended to run alongside the river but that the water was reclaiming the land. And very soon now, the Rails to Trails path is going to require another footbridge where my favorite bench used to be.

* * *

The Georgia Ports Authority intends to deepen the Savannah River channel from its present depth of 42 feet to as much as 48 feet to better accommodate the next

280

generation of super tankers currently under construction by companies who have yet to figure out how to transport oil safely in the old models. The harbor-deepening project has gotten thumbs up from the Army Corps of Engineers, but before it can go forward it must meet the ever-shifting criteria of environmental laws and take into consideration any and all impacts. Final approval rests in the hands of the Secretary of the Interior, the Secretary of Commerce, and regional administrator of the Environmental Protection Agency.

The harbor-deepening project qualifies for federal funding under the 1999 Water Resources Development Act, and $230 million has already been set aside to make it happen. The U.S. Army Corps of Engineers and paid consultants to the Port Authority are anxious to get underway, seeing no adverse impact on the environment. All they have to do now is find some way to silence a group of pesky do-gooder watchdog crackpots who hold regular monthly meetings to talk about erosion, flooding, endangered species, and the likelihood that our drinking water will take on a decidedly saline flavor once the U.S. Army Corps of Engineers turns the Savannah River into the Panama Canal.

Unless the idea of fishing from a park bench in Reynolds Square appeals to you, perhaps you should be more concerned about the Georgia Port Authority's harbor-deepening project.

I'm not the smartest guy in the world in these matters—and elsewhere you will find a more scholarly approach to this same subject—but it bothers me when people who are in a position to talk intelligently on the topic of deepening the harbor don't want to talk about it. Now, I'm looking at a map of the coastline and I notice that the Savannah River channel looks like a funnel, and it stands to reason that if the tides in Charleston average four to five feet deep and the tides in Jacksonville average three to four feet and we are already at six to seven, then

281

by deepening the channel the Atlantic Ocean will push farther and faster inward, won't it? And when it does, the Atlantic Ocean won't restrict itself to where the Georgia Port Authority wants it to go, will it?

No, it won't. If the Army Corps of Engineers trenches the Savannah River channel another six feet deep, it will wreak havoc on Savannah's antiquated drainage system and lay waste to the freshwater marsh that is the Savannah National Wildlife Refuge. The ocean will move in so far and so fast that they'll be surfing in Stillwell and catching fresh flounder for supper in Augusta.

The fancy term for this problem of height increase in average tides is called "tidal amplitude," and I used to hear it bandied about during the initial round of discussions on deepening the harbor. Some environmentalists said that deepening the harbor 6 feet would cause average tides to rise as much as 18 inches, and that figure doesn't even take into account fluctuations due to heavy rains and hurricane storm surges. But the environmental consulting company hired by the Port Authority to describe tidal amplitude changes argued that the effect on tides would be "insignificant," and fell back on a computer-driven mathematical model that fiddled with the figures and came up on dry land. There's a greater risk of flooding due to global warming than as a result of harbor deepening, they added. And then I didn't hear anymore about "tidal amplitude," as if the matter was settled.

Sweeping "tidal amplitude" under a rug is unsettling to local landowners who will tell you that their property never flooded prior to the first harbor deepening project that took the depth down to 39 feet in the late '80's, and then down to 42 feet in 1992. But during recent rainy seasons or when storms blow ashore, Springfield canal backs up like bacon grease in a kitchen sink and turns President Street into a moat. Now that these properties have a history of flooding, they cannot be sold or developed. And the landowners who are stuck with these bogs want to know if the Port Authority will send over their environmental consultant and his computer to pump out their property the next time the river turns it into a pool.

The deepening projects of a dozen years ago snuck by the watchdogs without allocating funds to study the impact on freshwater marshes. Had the U.S. Fish and Wildlife Service put long-term monitoring projects in place back in 1987 when this all started, it would be easier to determine whether further deepening will run off the striped bass now. But to tell the Georgia Ports Authority and U.S. Army Corps of Engineers that they must hold up a $230 million project until we find out whether it will inconvenience the endangered short nose sturgeon is to provoke peals of laughter, to say nothing of the plight of the Monkey People.

It's easy for the Port Authority to make fun of watchdog crackpots, but it's harder to ignore industries that are built on the banks of the Savannah River and rely on its fresh water for manufacturing processes. And there is nothing funny about saltwater flowing into Abercorn Creek tributary where the city's water treatment plant is located. The only thing more alarming to me than finding saltwater coming from my tap is that the Port Authority is still considering going forward with this half-baked scheme.

While walking on the beach at the south end of Tybee last fall I happened upon a man hiding in the bushes. He was sitting in the old metal scaffold that once was a shark tower and coast guard lookout, and he was twiddling the knobs on a piece of electronic equipment that looked like a stereo receiver. I watched him for a while and heard no music, so I asked him what he was doing.

He tried to brush me off, saying that the equipment was too difficult to explain. When I told him I was a writer and would like to hear the explanation if he wanted to take the time to make it, he took me to school on the subject of the Floridian Aquifer, Savannah's source for drinking water which lies 200 feet below ground level.

He told me that he was part of a scientific research team that was drilling four miles off shore into the Miocene Aquifer, which is 62 feet below sea level and is believed to feed fresh water into the Floridian Aquifer below. The purpose of his equipment was to provide the ship a fixed reference point so that it could stay atop the drill site.

If the Georgia Port Authority wants to dig within 12 feet of the rock layer that seals the Miocene Aquifer, there is a perilously small margin for error. A slip of the slide rule and we're looking at the kind of situation that makes for bad science fiction movies.

Now, I ask you: the source of your drinking water is covered by an ancient lid of rock covered by 60 feet of silt. Do you

A. Allow nature to add to the thickness of the silt layer
B. Leave it alone
C. Dig to within 12 feet of the rock so you can sail bigger boats over it

Is that your final answer?

Of course, the man in the shark tower had no findings to report; they were still drilling. The equipment remained in place and covered by plastic for several weeks, and then I noticed he cleared out around the time that we were expecting Hurricane Floyd. I never saw him again, and I never heard the first word about the drilling expedition in the Savannah Morning News or on local television news broadcasts. Whatever they found, they're not telling yet but I have a strong suspicion that owing to the vastness of the aquifer's size and scale that the findings are inconclusive.

What I think will happen is this: sometime between now and the election in November, the Tier II Environmental Impact Statement will deliver a guilty verdict on the effects of harbor deepening on erosion, wetlands, endangered species and the aquifers, and the Port Authority plan will be shot down. Bass fishermen will breathe a sigh of relief, the Monkey People will be saved, and Al Gore will take credit for the whole thing: "A vote for Al is a vote for the Monkey People."

A hard rain is gonna fall, sections of the city are going to flood, and some environmental consultant with a computer will blame it on global warming. I can see it coming a mile away.

And late at night when we gather around the campfire to tell ghost stories, when my turn comes, I won't be telling "The Tale of the Monkey People." I'll be telling an even scarier story: "The Tale of the Tidal Amplitude."

ADDENDUM TO
THE THIRD
EDITION

With the publication of the first edition of
"Behind the Moss Curtain" in November 2002, the
author nominated Shoeless Joe Jackson for inclusion
to the Greater Savannah Athletic Hall of Fame using
the story "In Search of Shoeless Joe" in support of
his petition. Founded in 1966, the Hall had
overlooked Jackson because they claimed he was
neither born in Savannah nor distinguished upon
her playing fields, but when the author placed the
revelations of his story before the board of directors
they were forced to admit the error of their
oversight. Embarrassed by an article in the local
paper in which its sports editor seconded Silver's
motion, the Hall's board of directors was placed in
the precarious position of having to admit the long-
standing mistake of excluding one of the greatest
baseball players who ever lived and an athlete more
famous than the Hall's 133 members combined.

Meeting behind closed doors, the Greater
Savannah Athletic Hall of Fame hammered out a
resolution that recognized Jackson and at the same
time saved face. Rather than enshrining Jackson with
full honors as an athlete, the Hall meted out a
Special Award, as if to say that he still failed in some
way to measure up to their requirements.

On May 5, 2003, at the 34th awards banquet,
acting on the suggestion of the author, the Hall of
Fame presented its plaque to Maggi Hall, Jackson's
88-year-old niece and a lifelong Savannah resident.

286